Celebrating 40 Years of
China-Australia
Diplomatic Relations



中澳

# 中澳关系大趋势：
## 利益共同体的构建与展望
## ——纪念中澳建交40周年

# China–Australia Relations:
## Towards a Community with Shared Interests

主　　编　常晨光　喻常森
特邀主编　曾筱龙（澳大利亚）

Edited by Chang Chenguang & Yu Changsen
Guest Editor: The Honorable Henry Tsang OAM

中山大学出版社
SUN YAT-SEN UNIVERSITY PRESS
·广州·
· Guangzhou ·

**图书在版编目（CIP）数据**

中澳关系大趋势：利益共同体的构建与展望——纪念中澳建交40周年/常晨光，喻常森主编．—广州：中山大学出版社，2012.11

ISBN 978-7-306-04376-4

Ⅰ.①中…　Ⅱ.①常…②喻…　Ⅲ.①中外关系—澳大利亚—文集　Ⅳ.①D822.361.1-53

中国版本图书馆CIP数据核字（2012）第276527号



**出 版 人：祁　军**
策划编辑：熊锡源
责任编辑：熊锡源
封面设计：林绵华
责任校对：刘学谦
责任技编：黄少伟
出版发行：中山大学出版社
电　　话：编辑部 020-84111996，84113349，84111997，84110779
　　　　　发行部 020-84111998，84111981，84111160
地　　址：广州市新港西路135号
邮　　编：510275　　　　传　真：020-84036565
网　　址：http://www.zsup.com.cn　　E-mail:zdcbs@mail.sysu.edu.cn
印 刷 者：佛山市南海印刷厂有限公司
规　　格：880mm×1230mm　1/32　8.5印张　200千字
版次印次：2012年11月第1版　2012年11月第1次印刷
印　　数：1~2000册　　　定　　价：35.00元

献给与中华人民共和国建立外交关系的澳大利亚前总理惠特拉姆

Dedicated to former Australian Prime Minister Gough Whitlam, who established diplomatic relations with the People's Republic of China in 1972

(Courtesy of Henry Tsang　曾筱龙摄)

**策划支持：**中国人民对外友好协会　澳中友好交流协会　侨鑫集团

**Supported by**

Chinese People's Association for Friendship with Foreign Countries

Association of Australia China Friendship and Exchange

Kingold Group

AACFE

僑鑫集團

KINGOLD GROUP

www.cpaffc.org.cn　　www.kingold.com

# 目　　录


序 …………………………………………………… 李小林　i

Preface …………………………………………… Chen Yuming　v

Introduction

……… Chang Chenguang，Yu Changsen & Henry Tsang　1

1　Australia in the China Century ………………… Bob Carr　15

2　中澳关系面面观：写在中澳建交四十周年之际
　　…………………………………… 喻常森　常晨光　37

3　中澳建交四十周年以来两国经贸关系发展述评
　　…………………………………… 蒋启良　张秋生　55

4　中澳天然气合作研究 ………………………… 侯敏跃　77

5　澳大利亚能源新战略评析 ………… 唐小松　许　嬉　97

6　试论澳大利亚海洋安全战略与中澳关系
　　………………………………… 甘振军　李家山　112

7　澳大利亚的南海政策解析 ………………… 王光厚　136

8　“融入亚太”背景下澳大利亚媒体视域中的中国
　　国家形象分析 ………………………… 刘　琛　154

9　澳大利亚公共外交探析 ………… 黄　忠　唐小松　170
10　澳大利亚：移民、多元文化与身份困惑
………………………………………………… 钱超英　192
11　澳大利亚对中国崛起的认知与反应……… 喻常森　214
12　悉尼与上海城市更新的发展特征比较
——案例分析与启示…………… 苏　宁　黄烨菁　235

编后记……………………………………… 曾筱龙　250

# 序

中澳地处北、南两个半球，历史背景、文化传统、社会制度不尽相同，但在当今全球化加快、科学技术日新月异、社会变革不断深入的世界里，中澳两国必须携起手来，共同应对各种挑战，共同开拓和分享新时代、新科技带来的巨大机遇，共同加强和巩固中澳友谊，为维护亚太地区和平、繁荣和稳定作出应有的贡献，造福两国人民。

40 年前，以高夫·惠特拉姆为首的澳大利亚工党政府作出了历史性抉择，承认中华人民共和国是代表全中国的唯一合法政府，与新中国建立正式外交关系。和其他许多西方大国一样，作出承认共产党政权与新中国建交的决定并非容易，甚至是迫于无奈。当时在美苏争霸的大的冷战格局下，苏联在军事上给西方世界施加了强大的压力，美国深陷越战的泥潭不能自拔，因此，团结中国反对苏联以缓和世界紧张局势、对抗苏联霸权主义就成为可行甚至是诱人的政策选项。

与新中国建交不仅仅是当时的国际形势使然，更是澳大利亚出于自身发展利益而作出的明智选择。10 年前，惠特拉姆在庆祝中澳建交 30 周年时说过这样一段话：“这样一种基于与中国合作的外交政策也将得到中国的理解和接受，国家荣誉与理性的自我利益能够如此紧密并行是非常罕见的。”

回顾过去，我们不得不佩服惠特拉姆先生那一辈政治家的远见卓识以及他们的智慧和勇气。事实证明，他的决策是对的，中澳同时站在了历史正确的一边。40年过去了，世界格局与过去截然不同。中国经过40年特别是改革开放30多年的发展，取得了举世瞩目的成就。中国经济高速发展并成为世界第二大经济体，中澳的交流与合作达到了前所未有的高度。中国已经是澳大利亚最大的贸易伙伴，第三大投资国，第一大留学生来源国；澳大利亚向中国提供其所需铁矿石的44%，向中国提供了大量的服务贸易，澳大利亚的产品在中国随处可见。

更紧密的经贸关系和人员往来这一趋势随着时间的推移进一步得到加强，这在40年前是不可想象的。从这个意义来说，面向未来40年，我们再一次站在了历史的十字路口。惠特拉姆先生正凝视着我们，他的睿智仍然在给我们以灵感和启迪，我们不应该犹豫、彷徨，不应该被一些杂音所困扰。40年前，为了世界和平、亚太稳定我们可以携手合作，为了同样的原因，更为了中澳两国的经济繁荣和百姓的福祉，为了亚太区域更紧密的合作及在全球经济竞争中同样立于不败之地，中澳两国将更加优势互补，共同开拓创新，力争取得互利共赢的良好佳绩。让事实证明，中澳再次同时站在了历史正确的一边。

惠特拉姆先生是澳大利亚唯一一位同我国三代领导人都打过交道的政治家，在从总理一职退下来后，仍然为中澳关系的发展而奔波。我会有幸曾多次邀请并接待过惠特拉姆先生访华，他睿智风趣，平易近人，令人感佩。

中国人民对外友好协会是我国致力于民间外交的全国性人民团体，代表中国人民与世界各国人民开展友好交流与合作，服务总体外交，服务祖国建设，维护世界和平。我会在做友好人士和友好城市工作的过程中，与澳中理事会、澳中友协、澳地方政府协会、澳姐妹城协会及社会各界人士保持着长期密切的友好合作关系，为促进中澳交流发挥着不可替代的积极作用。我会今年为庆祝中澳建交40周年，与澳大利亚中国友好交流协会联合主办了“中澳沙漠大穿越”活动，是我会采用多种形式开展对澳大利亚民间友好活动的创新举措。截至今天，中澳两国已建立了82对友好省州、友好城市关系。促进中澳地方政府的交流是我会的责任，也是我会今后要加大力度的方向。

我想再次强调，频繁、深入的中澳友好往来和交流，对增进相互了解和友谊是至关重要的。只要中澳两国人民之间的相互了解加深了，交往增多了，我们才会不相互存有偏见，才会建立信任；只要我们的共同利益拓宽了，我们就更有可能拥有一个共同的目标；只要我们都成为朋友了，我们就能做到休戚与共，命运与共。

要做到这一点有赖于像惠特拉姆、毛泽东、邓小平等老一辈政治家的远见卓识，也有赖于像本书主编这样的各领域的杰出领袖的贡献。在此，我愿特别提到并感谢澳大利亚中国友好交流协会会长周泽荣博士的杰出贡献，作为一名成功的企业家，他深感中澳良好的双边关系对国家和普通民众的重要性，在生意繁忙之时，也不忘作为普通民众为促进两国关系尽一份责任，作出了很好的榜样。

澳大利亚现任总理杰拉德2012年10月28日发布了《亚洲世纪中的澳大利亚》白皮书，并于当天发表讲话说："亚洲正走在重返全球经济和政治主导地位的道路上，这不仅不可阻挡，而且正在加速。"展望未来，我们充满信心。有中澳两国领导人的关心支持，有两国政府、经济界、学术界、地方政府及普通民众的共同努力，面向未来40年，中澳友谊必将充分发挥出巨大潜力，创造出更加美好的未来。

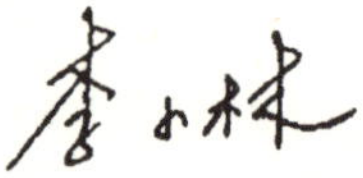

中国人民对外友好协会会长

# Preface

## by His Excellency Ambassador Chen Yuming

Professor Chang Chenguang, Professor Yu Changsen and Mr Henry Tsang are to be congratulated on their initiative and effort in putting together this special collection of papers in commemoration of the $40^{th}$ anniversary of China-Australia relations.

Forty years ago, with extraordinary political wisdom, vision and courage, statesmen from China and Australia made the strategic decision to establish diplomatic relations. Over four decades, China-Australia relations have sailed through the wind and waves and achieved leapfrog development.

The relationship between our two countries has gained more maturity. Close exchanges have been conducted at the leadership and other levels and in wide ranging areas. Our leaders exchange visits or meet at multilateral settings on an annual basis. More than ten bilateral dialogue mechanisms have been established. A mutual respect for road of development and each other's core interests and major concerns is taken as an important principle guiding the bilateral relations.

The two countries have a closer integration of interests. We have given full play to our economic complementarity, focused on mutual benefit, and produced fruitful outcomes in trade and investment cooperation. It has become a simple fact that we need each other and are interconnected. Two way trade volume topped 110 billion dollars last year. Our mutually beneficial cooperation is moving beyond the traditional energy and resources sector. It is diversifying into emerging areas like agriculture, services, finance and low-carbon economy. Bilateral cooperation in education and science has added impetus to our respective economic and social growth.

The popular foundation has become more solid. Chinese books dating back more than 2,000 years described indigenous Australians, the boomerang and kangaroos. It is said that the first Chinese person, a carpenter, migrated to Australia in 1803. For over two centuries, the Chinese community has grown and developed together with Australia. Prosperity of Australia is also attributed to the contribution from a million Chinese migrants through the history.

In 1972, there were no Chinese students in Australia, and two-way visitors were fewer than 500. Today, more than 120,000 Chinese students are studying in Australia, and 1.37 million visitors travel between the two countries. Students and tourists from China make more contribution to Australia's economy than any other groups. The two countries have 81 pairs of sister states and cities. With hundreds of events, the successful Chinese and Australian Cultural Years have enhanced mutual understanding and friendship between our peoples. The cross-society, all-dimensional people-to-people exchanges form the bedrock for long term and stable growth of China-Australia relations.

It is in this context that I find this volume on China-Australia relations highly commendable. The contributors are mostly scholars working in the areas of Australian studies, international relations, diplomacy, history, economy and trade. The papers provide an overview of the development of Sino-Australian relations in the past 40 years and discuss some of major current issues and challenges concerning bilateral relations, sometimes with a unique Chinese perspective. I believe that this new volume will contribute to increasing awareness and understanding in China of different aspects of Australia, and help stimulate discussion in both countries of current issues in China-Australia relations, so that we can all work together to open a new chapter in China-Australia relations, towards more comprehensive and stable cooperation for the common prosperity of our two countries.

Chen Yunming
Chinese Ambassador Extraordinary and Plenipotentiary
to the Commonwealth of Australia

［译文］

# 序

经过常晨光教授、喻常森教授和曾筱龙先生的积极努力，这本纪念中澳建交40周年的论文集得以出版，值得祝贺。

40年前，中澳两国政治家以非凡的政治智慧、远见与勇气，作出了建立外交关系的重大战略抉择。40年来中澳关系斩风破浪，实现了跨越性发展。

中澳关系渐趋成熟。两国高层和各级别、全领域交往密切，领导人年度互访或在多边场合会晤，两国建立起10多组对话磋商机制。相互尊重发展道路，彼此尊重核心利益和重大关切，成为指导双边关系的重要准则。

两国利益日益交融。中澳发挥经济互补优势，着眼互利共赢，经贸、投资合作成果丰硕，彼此需要、我中有你已是不争事实。去年双边贸易额超过1100亿澳元，中澳互利合作在传统能资合作之外，正向农业、服务、金融、低碳等新兴领域多元拓展，教育、科技合作对彼此经济、社会发展形成了强有力支撑。

两国关系民意基础更加坚实。两千多年前中国典籍就记载了澳洲土著人、回力镖和袋鼠。1803年就有中国的木匠移民澳洲。200多年来华人与澳共同成长，这片土地的繁荣离不开百万华人的贡献。

1972 年，中国在澳留学生是零记载，两国每年互访人数不足 500 人。而今，中国在澳留学生超过 12 万人，双向游客 137 万人。来自中国的国际留学生和游客对澳经济的贡献排在首位。两国已有 81 对友好省州和城市。中澳成功互办文化年的数百场活动增进了两国人民的互相了解与友谊。全社会、全领域的人文交流为中澳关系长期稳定发展提供了重要基石。

正是在这个意义上，我认为这本有关中澳关系的文集非常值得称赞。文集中的论文作者大多是从事澳大利亚研究、国际关系、外交、历史、经济和贸易等领域研究的学者。文集回顾了中澳关系 40 年的发展历程，并讨论了双边关系中的一些热点问题和存在的挑战，有些文章还具有独特的中国视角。我相信，这本新书将有助于促进国内读者对澳大利亚的了解和认识，同时激发中澳两国对目前双边关系相关议题的讨论，大家携手努力，为了中澳两国的共同繁荣构建更全面、更稳定的合作关系，开启中澳关系的新篇章。

中华人民共和国驻澳大利亚大使　陈育明

# Introduction

## Forty Years of China-Australia Relations: Towards a Community with Shared Interests

Chang Chenguang, Yu Changsen & Henry Tsang

On December 21, 1972, China and Australia established diplomatic relations. At that time, no one could have ever anticipated the tremendous progress made in the development of bilateral relations since. Today, after forty years of increased exchanges and cooperation, the bonds between our two countries are much stronger and more broadly-based. China is now Australia's largest trading partner—two-way trade volume has increased by 1,000 times over 40 years, from less than $100 million to over $105 billion in 2011. [1] China is also Australia's biggest export market by far, the biggest source of tourist revenue, the biggest source of full-fee paying students, and the fastest-growing source of foreign investment. [2]

As His Excellency Ambassador Chen Yuming rightly points out, the fundamental reason that China-Australia bilateral relations have developed so rapidly in the past 40 years is that we have broad and important common interests. [3] Since our two countries established diplomatic relations in 1972, especially after China started its opening up and reform policy in the late 1970s and early 1980s, China's economy has seen extraordinary growth and has become the second largest economy in the world. Some predict that the trend is set to continue and its size is likely to quadruple in the next 20 years. [4] By 2030, China is expected to become the major driver of economic activity both regionally and globally, and it has the potential to overtake the United States as the world's largest economy and a leading stakeholder in the development and stability of the global economic and political system. [5] China is, and for the foreseeable decades ahead will be, Australia's most important economic partner. As our two economies are highly complementary to each other, both China and Australia have benefited, and will continue to benefit, from our expanding economic and trade relations.

Of course, economic and trade relations do not develop in isolation. The achievements in the areas of economy and trade are due to the longstanding commitment by the governments of both countries to create the environment in which business and commercial links can flourish. [6] Over the years, both governments have placed great importance on bilateral relations and have maintained regular exchanges at the leadership and other levels and in wide ranging areas. The two sides have established a full set of dialogue platforms which include strategic dialogue, inter-party exchanges, high-level economic dialogue, strategic defense consultation and human rights dialogue. [7] Leaders of the two countries exchange visits or meet at multilateral settings on an annual basis. Both China and Australia recognize shared interests and differences, and agree to pursue bilateral relations on the basis of mutual respect and to manage differences in a way that does not hinder the achievements of the many goals both countries have in common.

More importantly, robust people-to-people exchanges have contributed enormously to enhancing mutual trust and ensuring the continual growth of the bilateral relationship. Each year, over a million visits are made between our two countries. In 2011, for example, nearly 500,000 Chinese people visited Australia and there were more than 126,000 Chinese students who chose to study in Australia. With hundreds of events, the successful Chinese and Australian Cultural Years have enhanced mutual understanding and friendship between our peoples. The cross-society, all-dimensional people-to-people exchanges have laid a more solid popular foundation for the long term and stable growth of China-Australia relations.

As we celebrate the 40th anniversary of China-Australia diplomatic relations, it is important to look to the future as well as review past achievements. We also have to recognize that, despite the enormous achievements made in many aspects of bilateral relations, there is still much room for improvement, given the many misconceptions and misunderstandings between the two sides, as reflected in opinion surveys. [8] Some even argue, for example, that Australia is now more conflicted about Australia-China relationship than at any time since 1972. [9] Both countries have realized that we need to do more to foster better understanding of each other and are taking measures to do so.

As we are writing this introduction, the White Paper on Australia in the Asian Century has just been released. This document emphasizes the importance of becoming a more Asia-literate country and building Australia's "Asia-relevant capabilities". As the Prime Minister Julia Gillard points out in the Foreword, "The transformation of the Asian region into the economic powerhouse of the world is not only unstoppable, it is gathering pace", and Australia needs to "seize the economic opportunities that will flow and manage the strategic challenges that will arise." China is naturally at the centre of almost every facet of the policy, which calls for deepening Australia's "already close and cooperative relationship with China at every level", as "China's importance to Australia, economically and politically, will only grow in decades to come." [10]

The White Paper, coordinated by Dr Ken Henry, former Secretary of Federal Treasury, has also generated public discussion in Australia during its formation about relationships with China – politically, socially, economically and culturally. Such discussion is also needed in China as we try to move China-Australia relations to another level. We believe that the academia will have an important role to play here, and candid, scholarly discussions of relevant issues will help clear the misunderstandings and enhance mutual trust, which is the motivation for the compilation of the present volume.

In this special collection, *China-Australia Relations: Towards a Community with Shared Interests*, we try to bring together the most recent studies of leading scholars in the areas of international relations, diplomacy, Australian studies, history, economy and trade. The contributions range from China-Australia trade and political relations, energy cooperation, Australia's energy strategy, to Australian culture and identity, and people-to-people exchanges between China and Australia, and provide an overview of the development of Sino-Australian relations in the past 40 years and discuss some of major current issues and challenges concerning bilateral relations with a Chinese perspective.

We are most honored to have been able to include a contribution from Senator the Honorable Bob Carr, the Foreign Minister of Australia in Chapter 1. This was originally a speech by the foreign minister at the "*The Australian* and *Wall Street Journal* China Conference" held in Sydney, September 14, 2012, where he reviewed the growth and development of Australia-China relations over the past 40 years and made forthright comments on issues that have been causing debates on both sides – Australia-US Alliance and China investment, which serves to clarify Australian government's position on Australia-China relations.

In Chapter 2, Yu Changsen and Chang Chenguang's paper reviews the 40 years of China-Australia relations in political, economic and security spheres. It shows how the relationship has developed from political hostility and isolation to mutual adaptation and accommodation, from mutual economic benefit to greater interdependence, from military confrontation to security exchanges, cooperation and dialogue. The authors argue that, with the rise of China, it is even more important for both governments of Australia and China to recognize the differences between them and show concern and respect for each other's core interests, so that these differences are managed in a way that does not adversely affect our shared interests.

In the third chapter, Jiang Qiliang and Zhang Qiusheng look at the ups and downs in the economic and trade relations between China and Australia. The paper divides the forty years of economic and trade relations into four periods and analyses the remarkable achievements and characteristics. The authors believe that the bilateral economic and trade relationship has exhibited all-dimensional, multi-tiered and wide-ranging interaction patterns, and that the development of bilateral economic and trade relations is closely related to the geopolitical environment and market factors. It is concluded that the general trend of this relationship has been harmonious and stable, although there are problems, such as the "asymmetric interdependence" between the two economies.

Hou Minyue's paper looks at the cooperation between China and Australia in LNG. The arrival of the first shipment of Australian LNG in May 2006 at Dapeng LNG Co. Ltd., in Guangdong heralded the commencement of China's imports of natural gas on a considerable scale. Australia has provided approximately 50% of China's total LNG imports over the past few years. Hou predicts that Australia will remain a major LNG supplier to China in the years to come and play a positive role in improving China's primary energy consumption structure, energy security and the quality of environment. The paper also points out that, while increasingly yielding tremendous economic and social benefits, China-Australia gas collaboration is also facing some issues, which need to be dealt with properly.

Chapter 5 reviews Australia's new energy strategies. In this paper, Tang Xiaosong and Xu Xi analyze some of the new shifts in Australia's energy strategy and policy, based on documents such as the *National Energy Security Assessment*, and *Strategic Directions for Energy White Paper*, and the reasons behind these shifts, and discuss the implications for China by looking at the opportunities and challenges posed by these shifts.

In Chapter 6, Gan Zhenjun and Li Jiashan review Australia's ocean security strategy and its implications for China. The authors believe that the main elements that affect Australia's ocean security strategy have been its geopolitical security and its outlook on ocean, which is a result from its history and culture.

Wang Guanghou's paper in Chapter 7 discusses Australia's policy regarding the South China Sea. As Australia is beginning to pay attention to the situation of the South China Sea, it has become a new external factor which affects the development of the

South China Sea issue. The paper analyzes what motivated Australia's concern over the South China Sea and some of the contradictions between Australia's interests in South China Sea. Wang argues that Australia's fear of China has no basis, and its involvement in the South China Sea will only complicate the issue and affect the development of the regional security pattern. The paper calls for enhancing mutual trust in political and security fields between China and Australia, maintaining the stability of Sino-US relations and carefully handling of the relationship with the related claimers of the South China Sea.

Liu Chen's paper assesses the evolution of China's image on the mass media in Australia in the context of Australia's "Enmeshment with Asia". The paper focuses on China's image interpreted by Australian mass media since the 1990s to examine the principles, genres and techniques implemented. It then goes on to discuss the strategies China should consider. The paper concludes that (1) the political image of China in the mainstream media in Australia has been presented based on obvious agenda-setting; (2) the economic image seems generally more positive and acceptable; and (3) the cultural image has been presented in a stereotypical manner. It is suggested that China should invest more efforts into the cultural communication and the improvement of its political image by taking advantage of the economic bonds between the two countries.

In Chapter 9, Huang Zhong and Tang Xiaosong review the achievements of Australia's public diplomacy. The authors argue that the main reasons of the development of Australia's public diplomacy include the inherent requirements of Australia's "Middle Power" status and particularly its adaptation to the changing regional strategic situation, the demand for the establishment of a positive and responsible national image, and the result of stimulation by global public diplomacy. The paper also analyzes some of the problems in Australia's public diplomacy.

Qian Chaoying's paper focuses on the Australian national identity. Qian discusses this issue in relation to modern international geopolitics, and cultural-political practices in Australia regarding issues of immigrants, aborigines and multi-culturalism. Australia's exploration of her own national identity is shaped by historical factors and the combined effects of domestic and international situations. The paper argues that the ambiguity and indeterminacy regarding identity provide the country with a special adaptability, and serve as a showcase to inform our understanding of "diverse postcolonial situations and multiple identity issues".

In Chapter 11, Yu Changsen analyzes the Australians' perception of and response to the rise of China. It is true that bilateral relations between China and Australia have made tremendous progress, especially in the economic sphere, yet as the author argues, with China's re-emergence as a big regional power, Australia has gradually adjusted its policy towards China, thus leading to a series of frictions. The paper tries to analyze the perceptions of and attitudes towards the rise of China from three different sectors in Australian society: the academia, media and the general public, and the government policy circle. The paper argues for the need of strengthening mutual trust and understanding of each other's concerns and core interests, so as to ensure a healthy development of bilateral relationship, which will contribute to China's peaceful rise and the stability and prosperity of the Asia-Pacific region.

In Chapter 12, Su Ning and Huang Yejing compare the processes of "urban renewal" of Sydney and Shanghai. The paper also discusses the implications for other cities in China and Australia that are going through the same process. It is hoped that such a comparative study will present some important principles for urban renewal, and contribute to our understanding of metropolitan city development under the urbanization process.

We hope the brief synopsis above will serve to introduce the scope and contents of the papers in this volume. What emerges clearly in all the papers is the emphasis on China and Australia being a community with shared interests and that it requires more conversation and discussion to bring this bilateral relationship to a new level. As we celebrate 40 years of diplomatic relations between China and Australia, it is hoped that this collection will contribute to increasing awareness and understanding in China of different aspects of Australia, its foreign policy, society and culture, etc., and help stimulate further discussion in both countries of current issues in China-Australia relations, so that we can all work together to open a new chapter in China-Australia relations, towards more comprehensive and stable cooperation for the common prosperity of our two countries.

The publication of this book is generously supported by Chinese People's Association for Friendship with Foreign Countries, Association of Australia China Friendship and Exchange, and the Kingold Group. We would like to acknowledge our gratitude to Dr. Chau Chak Wing, President of Association of Australia-China Friendship and Exchange, for his support to this publication and to Australian Studies at Sun Yat-sen University. We are greatly indebted to the Honorable Bob Carr, the Foreign Minister of Australia, who agreed to have his speech at the "*The Australian* and *Wall Street Journal* China Conference" included in this special collection. Senator Bob Carr has been a strong proponent of Australia-China friendship and has always been very supportive of the activities of Australian Chinese communities. We are honored to have included a special preface from Ms Li Xiaolin, President of Chinese People's Association for Friendship with Foreign Countries. We are also especially grateful to His Excellency Ambassador Chen Yuming, who has shown his support to our initiative and written a preface for this volume.

Chenguang and Changsen would like to thank the Honorable Henry Tsang OAM, who first initiated this project and has agreed to be the guest editor of this collection. Heartfelt thanks also go to Mr Jim Zheng and Mr Michael Harkins from Kingold for their coordination, and to all our contributors for their cooperation and understanding. We should thank our copy editor from Sun Yat-sen University Press, Dr Xiong Xiyuan, for his efficiency and tolerance, as we have been working to a very tight schedule to get this volume published before December 2012 for the $40^{th}$ anniversary celebration of China-Australia diplomatic relations. We also appreciate Dr Zhao Jing's help in the translation of Bob Carr's paper.

As we celebrate this important milestone in China-Australia relations, it is important to remember all those who have made significant contributions to the development of this relationship. The most important person is of course Gough Whitlam, former Labor Prime Minister of Australia, who, with extraordinary political insight and courage, first visited China in 1971 in the darkest days of the Cold War, and subsequently established diplomatic relationship with China in December 1972 after his election as the Prime Minister. It is Whitlam who marked the beginning of China-Australia relations. We therefore dedicate this collection to Gough Whitlam.

## Notes

[1] Great Transformation, address by His Excellency Ambassador Chen Yuming at the 63rd National Day reception, 28 September, 2012. http://au.china-embassy.org/eng/sgjs/sghd/t974129.htm. See also Geoff Raby, Australia and China Forty Years on. *Meanjin* (Melbourne), 2012, pp90 – 97.

[2] Geoff Raby, Australia and China Forty Years on. *Meanjin* (Melbourne), 2012, pp90 – 97.

[3] Speech by His Excellency Ambassador Chen Yuming at the Conversations in Diplomacy with Coalition Members and Senators, 29 May, 2012. ht-

tp: //au. china-embassy. org/eng/sgjs/sghd/t938496. htm.

[4] Geoff Raby, China's economy: ever upwards, *Australia-China Business Insight* (*The Journal of the Australian Chamber of Commerce in China*). 2012, Vol. 2, Issue 1, p20.

[5] Susan Bliss, Australia's engagement with Asia. Part B: Rising China and flourishing China-Australia relationships, *Geography Bulletin*, 2012, Vol. 44, No. 2, p24. See also Ken Henry's speech at Australia National Conference on Resources and Energy, "Australia's Place in Asia Session", 18 September, 2012. Dr Ken Henry predicts that China will be the largest economy in the world by 2025.

[6] Julia Gillard, Foreword, *Australia-China Business Insight* (*The Journal of the Australian Chamber of Commerce in China*). 2012, Vol. 2, Issue 1, p3.

[7] Speech by His Excellency Ambassador Chen Yuming at the Conversations in Diplomacy with Coalition Members and Senators, 29 May, 2012. http: //au. china-embassy. org/eng/sgjs/sghd/t938496. htm

[8] Australia's relationship with China is subject to a great deal of debate in the media in Australia, often with an overtone of fear. The Lowy Institute Poll 2010, for example, shows that 69% of Australian respondents believe that China's aim is to dominate Asia, 46% interviewees consider China to be a military threat to Australia in the next 20 years, and 55% think that Australia should join with other countries to limit China's influence. http: //www. lowyinstitute. org/ See also Fergus Hanson's discussion on current Australian attitudes towards China in "How your attitudes help shape relations with China", in James Reilly & Jingdong Yuan (eds.), *Australia and China at 40*. Sydney: University of New South Wales Press Ltd. 2012.

[9] Geoff Raby, Australia and China Forty Years on. *Meanjin* (Mel-

bourne), 2012, pp90 – 97. See also David Uren, *The Kingdom and the Quarry: China, Australia, Fear and Greed.* Black Inc. 2012.

[10] The White Paper, released on 28 October, 2012, outlines 25 objectives for Australia to achieve by 2025. http://asiancentury.dpmc.gov.au/sites/default/files/white-paper/australia-in-the-asian-century-white-paper.pdf

# 1

# Australia in the China Century*

Bob Carr

---

I would like to congratulate the Australian Studies Centre, Sun Yat-sen University on the publication of the book *China-Australia Relations: Towards a Community with Shared Interests*, dedicated to the Honourable Gough Whitlam.

On Monday July 5, 1971, Gough Whitlam had his historic meeting with Premier Zhou En Lai – a very public affair, in the great Hall of the People, from 9pm to midnight, before a large audience of Chinese officials and Australian journalists.

Four days later, in deepest secrecy, Dr. Kissinger arrived in Beijing for his own talks with Premier Zhou. He rightly reported back to President Nixon: "Our announcement will shake the world." Gough was, typically, more modest. When President Nixon revealed all, on world-wide television on July 15, the most

---

* This paper is based on the keynote address by Senator the Honourable Bob Carr, the Foreign Minister of Australia at the "The Australian and Wall Street Journal China Conference", Sydney, September 14, 2012.

he would claim was "at least it made Australia look less flatfooted, less imitative".

Mentioning these events of 41 years ago – perhaps the Chinese might say a mere 41 years ago – I don't want to assert some kind of political ownership of Australia's China Policy. Indeed, the continuity under successive governments, Labor and Liberal, underwrites its success.

But I make two points: the Whitlam visit of 1971 cleared the way for Australia's recognition of the People's Republic of China on the basis of the clear and firm undertakings spelt out on that night in the Great Hall of the People. And second, the visit, and the interview with Premier Zhou En Lai, expressed certain fundamentals about the relations between China and Australia which grow in relevance by the year.

The first of these fundamentals was, simply, facing the realities of China's existence, its place in the region and the world as the home of a quarter of the world's population and a unique civilisation. The second fundamental was that China could and should return to its rightful place as a constructive member of the international community. The third fundamental was that China's return would open immense opportunities – mutual opportunities – for the region, by no means limited to trade.

In 2012, all this may sound trite. It certainly wasn't 40 years ago.

One of the great achievements of the Nixon-Kissinger initiative was to strip away the Cold War attitudes which saw China merely as an extension of a communist monolith from the Baltic Sea to the South China Sea. The more powerful and decisive precisely because the initiative came from Richard Nixon, with peerless Cold War credentials.

Let me state a fourth fundamental which was clearly put forward by Whitlam in Beijing in July 1971. It is the primary importance of our relationship with the United States and of a strong American presence in Asia and the Pacific. Remember that the United States and Australia were still in Vietnam. Australia had entered that war on the spurious argument advanced by Sir Robert Menzies that it was "part of the downward thrust of China between the Indian and the Pacific Oceans".

My party's opposition to Australia's involvement was based partly on the belief that defeat or humiliation would weaken, not strengthen, America's position in the region.

In Beijing in 1971, Premier Zhou did in fact - very skilfully and politely - invite Whitlam to repudiate the alliance by "suggesting that America would prove an unreliable ally" as the Soviet Union was proving an unreliable ally for China.

We sometimes hear echoes of this argument today from Chinese commentators. But note Whitlam's immediate reply - and remember this was back in 1971 -

> "I must say with respect I see no parallel in the Sino-Soviet Pact and the ANZUS Treaty. There has been no similar deterioration between Australia and the United States as

between China and the Soviet Union".

I mention this only to emphasise – as I have emphasised to Chinese interlocutors – that the Australia-US alliance is a very long-term, fundamental fact of life. Those fundamentals must include a prospering and outward-looking China and a confident and forward-looking America. Australia is well-placed to help effect those outcomes in our region.

In charting our future course, we will draw on our very positive experiences of the past 40 years. We are accumulating resources of experience and knowledge over a wide range – in business, diplomacy, education, health services, technology, agriculture, language and the arts – which will prove as important, in their own way, as the minerals and the products we export to China. We talk about 40 years ago and call it history. The Chinese, of course, take a longer view.

In my own visits to China, not so spectacular but always rewarding, I've been struck by how quickly conversations with officials in government and people in the capitalist sector turn to the parallels of Chinese history. On one occasion, a party official spoke to me about how "China had opened to the world", and the world had opened to China.

He was talking about what happened during the Tang Dynasty 618 – 907. Coming to more recent times that parvenu Westerners might be more familiar with, Chinese officials will refer to the 19th century – the years of the Opium Wars, the unequal treaties and territorial concessions forced by the European powers on the Ching dynasty in its fatal decline. And this is important for anyone who wants to understand China today.

China will never again submit to the humiliations, the unequal treatment, the crushing indignities, and the loss of sovereignty that came from the weakness of the Chinese State and the impotence of its rulers in the 19th century. This remains a very real factor in Chinese thinking.

But, of course, the overwhelming factor for us to consider today is the Chinese revolution. Not Mao's revolution. Not the Cultural Revolution, its dire effects still at work when Nixon and Kissinger and Whitlam made their first visits. I mean the revolution set in train by Deng Xiaoping after 1978. And, in particular, by the new impetus given to reform policies by Deng's southern tour of 1992. The Chinese themselves recognise its historic significance. They marked its 20th anniversary this year. I've called it, with deliberate provocation, Deng's revolution of 1978, the only successful revolution of the 20th century.

But just look at its scope. It has resulted in a faster and longer modernisation, urbanisation and industrialisation than anything before it in history. More dramatic than Europe's Industrial Revolution beginning in Britain in the 1780's – just about the time when the 700 convicts were struggling to stay alive on the shores of Sydney Cove. It's a faster industrialisation on a bigger scale than that of the United States in the 70 years after the Civil War. China is truly globalising, becoming part of the world around it. A huge middle class is emerging. A consumer market bigger than anything world has ever seen.

By 2030, China should have approximately 1 billion middle class consumers compared to 365 million in the U. S. and 414 million in Western Europe. Of course – its transformation is still underway – and change is patchy. But many of the material changes in peoples' lives are dramatic. We can see those changes through our four diplomatic missions in China – Beijing, Shanghai, Guangzhou, and Hong Kong.

I asked each of our diplomatic posts to provide me with a picture of what's occurring on the ground – this is what they sent back. Twenty years ago, one powerful image of China was cities like Beijing and Shanghai teeming with millions of bicycles in the streets. In 1978, private cars were unheard of. By July 2012, according to the China Association of Automobile Manufacturers, 5 million people in Beijing had their own car. In 2007, the Chinese high speed rail system didn't exist. By mid-2011 – the space of only four years – there was nearly 10,000km of high speed track. Guangzhou will build more than 300 kilometres of metro railway over the next decade.

The pace of economic and social change in China is intense. China's massive urbanisation – a faster rebalancing of the city/rural divide than the world has ever seen – has made moving to find work a way of life for many Chinese. In 1994, there were only 2.64 million internal migrants in China, according to the Chinese Academy of Social Science. But by the end of last year, there were 250 million. Higher incomes are inevitably transforming Chinese life. Many of the restrictions associated with Communist rule have been wound back, as economic success has reached more and more of China.

It's the details that fascinate. China is now the world's fastest growing wine consumption market. In 1999, retail wine sales were only 3.76 billion RMB. By 2008, this increased to about 20 billion RMB, an average annual increase rate of about 20 per cent. Shopping habits have changed too – driven by the emerging middle class that will, at some point, dwarf the American consumer. In less than 10 years, the volume of fine art sales at public auctions in mainland China has rocketed from next to nothing to 41 per cent of the global market.

Travel is playing its part in China's opening to the world. Tourism in and out of China has soared. There are now as many Chinese tourists abroad as there are foreign tourists in China. Many more international visitors now go to Shanghai – from just 240,200 international visitors in 1978 to 8.5 million in 2010. (In 2000, this figure was 1.8 million). In 2011, mainland visitors numbered more than 1.7 million and constituted nearly a third of the total foreign visitors to Taiwan that year. Mainland tourists have revitalised Taiwan's tourism industry and there are now more than 550 flights per week between the Mainland and Taiwan. Life expectancy has grown dramatically. Women in Hong Kong now have the second highest life expectancy in the world – nearly 87 years. In Shanghai average life expectancy has grown from 73 in 1975 to 82 in 2010.

Sport is perhaps the clearest emblem of China's integration with the world. In just 12 years, we have seen China emerge as an Olympic powerhouse. And Australia helped. The Australian Olympic Committee gave generous support to China to ensure the success of the 2008 Beijing Games. Before the Sydney Olympics, China was simply not in the race. What a different story in London. Sport has become an increasingly important part of everyday Chinese life. The Asian Games were held in Guangzhou in 2010. Fifty three facilities were built or refurbished for competition, 17 for training. They have now become part of the Guangzhou's sporting landscape, including China's first cricket stadium.

I recalled that Neville Wran established a sister-province relationship between NSW and Guangdong, back in 1979, when Guangzhou, the capital of Guangdong was known as Canton. It was a world first. I might point out that Guangzhou provides an interesting example of the increased openness in China. In July, Guangzhou broadcast the Municipal People's Congress Standing Committee meeting live, the first broadcast of its kind. The webcast was on the official website of the Guangzhou city People's Congress, as well as several other local websites. Live broadcasts will help citizens better understand the People's Congress system and increase government transparency. Guangzhou plans to webcast 15 such meetings this year. Small steps, but China is opening up.

China's economic gains are certainly impressive, but as the World Bank warned earlier this year, China by 2030 risks falling into the "middle-income" trap – languishing on low incomes and low rates of growth. To avoid this trap, the World Bank calls for a burst of economic reform to strengthen the foundations of a market based economy – enhancing human capital, protecting the environment and creating the systems, rules and policies to increase competition. The most important of these reforms will be to integrate the Chinese financial sector into the global financial system. China is already taking the necessary first steps – in August the government handed out US $1.34 billion of new quotas to allow foreign fund managers to invest in Chinese financial markets. If it can accelerate these reforms, China will achieve the goal of high-income status by 2030.

So where's Australia in this picture? Everybody knows about Australia's resources trade with China. We are its biggest supplier of iron ore. Its second biggest supplier of coal. And its third biggest supplier of LNG. But we are working together in other areas as well.

As it grapples with the expectations of its new middle class, and its ageing population, China has been increasingly interested in Australia's social security, health and welfare systems. Australia is working with Chinese auto companies to develop new, green technologies – including a strategic cooperation agreement in Guangzhou to develop the infrastructure for electric vehicles.

Australia's services exports to China, valued at A $5.7 billion in 2011, are dominated by educational and recreational travel and have averaged annual growth of 11.3 per cent over the past five years. Our higher education sector is doing an impressive job in attracting Chinese students. China is Australia's largest source of overseas students, with almost 160, 000 enrolments in Australian educational institutions in 2011. And China itself is taking the improvement of its own education sector seriously – it now has 22 universities ranked in the world's top 500, up from 12 just eight years ago.

By 2030, China is expected to have up to 200 million graduates, more than the entire workforce of the United States. In the past 5 years, virtually all leading Australian cultural institutions have established Chinese art programs or collaborations with Chinese counterparts.

The Australian Ballet's 50th Anniversary will include a performance by China's National Ballet. The National Portrait Gallery will host the largest exhibition of contemporary Chinese portraits to be ever held in Australia from September 2012 to February 2013. Of course, we want to see more. We particularly want to see more investment between our two countries. And we should resist the temptation of falling back on narrow, nationalistic sloganeering when it comes to Chinese investment in Australia. The fact is, foreign direct investment from China equated to just 2.6 per cent of the total FDI stock in 2011. The top four source countries were the United States, the United Kingdom, Japan and the Netherlands. The European Union, as a region, remains Australia's largest source of foreign investment, accounting for close to 34 per cent of total FDI.

As my predecessor Alexander Downer wrote in the *Adelaide*

*Advertiser* this week (Sept. 10), "Asian money is just as good as US or British money". China has made progress in opening up its economy, but there is still more to do – on currency, capital controls, and investment. And it is true that there are still many barriers to investment. But the idea that foreign ownership of Australian mines or farms will somehow limit our control over production or undermine our food security is simply not correct. Australian Federal, State and Local governments make decisions about land zoning; they set the environmental standards; they legislate the investment rules. As former NSW Premier Neville Wran once said, when pressed on questions about foreign investment in real estate, "they can't take it with them".

As I began with Henry Kissinger, I might conclude by quoting from someone whose actions and thoughts on this subject over four decades entitle him to be heard with respect. In his latest book on China – and that is its simple title, *On China*, Kissinger writes:

> The question ultimately comes down to what the United States and China can realistically ask of each other. An explicit American project to organise Asia on the basis of containing China on creating a bloc of democratic states for an ideological crusade is unlikely to succeed – in part because China is an indispensable trading partner for most of its neighbours. By the same token, a Chinese attempt to exclude American from Asia economic and security affairs will similarity meet serious resistance from almost all other Asian states, which fear the consequences of a region dominated

by a single power (p. 256).

That seems to me a wisely balanced statement of the realities we face in our region in this century. It recognises the fundamentals that have shaped Australian policy over the past 40 years. Within those realities and fundamentals there is ample scope for Australian action and influence, for what Henry Kissinger calls "co-evolution", whereby "both countries pursue their domestic imperatives, co-operating where possible and adjusting their relations to minimise conflict".

The South China Sea is one arena where the United States, China and the ASEAN countries will need to find a peaceful co-evolution. Our national interest is to ensure the great success story of this century, the Asian economic transformation, is not distracted by strategic competition in the South China Sea.

At the very least, because we got the fundamentals right from 1972 on, I believe Australia can approach the exciting and challenging developments in our region – including the evolution of US-China relations – with clarity, consistency and confidence.

Finally, I would like to congratulate the authors again on their initiative. As we celebrate the 40th anniversary of diplomatic relations between Australia and China, I find the publication of this book highly significant in that it will further stimulate discussion in both countries about how we can better move our bilateral relations to a new level in this new era, which will help enhance our mutual understanding and trust.

[译文]

# 置身中国世纪的澳大利亚*

## 鲍勃·卡尔

首先我要祝贺中山大学澳大利亚研究中心正式出版特别献给高夫·惠特拉姆阁下的《中澳关系大趋势：利益共同体的构建与展望》一书。

1971 年 7 月 5 日星期一，高夫·惠特拉姆与周恩来总理在人民大会堂进行了具有历史意义的会晤。这次非常公开的会晤从晚上九点一直持续到深夜，众多的中国官员与澳大利亚记者也在会晤期间列席。

四天后，在绝对保密的情况下，基辛格博士到达北京与周恩来总理进行会晤。正如基辛格向尼克松总统的汇报中所说："这个消息将震撼全世界。"高夫则更为谦逊低调。当尼克松总统在 7 月 15 日通过电视向全世界宣告此消息时，高夫只这样回应："这至少让澳大利亚显得没那么措手不及，亦步亦趋。"

---

* 本文基于澳大利亚外长、参议员鲍勃·卡尔阁下在 2012 年 9 月 4 日《澳大利亚人报》与《华尔街日报》联合在悉尼举办的"置身中国世纪的澳大利亚论坛"上发表的主旨演讲。

回顾41年前的往事（或许中国人会说那仅仅是41年前而已），我并不是想宣称我们对澳大利亚对华政策的政治所有权。事实上，历届政府对华政策的持续性，不论是工党或是自由党，保证了中澳关系的成功与发展。

但我要提出两点：第一，惠特拉姆1971年访华，在那天晚上人民大会堂里所做的清晰而坚定的承诺的基础上，为澳大利亚承认中华人民共和国的国际地位扫清了障碍。第二，那次访问以及与周恩来总理的会晤，明确表达了中澳关系发展的一些基本原则，这些原则越来越具有现实意义。

第一条原则，很简单，面对现实，即中国的存在、中国在本地区的地位、中国作为全球四分之一人口的家园以及中国是一个独特的文明这些现实。其次，中国作为国际社会中有建设性的一员能够并且理应回归到国际社会中。第三，中国的回归将给该地区带来不可限量的机遇——相互的机遇——而这些机遇绝不仅限于贸易领域。

在2012年，这些话听起来都是老生常谈。但40年前却完全不同。

尼克松与基辛格倡议的重要作用之一在于破除了冷战偏见。这种偏见将中国仅仅视为从波罗的海到南中国海的共产主义庞然大物的延伸。这一倡议之所以显得更加有力、更加关键也在于它是由理查德·尼克松这位具有不可比拟的冷战资历的总统提出来的。

让我再阐述一下惠特拉姆1971年7月在北京时就已经清楚明确地表达过的第四个基本原则，即美澳关系的重要性以及一个强大的美国在亚太地区存在的重要性。要记住，当年美国与澳大利亚都身处越战困境。当时罗伯特·孟席斯先生声称，越战是“中国在印度洋和太平洋之间的南侵”，由于受到其谬误的言论的影响，澳大利亚参与到战争当中。

我的政党反对澳大利亚参战，部分原因是因为我们认为，无论是战胜还是战败蒙羞，都只能削弱而非加强美国在这一地区的地位。

周恩来总理1971年在北京确曾非常巧妙且礼貌地建议惠特拉姆与美国终止联盟关系。周总理暗示“美国将被证明是一个不可靠的盟友”，就如当时已经证明苏联不是中国可靠的盟友一样。

我们有时会从中国评论员那里听到类似的观点。但是，应当注意惠特拉姆的立即回应，而且要记住那是在1971年：

> “恕我直言，我并不认为《中苏条约》与《澳新美安全条约》具有可比性。美澳关系中不曾出现过类似中苏关系的恶化情况。”

我提到这一点只是想强调，就像我向中方对话者所强调的，美澳联盟关系由来已久且意义重要。那些基本原则中必须涵盖一个日渐繁荣且开放的中国与一个自信也具有远见的美国。澳大利亚所处的地位正好能促使这些目标在亚太地区成为现实。

在描绘我们未来的前景时，我们将从过去40年的积极经历中吸取经验。我们在包括商业、外交、教育、医疗服务、技术、农业、语言以及艺术等多个领域已经积累了丰富的交流经验与知识资源。这些领域都以他们各自的方式证明它们与我们对中国的矿石与产品出口一样重要。我们谈到40年前即称之为历史，而中国人看得更为长远。

我个人对中国的访问没有像惠特拉姆访华那样意义非凡，但也总是成果丰硕。给我印象深刻的是，与政府官员及商业领域的人士之间的谈话总能被迅速地转到中国历史上并加以对比。有一次，一位共产党官员跟我聊起“中国是如何向世界开放的”，以及世界向中国的开放。

他说的是唐代（公元618—907年）发生的事情。如果是谈到西方新贵可能更熟悉的近代，中国官员会提到19世纪，也就是鸦片战争时期，欧洲列强逼迫衰弱的清政府签订一系列不平等条约和割让土地。了解这一点，对每一个想了解当今中国的人来说都是十分重要的。

中国绝对不会再次屈服于外来的凌辱、不平等的待遇以及主权的丧失。19世纪发生的一切都是因为中国的衰弱和统治者的无能。这在中国人的心目中依然是一个非常实在的因素。

当然，现在最需要我们考虑的因素是中国的革命。这里，我不是指毛泽东发起的革命，也不是“文化大革命”，其可怕的影响在尼克松、基辛格和惠特拉姆首次访问中国的时候仍在蔓延。我指的是1978年以来由邓小平带领的革命，尤其是1992年邓小平南巡之后，为中国注入巨大活力的改革开放政策。中国人明白改革开放的历史意义，并于今年纪念邓小平南巡20周年。我故意将之称为邓小平1978年的革命，这是20世纪唯一成功的革命。

让我们看看它的规模。它带来了史无前例的快速持久的现代化、城市化和工业化。它比18世纪80年代源于英国的欧洲工业革命更加引人注目，那时700个被放逐澳洲的囚犯正在悉尼湾上艰难求生。它比美国内战结束后70年里开展的工业化规模更大、速度更快。中国的确正在全球化，成为周边世界的一部分。庞大的中产阶级正在形成。其消费市场更是前所未有地巨大。

到2030年，中国将会有大约10亿的中产阶级消费者，而美国数字是3.65亿，西欧则是4.14亿。当然，中国的转型仍在进行中，而且变化参差不齐。但是中国民众生活的实际变化是巨大的。我们可以通过在北京、上海、广州、香港这四个城市的外交使领馆见证这些变化。

我要求我们的外交使领馆给我提供当地正在发生的事件的概貌，下面是他们给我的反馈。20年前，中国一个鲜明的形象就是北京和上海这样的城市塞满成千上万的自行车。1978年，人们还没有听说过私家车。至2012年7月为止，根据中国汽车制造商协会的数据，北京私家车拥有量达到5百万辆。2007年，中国还没有高速铁路系统，而仅仅四年后，到了2011年中期，中国的高速铁路已经建设到将近1万公里。广州将在接下来的十年中修建超过300公里的地铁。

中国的经济社会变化的速度非常快。中国在进行大规模的城镇化，以前所未有的速度重新平衡城乡差异，这也使迁徙寻找工作成为许多中国人的一种生活方式。根据中国社会科学院的统计，1994年，中国仅仅有大约264万的国内流动人口。但是到去年底，这个数字达到了2.5亿。更高的收入不可避免地改变着中国人的生活。随着经济发展的成果惠及越来越多的中国人，许多与共产主义管制相关的限制已经被取消。

真正令人叹为观止是一些细节。中国现在是世界上发展最快速的红酒消费市场。1999年，红酒零售额只有37.6亿人民币。到2008年，这个数字增加到了大约200亿元，年均增速大约是20%。由于中国的新兴中产阶级的增长，消费习惯也在改变，他们在未来的某一天会超过美国消费者。在不到十年的时间里，中国大陆公开拍卖的艺术品的数额从几乎为零，飞速增长到了现在占全球市场的41%。

旅游对中国对外开放起着重要的作用。境内外旅游发展迅猛，到境外旅游的中国人与到中国旅游的外国人一样多。到上海的境外游客已从1978年的240,200人增长到了2010年的850万人（2000年境外游客数量为180万人）。2011年，到台湾的大陆游客达到170万人，占当年赴台境外游客总人数的三分之一。大陆游客使台湾旅游业重获新生。现在，每周超过550班航班来往于大陆和台湾。中国人预期寿命大幅增长。香港女性预期寿命近87岁，位居世界第二。上海人的平均预期寿命已从1975年的73岁增长到了2010年的82岁。

体育或许是中国融入世界最显著的标志。在12年中，我们目睹中国发展成为奥林匹克强国。这其中有澳大利亚的帮助。为确保2008年北京奥运会的成功举办，澳大利亚奥组委向中国提供了慷慨的支持和帮助。就在悉尼奥运会之前，中国在奥运会上的表现仍是差强人意。到伦敦奥运会，中国的表现就完全不一样了。体育运动在中国人生活中已占据日益重要的地位。广州于2010年举办了亚运会，新建或修缮了53处用于比赛的场馆和17项用于训练的设施，它们已经成为广州运动景观的一部分，其中包括中国首个板球馆。

我记得耐威尔·冉早在1979年就缔结了新南威尔士州和广东省的姐妹省州关系，那时，广东的省会广州还被称为Canton。这在世界上是首例。广州是个有趣的范例，它展现了不断开放的中国。今年7月，广州对广州市人民代表大会常务委员会会议进了现场直播，此举尚属首次。这次直播是通过广州市人大的官方网站和其他几家地方网站进行的。这种现场直播不仅能加深市民对人民代表大会制度的认识，也能增加政府透明度。广州今年计划网络直播15场人大常委会会议。步子虽然不大，但显示了中国正在开放。

中国的经济增长的确令人钦佩，但世界银行早在年初就提到中国有可能在2030年陷入“中等收入”陷阱，也就是在低收入，低增长率中徘徊。为避免这种陷阱，世界银行呼吁通过一系列经济改革来稳固以市场为基础的经济，提高人力资本，保护环境，创立鼓励竞争的规则、条例和政策。改革的关键是将中国的金融业融入全球金融体系。中国已迈出了关键的第一步，8月，政府新发放了价值13.4亿美元的份额，让外国基金经理来中国金融市场投资。如果能加快这些改革，中国将会在2030年跻身高收入国家。

那么澳大利亚在此之中发挥什么作用呢？中澳两国的资源贸易已众所周知。我们是中国铁矿石进口的第一大供给国，煤炭进口第二大供给国，液化天然气进口第三大供给国。然而我们在其他领域也有合作。

为应对新兴中产阶级的期待和老龄化的人口，中国对澳大利亚实行的社会保障、医疗和福利制度的兴趣逐渐增长。澳大利亚正同中国汽车公司一起研发新的绿色环保技术，其中包括在广州签署的为发展电动车辆进行基础设施建设的战略合作协议。

澳大利亚对中国的服务出口的总价值2011年已经达到57亿澳元，这其中主要包括教育和休闲旅游，在过去五年内的年均增速为11.3%。我们的高等教育部门在吸引中国留学生这方面很有建树。中国是澳大利亚最大的留学生来源国，2011年就有将近16万名学生在澳大利亚的教育机构登记入学。而中国自己的教育部门也正在不断改善——8年前，中国只有12所大学挤进世界前500名，而如今已经增长到了22所。

到2030年，中国预期会有2亿大学毕业生，比整个美国的全部劳动人口还多。在过去五年里，几乎所有主要的澳大利亚文化机构都开设了中国艺术项目或是与中国对应的机构建立合作关系。

澳大利亚芭蕾舞团50周年庆典将会包括中国国家芭蕾舞团的表演。2012年9月至2013年2月，澳大利亚国家肖像美术馆将会举办澳大利亚有史以来最大的当代中国肖像展。当然，我们期待着更多的交流，尤其是两国间更多的投资。在有关中国在澳大利亚投资的问题上，我们要拒绝回到狭隘民族主义当道、人们空喊口号的那种状态。事实上，2011年来自中国的投资只占据了外商直接投资总额的2.6%。名列前四位的分别是美国、英国、日本和荷兰。欧盟作为一个地区，依然还是澳大利亚最大的外商投资来源，占据外商直接投资总额的34%。

正如我的前任亚历山大·唐纳这周（9月10号）在《阿德雷德广告报》上所说的那样，“亚洲的钱和美国或英国的钱一样值钱”。中国在打开经济大门上已经取得很大进步，但在货币、资本控制和投资等方面仍需提高。诚然，投资壁垒还有不少，有人担心，外资占有澳大利亚的矿藏或农场多少会限制我们对生产的控制或者威胁到食品安全，这样的想法是不正确的。澳大利亚联邦政府、州政府和地方政府会决定不同区域的划分；他们会设定环保标准；他们会制订投资的相关法律法规。正如新南威尔士州前州长耐威尔·冉在被逼问关于外商投资房地产的问题时所说，“反正那些房地产他们也带不走”。

我用亨利·基辛格的故事开头，我想再引用他的一段话作为结尾。基辛格在中国问题领域有40多年的经验和思考，我们应当满怀敬意地聆听他的看法。在他最新的一本论中国的书中，而这本书的书名就是简简单单的《论中国》，他写到：

> 最终的关键是美国和中国究竟能现实地向对方索取多少。美国企图通过在亚洲建立一个民主国家集团来遏制中国、进行意识形态圣战的计划是不太可能成功的，这部分是因为中国是其大部分邻国不可或缺的贸易伙伴。同样，中国若试图把美国排除在亚洲经济和安全事务之外，也会遭到几乎所有其他亚洲国家的反对，因为他们害怕出现某单一霸权统治整个地区的结局（p. 256）。

在我看来，这似乎是对本世纪本区域现实状况明智而平衡的论述。它体现了过去40年来影响澳大利亚政策的基本原则。在此现实和原则之下，澳大利亚有足够的空间去采取行动，施加影响，以实现基辛格所说的“协同演变”，即“两国都努力处理好国内事务，并在可能的情况下进行合作，并调整关系将冲突减至最小”。

在南中国海，美国、中国和东盟国家需要找到一种和平的“协同演变”。我们的国家利益就是确保本世纪的成功，即亚洲经济转型，不受到南中国海的战略竞争的干扰。

自1972年起我们便正确把握住这些基本原则，我坚信澳大利亚必将以明确、一致和自信的姿态去迎接包括中美关系演变在内的本地区令人激动而又富于挑战的发展。

最后，我想再次祝贺本书作者们的努力。在我们庆祝澳中建交40周年之际，我认为本书的出版具有重要意义，因为它将进一步激发双方讨论如何在这个新的时代更好地将双边关系推向新的水平，这将有助于增进相互理解与信任。

# 2

# 中澳关系面面观：写在中澳建交40周年之际*

喻常森　常晨光

中华人民共和国政府与澳大利亚联邦政府于1972年12月正式建交，至今40周年了。中澳关系在这40年期间发生了重大的变化。特别是在进入21世纪以后，两国在各自的对外战略地位明显上升。随着近年来中澳两国经济贸易关系的飞速发展，两国之间的相互依存程度日益加深。目前，澳大利亚是中国主要的外部能源供应地，中国是澳大利亚最大的对外贸易伙伴。两国均从这种产业分工中获得极大的比较利益。但是，由于中澳两国存在着明显的主流传统价值观和政治文化差异性，反映在对外政策问题上有着各自不同的理解和考虑。随着中国的强势崛起，中澳关系处于重要的调整和转换时期。未来发展既取决于国际格局的变化，也取决于两国政治家对共同利益的认知，对分歧的妥善处理。本文将

* 本文为中山大学大洋洲研究中心2012年度招标项目“中国与澳大利亚建交40周年：历史经验与发展现状研究”的前期成果。

通过简单的历史回顾，重点从政治、经济和军事安全等三个方面透视中澳关系的现状与特点。

## 政治上：从相互隔离到相互调适

20世纪70年代初，中澳成功实现建交，这既是中国和平共处外交战略的实际运用，也是澳大利亚外交政策重大调整的结果。

从20世纪50年代至60年代中期，中国与澳大利亚分属东方和西方两个不同的“冷战”阵营，双方采取针锋相对的外交政策。中国官方的宣传报道倾向于将追随美国政策的澳大利亚政府称作为“美帝国主义的反动走狗”，并在舆论上支持澳大利亚共产党活动。澳大利亚联邦政府则与盘踞台湾地区的“中华民国”政府保持官方外交关系，与大陆地区的中华人民共和国则处于政治隔离状态。

20世纪60年代中期以后，中国由原来的社会主义阵营中的重要支柱国家演变为奉行独立自主外交政策的中间力量。中苏由意识形态盟友走向明显分裂，使西方国家认识到社会主义阵营并非铁板一块。此后，中国的外交政策表现出更大的灵活性与多元化，从而给中国与西方国家的接触以及关系的正常化打开了大门。1971年11月，中华人民共和国取代“中华民国”成为联合国会员国和安理会常任理事国。1972年春天，美国总统尼克松访华，两国签署了《联合公报》。新中国国际地位的提高和中美关系的缓和，极大地消除了西方及部分周边国家对中国的敌意和怀疑，中国迎来了一个新的建交高峰。澳大利亚及时把握住这一有利时机，积极开拓与中国的关系。

而恰在此时，澳大利亚也正在经历一次内政外交政策的重大转向。1971 年英国签署加入欧共体条约以后，逐步取消了英联邦特惠制，[1]使传统上依靠英联邦市场的澳大利亚经济受到严重影响。没有英国的保护，对于没有自己自然区域的澳大利亚来说，很难在大洋洲生存下来，更不用说发展。1971 年 7 月，应中国人民外交学会邀请，澳大利亚工党领袖高夫·惠特拉姆率领的澳大利亚工党代表团对中国进行了历史性的访问，受到了中国国务院总理周恩来、外交部部长姬鹏飞、外贸部部长白相国和中国人民外交学会会长张奚若等的友好接待。在 1972 年的大选中，工党击败自由—国家党联盟而实现组阁，惠特拉姆成为澳大利亚新总理。惠特拉姆执政后，首先废除了推行半个多世纪的“白澳政策”，实行开放平等的移民政策，这是一个向包括中国在内的广大亚洲国家示好的重大举措。随即，澳大利亚在经济上加速向亚洲靠拢，在外交上加大与亚太国家的联系。在这个背景下，中澳建交乃是大势所趋。

1972 年 12 月 21 日，中国驻法国大使黄镇与澳大利亚驻法国大使雷诺夫分别代表两国政府签署《中澳关于建立外交关系的联合公报》（以下简称《联合公报》），宣布两国建立正式外交关系。《联合公报》指出：“（中澳）两国政府同意，在互相尊重主权和领土完整、互不侵犯、互不干涉内政、平等互利和和平共处的原则的基础上，发展两国之间的外交、友好和合作关系。”“澳大利亚政府承认中华人民共和国政府是中国的唯一合法政府，承认中国政府关于台湾是中华人民共和国的一个省的立场，并决定于一九七三年一月二十五日前从台湾撤走其官方代表机构。”[2] 1973年4月24日，澳大利亚首任驻中华人民共和国特命全权大使斯蒂芬·菲茨杰拉德向中华人民共和国代主席董必武递交了国书。5月17日，中华人民共和国首任驻澳大利亚特命全权大使王国权向澳大利亚总督保罗·哈斯勒克递交了国书，从而，标志着中澳两国完成了官方建交程序。1973年10月，澳总理惠特拉姆对中国进行正式访问，周恩来总理亲自主持会谈，毛泽东主席和邓小平副总理分别会见了澳大利亚代表团一行。

建交以后，中澳两国签署了一系列促进经济文化交流与合作的协定，双方关系发展比较平稳。但是，两国由于传统文化差异、政治制度分野以及现实国际政治结构制约，难以迅速成为志同道合的朋友，在政治上经历了一个相互调适的过程。

中国是一个以儒家文化为主体文化价值观的东方大国，儒家文化主张集体主义、等级观念、尊崇权威。而澳大利亚是属于西方盎格鲁－撒克逊文化的继承者，主张实用主义、竞争意识、权力意识与平等思想。在政治制度上，中国是共产党领导下一党长期执政的社会主义国家，而澳大利亚继承了英国式的君主立宪之下的议会民主制国家，多党制在实际中体现为两党轮流执政。中澳两国在民主、人权、宗教自由等方面有着不同的理解和观念分歧。由于两国主体价值观和政治理念差异而导致现实政策冲突是中澳关系历史上最突出的深层次本质问题。虽然双方都试图在平等基础上开展友好对话，但是分歧和摩擦难以在短期内消弭。例如，在澳大利亚的要求下，从1997年开始，中澳建立人权对话论坛，目前已经举行了13届。在人权问题上，中国始终认为，人权必须建立在各国人民基本的生存与发展状况基础之上，而且必须与整个国家的经济社会发展水平相适应。澳大利亚主张天赋人权观，把政治平等与宗教自由看成是最崇高的人权，而且，倾向于认为人权高于主权。正是由于这些基本价值判断差异，澳大利亚政府允许中国西藏分裂分子达赖喇嘛以宗教人士的身份，允许新疆分裂分子热比娅以政治民主派人士身份访问澳大利亚。而中国坚持认为，澳大利亚政府这样做是在纵容中国的分裂势力，是对中国内政的严重干涉和不友好行为，因而对澳大利亚提出强烈批评。相应的，中国对澳大利亚的这些指责，又反过来被澳大利亚认为是对它的内政干涉，因为，澳大利亚认为，它有权决定该怎么做和不该怎么做。另外一个典型事例是，2008 年 4 月，澳大利亚总理陆克文访华期间，自告奋勇地提出要做中国的“诤友”，[3] 提出双方进行开诚布公的政治对话，但并没有得到中国方面的积极反应。中国倾向认为，在目前西方占据国际政治话语优势的情境下，“诤友”很容易被理解为“老师”或者“教父”，中国只能是学生或者门徒，从而掉进“西方优越论”的窠臼。这对目前综合国力迅速上升时期的中国民族主义者和政治精英们来说是无论如何难以接受的。而且，“诤友”的前提条件是心心相印，但就目前中澳双方的政治信任程度来说，很难做到这一点。

由于中澳两国存在的政治和文化差异及误解在短期内难以消除，遇上突发事件，就会点燃不满情绪，处置不当就会危及双边关系的健康发展。例如，2009 年，中澳关系因一系列事态发展而几至跌入底谷。先是 2009 年春天，澳大利亚国防部公布新版《国防白皮书》，明确将中国当成是澳大利亚的潜在威胁。无独有偶，该年夏天，中国政法部门以违反国家安全罪名逮捕了澳大利亚力拓矿业集团驻上海办事处主任胡士泰，随后又改为以经济贿赂罪对其进行起诉，并判处其有期徒刑10年。而澳大利亚民众普遍认为，此举是中国政府对中国铝业公司稍前并购力拓股份遭拒所实施的打击报复，是一种明显的恃强凌弱行为。[4]同年秋天，中国新疆分裂分子热比娅前往澳大利亚，受到澳大利亚媒体的热捧，引起中国的强烈不满。中澳两国主流媒体在当年围绕上述事件展开了一场舆论大战，相互指责对方干涉内政，攻击对方的社会制度和文化。澳大利亚学术界也加入了这场大辩论。主流学者们相对理性地认为，中国崛起已经是不争的事实，但是，对于中国未来发展走向无法做出明确的积极预测。也有部分澳大利亚保守派学者从意识形态和“冷战”思维出发，对社会主义中国怀着非常强烈的不信任感和偏见，从消极的立场审视中国的崛起。他们将中国崛起看成是一种挑战和威胁，甚至认为，中国的崛起不仅影响澳大利亚的国家安全，而且将严重冲击和动摇整个世界自由资本主义体系。[5]由于澳大利亚自立国以来，已经习惯、而且业已从西方主导的亚太秩序中获得安全与发展，因而，对中国这样一个社会主义大国的崛起感到恐惧，更难以接受可能由中国主导的地区秩序。同样，中国对澳大利亚的这种浓烈的西方价值观和思维方式怀着极大的不满。澳大利亚对中国崛起的恐惧和抵触反应，妨碍了中国营造一个和谐的周边及地区环境的努力，甚至有可能把两国引入不利的纷争，甚至不排除恢复到历史上曾经发生过的间接对立状态。与此同时，随着中国的全面崛起，国内激进民族主义情绪上升，很容易演变为仇外主义并左右到国家外交决策判断，从而影响到中国与包括澳大利亚在内的西方国家的关系。由此可见，中澳建交40年以来，尽管双方的联系非常紧密，但政治上的互信关系还比较脆弱，今后还需要着力继续加以精心培养，妥善处理。

## 经济上：从相互获益到相互依赖

中澳两国由于各自的自然禀赋、产业结构和发展水平的差异，存在较为明显的经济上的互补性，双方日益发展成新的利益共同体。

中澳建交以来，双边贸易关系发展十分迅速。1972年中澳建交时，双边贸易额不到1亿美元，仅为8655万美元，接近9000万美元。8年以后，至1982年，中澳双边贸易额达到11.2亿美元，增长了12倍。从1982年到1992年的第二个10年中，中澳双边贸易额又翻了一番，达到23.3亿美元。进入21世纪以后，中澳贸易出现了跨越式的发展。2002年，中澳双边贸易首次突破100亿美元大关，达到104亿美元。10年以后，至2010年，中澳双边贸易达到880亿美元，逼近千亿美元大关。2010年的中澳贸易额较之2002年增长了8.5倍多，是1992年的近40倍，是1982年的近80倍。至2010年，中国位居澳大利亚第一大贸易伙伴，澳大利亚成为中国第七大贸易伙伴。

从进出口货物贸易结构分析，中国出口到澳大利亚的商品以劳动密集型的轻工业制成品为主，中国从澳大利亚进口的商品主要是资源性产品为主。以2010年为例，中国对澳大利亚主要出口商品为机电产品、纺织品和家具、玩具制品，此类产品当年合计出口239.6亿美元，占中国对澳大利亚出口总额的66.1%。除上述产品外，贱金属及制品、塑料、橡胶、化工产品等也为中国向澳大利亚出口的主要大类商品。而中国从澳大利亚进口的主要是矿产品，2010年进口额为422.8亿美元，占中国从澳大利亚进口总额的78.6%；贱金属及制品是中国从澳大利亚进口的第二大类商品，进口额19.8亿美元，占中国从澳进口总额的3.7%；纺织品及原料是中国从澳大利亚进口的第三大类商品，进口额18.9亿美元。从进出口商品结构分析，中国处于明显不利地位。中国出口为劳动密集型产品，尽管这些产品占据澳大利亚很大的市场份额，但是此类产品的特点是技术含量不高，市场替代性较强，消费刚性小。而中国自澳大利亚的进口商品中，绝大多数为资源性产品，中国对这些产品的依赖性很强，替代性较弱。澳大利亚能源和矿产资源储量丰富，距离中国只有9天的海上运程，出口增长甚快。中国目前已成为澳大利亚铁矿砂第一大进口国，除铁、铜、铝以外各种矿砂的第二大进口国，铜矿砂、原油、镍的第三大进口国，金属铜的第四、铝的第五大进口国。矿产品消费与经济关系直接挂钩，是一种很强的刚性消费品。矿产品全球市场的垄断状况以及卖方谈判机制使中国相关能源型生产企业处于被动局面，并将这种被动局面传导给了下游产业。除了矿产品外，农产品是中澳货物贸易的另外一个重要领域。澳大利亚在农产品出口方面具有较强的竞争力，是发达国家中对农产品补贴最低的国家。中国在加入WTO时在农业问题上已经作出很大让步。兑现加入WTO的承诺，对于中国来说已经是严峻的挑战。中国有12亿农民，农产品贸易自由化关系到中国的社会稳定和国家安全。目前对中国农产品出口来说，最大的障碍并非关税，而是澳大利亚海关苛刻的动植物检验检疫程序。虽然从自然禀赋的条件（如可耕种土地面积和气候条件）来看，澳大利亚并不占太大优势，但由于人口稀少（全国只有2000多万人口），所以澳人均土地占有面积比中国多很多。另外，澳大利亚农业劳动力的综合文化素质普遍较高，农业机械化程度也相当高，高科技的应用也非常广泛，所以其人均劳动生产力比中国要高出很多。由于中国对澳大利亚资源产品的高度依赖，使得在中澳双边贸易中，中方长期处于贸易逆差地位。根据中国的计算，2010年中国对澳大利亚贸易逆差为336亿美元。而根据澳大利亚的统计，中国对澳大利亚的贸易逆差为175.5亿美元。中国是仅次于日本的澳大利亚第二大贸易顺差来源国。

在相互投资方面，近年来，中澳相互投资不断扩大，中澳互为重要的投资伙伴。澳大利亚对华投资始于1979年，是最早进入中国进行投资的国家之一。截止2010年底，澳大利亚在华累计设立投资项目9582个，实际投资超过65亿美元，澳大利亚是中国吸收外资的主要来源地之一。澳大利亚在华投资行业主要涉及建筑、交通、销售、机场着陆系统、债券交易软件、车辆控制系统、医疗设备、制药、制造业、环境管理、食品加工、信息技术、电讯、广告和设计、法律、金融、保险等。与其他外来投资相比，澳大利亚对中国的投资起步早但实际到位资金不多。由于中国过去对服务业市场开放限制较多，在一定程度上阻碍了澳大利亚的投资。与此同时，中国对澳投资规模近年也不断扩大。到

2010年底，中国企业对澳非金融类直接投资接近88亿美元。中国对澳投资领域主要有远洋运输、航空、金融、铁砂矿、有色金属、农牧场、产品加工、房地产和餐饮业等，但绝大部分集中在矿业领域。中澳双边投资规模总体不大，投资障碍主要制度和规则方面。同时，两国的外交关系好坏也直接影响到双边投资。例如2009年发生的力拓案就是中澳能源合作关系的一个缩影，该案在一定程度上恶化了两国政治关系和投资环境。澳大利亚近年来经济民族主义盛行，联邦政府以国家安全为由，采取了一种类似“资源民族主义”（resource nationalism）的做法，有意限制来自中国的投资，特别是具有国有企业背景的投资。[6]根据最新澳大利亚民调显示，越来越多的人认为澳大利亚政府允许过多的中国投资。[7]这是一种极不正常的现象，是中国威胁论的一种翻版。

由此可见，建交40年来，中国与澳大利亚两国之间的经济关系，由过去的简单相互获益，逐渐发展到密切的相互依赖。一方面，澳大利亚对中国的大量出口，拉动了该国GDP增长，扩大了就业机会；另一方面，中国从澳大利亚大量的原料与能源进口，驱动了中国经济高速发展的列车前进。从政治经济学国际相互依赖理论中的敏感性和脆弱性两个变量衡量，针对中澳双边进出口贸易产品结构和替代性而言，中国对澳大利亚经济上的依赖程度明显高于澳大利亚对中国的依赖，其中产生的权力明显倾向澳大利亚一边。[8]但是，与中国观点截然相反的是，澳大利亚害怕中国控制澳大利亚的经济，认为目前中澳的经济相互依赖关系已经或者可能将澳大利亚置于不利的附属境地。[9]因此，澳大利亚政治家和战略研究专家纷纷主张，要充分利用未来10～15年的中国经济高速发展带来的战略机遇期，在与中国开展经济交往过程中，进一步讨价还价，以获得更多的实际利益。

## 军事安全上：从相互对抗到相互交流合作

中澳建交以前，特别是“冷战”前期，中澳分属不同的政治阵营，军事安全上也一度处于间接对立甚至直接对抗状态。1950年初，中国与苏联结盟，成为社会主义阵营的骨干成员。澳大利亚于1951年8月与美国、新西兰正式缔结澳新美同盟条约，成为美国的重要盟国以及亚太安全体系的南部之锚。由于分属对立的两大军事同盟，在20世纪50年代的朝鲜战争和60年代中后期的越南战争中，中国和澳大利亚两度成为战场上的敌人。

中澳建交以后，双方的地区战略目标进行了调整，反对苏联霸权主义及其在亚太地区的扩张，维护地区安全与稳定，成为两国进行安全合作的基础。两国由对抗逐渐走向合作。例如在20世纪八九十年代，中澳两国联手，反对越南入侵和占领柬埔寨，共同推进在联合国框架下政治解决柬埔寨问题。为此，澳大利亚提出了解决柬埔寨问题的相关方案，并进行了卓有成效的外交斡旋活动，积极参与联合国主持下的柬埔寨和平进程和重建工作。[10]中国对越南进行了军事打击，并大力支持柬埔寨境内外的各种政治和军事反对派，致力于推翻越南扶植的柬埔寨傀儡政权。“冷战”结束后，中国与澳大利亚在维护地区安全稳定的目标上具有共同的利益。两国积极参与和推进亚太地区多边安全合作，支持以东盟为框架的安全合作机制——东盟地区论坛。在亚太地区非传统安全合作中，中国与澳大利亚也有着相近的立场。在1998～1999年联合国主导下的东帝汶维和行动中，中国与澳大利亚并肩作战，相互支持。近年来，中澳两军交流与合作也逐步展开。如2010年9月23日，中国海军北海舰队“洛阳”号导弹护卫舰、“北拖725”船与来访的澳大利亚海军“瓦拉蒙加”号护卫舰在中国黄海某海域举行了联合军事演练。这种两军联合演练，有效地推动了两国海军之间的务实性交流与合作，增进了两国军队之间的相互了解和信任，促进了两国的关系发展。[11]与此同时，中国海军舰艇也对澳大利亚悉尼港进行友好访问。中澳两军还一道参与过亚太地区多边军事演习。

但是，必须看到，中澳双方的安全目标和战略定位存在明显分歧甚至对立。特别是在进入21世纪以后，随着中国的强势崛起，两国的军事安全战略出现严重碰撞。澳大利亚的一贯政策是，随着中国的进一步崛起，澳大利亚一方面继续积极保持与中国的友好关系，并尽量分享中国发展带来的红利，但同时必须谨慎防止中国单独主导亚洲事务。澳大利亚尽管算得上是一个相当富裕的中等强国，但在大国竞争中，尚不具备独立的抗衡能力。无论在亚洲还是在其他地方均是如此。也就是说，仅仅依靠自己的力量，澳大利亚无法与崛起的中国进行竞争，更不用说与其抗衡。为此，澳大利亚主要奉行的国家战略可以用“两面下注”来形容：一方面，努力营造一个对自己有利的国际和地区环境，依靠自己的力量追求最大化的国家利益；另一方面，借助与美国联盟的力量，防范任何可能对澳大利亚国家安全和社会价值带来冲击的严重挑战。中国作为一个负责任的利益攸关方参与亚洲秩序建设，符合澳大利亚的地区政策。但是，如果中国未来作为一个修正主义的侵略性大国崛起的话，澳大利亚就要和盟国一道加以围堵和制衡，就像“冷战”时期对待苏联那样。[12]鉴于国际政治中权力转移的一般规律，未来中美冲突可能难以避免。澳大利亚与美国的安全同盟关系，及其与中国紧密的经济合作关系，使之陷入极大的困境——甚至毫不夸张地说，是该国自建国以来面临最大的选择困境——它需要堪培拉政府更加周密的考虑。[13]澳大利亚担心，随着中国实力上升，中国在东南亚和朝鲜半岛的影响力将超过美国。在国内民族主义的驱动下，中国极有可能采取对外扩张政策。随着中国政治和军事力量的增强，它就可以随心所欲地对台湾、南海周边国家及争议岛屿地区使用武力，从而威胁美国海军的存在。对澳大利亚来说，“最大的挑战是，确保东亚地缘政治平衡关系转换不至于损害地区的基本安全环境。最严峻的威胁是，一个专政而野心勃勃的中国的崛起成为东亚的主导力量，从而限制澳大利亚的行动自由。另外一个严峻挑战是，虚弱的美国没有作好遏制中国崛起的准备，导致包括日本和澳大利亚在内的盟国对美国维护地区战略秩序承诺信心的丧失。所以，澳大利亚必须为东亚地缘政治发展做好足够的准备”[14]。澳大利亚学者主张，鉴于中国军事现代化的步伐和规模可能给地区造成误判和不稳定，澳大利亚必须加强与美国、日本等民主国家之间团结与合作，建立和加固美、日、澳三边对话机制，强化三方政策协调能力，共同应对中国崛起的挑战。[15]

正是在上述思维模式主宰下，澳大利亚于2009年春天发表《国防白皮书》，公开把中国描绘为澳大利亚的潜在安全威胁。该白皮书甚至把中国当成为未来澳大利亚国防建设的假想敌。它大肆渲染“中国威胁”，称中国的军事现代化引发了周边国家的不安，推断随着中国等国军力的崛起，亚太地区在未来20年有可能发生战争。该白皮书继续强调美国仍将是澳大利亚“不可或缺的”盟友。为了应对中国崛起所造成的不确定性，白皮书表示，澳大利亚将在未来20年里计划投入700多亿美元用于改善军备，重点将潜艇数量扩充一倍至12艘，购入100架F-35战机，并希望购入8艘新型护卫舰和3艘驱逐舰。[16]对此，中国学者评论认为，澳大利亚《国防白皮书》所包含的“中国威胁论”，在“很大程度上是澳大利亚政治生态和安全观念的一种综合体现，同时也折射出澳大利亚对国际体系转型带来的不确定因素所感到的不安。”[17]

最近以来，随着南海争端日益升温，澳大利亚也希望借助美国的力量提升自己在这一地区的影响力，进一步扩大自己的防御空间。2011年11月中旬，为了纪念澳美安全同盟缔结60周年，美国总统奥巴马访问澳大利亚期间与澳大利亚达成协议，美国将从2012年开始在澳大利亚北领地首府达尔文地区驻扎250名海军陆战队员，并最终达到2500人的目标。达尔文基地将为美军提供了一个连接太平洋与印度洋的新立足点。美国选择这个地点的目的也十分明确，即加强在南海地区的军事存在，以防止地区冲突为借口，维护和扩大其在亚太地区的霸权。显而易见，澳大利亚北部相比日韩基地而言更接近南海，因此其矛头直指中国。[18]中国政府对此持强烈批评态度，认为：“当国际社会正在全力以赴应对经济危机，加强合作的时候，美澳两国此时加强安全同盟关系，明显是针对中国的一种‘冷战’思维。”[19]中国国防部发言人也明确表示：“军事同盟是历史形成的，任何强化和扩大军事同盟的做法，我们认为都是‘冷战’思维的体现，不符合和平、发展、合作的时代潮流，也不利于增进地区国家的互信与合作，最终受损的是各方的共同利益。希望有关各方多做有利于亚太地区和平稳定的事情，而不是相反。”[20]澳大利亚此举将进一步加剧中澳两国政治上的不信任和安全上的对立，严重违背两国建立心心相印的伙伴关系的长期努力。将美国力量引入该地区的争端，将进一步引发地区安全困境的加剧，也不利于澳大利亚的国家安全。中国方面将被迫对澳美同盟复活可能对未来亚太地区安全结构，特别是中国的周边环境带来的任何严重挑战做出反应。按照这一轨迹发展，中澳或许将成为下一场战争的敌人，至少是潜在的间接敌手。为此，我们同意这样一种观点，即，对澳大利亚来说，最明智的做法是，极力阻止中美冲突的发生，并积极充当中美合作的桥梁。稳定而富有建设性的中美澳三边合作关系，不仅符合各自的国家利益，而且将直接造福于21世纪的亚太地区各国。

## 小　　结

综上所述，自1972年至今，中华人民共和国与澳大利亚联邦自建交40年以来，双边关系发展大致比较平稳，没有出现重大的外交冲突或者关系逆转的事态。进入21世纪以后，中澳关系最大的特点是经济联系急速上升，形成了密切的相互依赖关系和利益共同体。但是，源于中澳双方的文化与价值观差异而产生的政治分歧并没有得到根本性改善。同时，受制于现实国际秩序与安全结构影响，中澳两国在军事安全领域的合作远远落后于经济文化教育领域的合作，甚至竞争性大于合作性。中澳关系的这种政经分离的双重性特征，反映了国际政治现实主义传统仍然在发挥关键作用，这对目前和今后中澳双方的外交政策都是一个严峻挑战。最后，我们认为，中澳关系目前仍然处于重大的历史转型期和调整期。如果各自能够进一步能把握机会，妥善处理各自的战略分歧和合理关切，努力避免矛盾激化，维护和扩大共同利益，中澳关系仍然具有较大的发展机会和空间。

## [注释]

[1] 帝国特惠制，是指英国和英联邦其他成员国间在贸易上相互优待的制度，1932年在加拿大渥太华英帝国会议上制定。主要内容是：对成员国间的进口商品，相互降低税率或免税；对成员国以外的进口商品，则征高额关税，以阻止美国及其他国家势力渗入英联邦市场。后改称英联邦特惠制。

[2]《中澳关于建立外交关系的联合公报》，《人民日报》1972年12月23日。附注：同日，中国与新西兰建立外交关系。

[3]《陆克文在北大用中文演讲，澳总理期待澳中成“诤友”》，《中国新闻网》2008年4月10日：http://news.sina.com.cn/c/2008-04-10/042013712560s.shtml.

[4] Greg Sheridan, Don't kowtow to Beijing bully, *The Australian*, July 23, 2009.

[5] Hugh White, Power Shift, Australia's Future between Washington and Beijing, *Quarterly Essay*, issue 39, 2010. Morry Schwartz, Australia.

[6] Jeffrey D. Wilson, Resource nationalism or resource liberalism? Explaining Australia's approach to Chinese investment in its minerals sector, *Australian Journal of International Affairs*, Volume 65, Issue 3, 2011, pp. 283 – 304.

[7] The Lowy Institute Poll 2011, Lowy Institute for Foreign Policy, Australia, p. 10.

[8] Yu Changsen & Jory Xiong, The Dilemma of Interdependence: Current Features and Trends in Sino-Australian Relations, *Australian Journal of International Affairs*, Vol. 66, Issue5, 2012.

[9] Michael Wesley, *Effects of the China boom on Australian Politics and Society*, Paper Presented to the Book Workshop of China-Australian Relations at Forty: Learning from the Past, Facing the Future, University of Sydney, 16 – 17Novernmber 2011.

[10] Allan Gyngell, Michael Wesley, *Making Australian Foreign Policy*, Second Edition, Cambridge University Press 2007, pp. 51 – 56.

[11]《中澳海军在黄海联合军事演练，双方均用实弹》，《中国新闻网》2010 年 9 月 24 日：http：//military. china. com/zh_ cn/05/11078235/20100924/16159791. html.

[12] Rod Lyon, Changing Asia, rising China, and Australia's strategic choices, *Policy Analysis*, ASPI, Australian Strategic Policy Institute, Friday, 17 April 2009.

[13] Michael Wesley, *The Howard Paradox*: *Australian Diplomacy in Asia*, 1996 – 2006, (ABC Books). 2007, p. 130.

[14] Paul Dibb, *The Future Balance of Power in East Asia* : *What are the Geopolitical Risks*? Strategic and Defence Studies Centre, Australian National University, Canberra, ACT 0200, Australia, January 2008, Defenses Studies Centre Working Paper No. 406.

[15] Paul Dibb, *Australia's Security Relationship with Japan*: *How much*

*further can it go*? Working Paper No. 407, April 2008.

[16] *Defending Australia in the Asia Pacific Century*: *Force* 2030, http://www.apo.org.au/sites/default/files/defence_ white_ paper_ 2009.pdf.

[17] 胡欣：《澳大利亚的战略利益观与“中国威胁论”——解读澳大利亚2009年度国防白皮书》，《外交评论》2009年第5期，第133页。

[18]《美国屯兵澳洲，“海空一体战”又一局》，《南方日报》2011年11月21日。

[19]《2011年11月16日外交部发言人刘为民举行例行记者会》，《外交部网站》：http://www.fmprc.gov.cn/chn/gxh/tyb/fyrbt/t877838.htm.

[20]《国防部回应美国在澳大利亚驻军：是“冷战”思维的体现》，《中国新闻网》2011年10月30日：http://www.chinanews.com/gn/2011/11-30/3498701.shtml.

# 3

# 中澳建交40周年以来两国经贸关系发展述评

蒋启良　张秋生

1972年12月21日，中国和澳大利亚签署《中华人民共和国政府和澳大利亚政府关于中－澳两国建立外交关系的联合公报》，标志着中澳两国正式建立外交关系。此后，两国在政治、经济、文化、社会等各个领域深化合作，取得了丰硕的成果，在经贸上的双边合作更是尤为突出。两国贸易总额从建交初期的8600万美元到2012年的1000亿美元，实现了跨越式的发展。两国经贸合作呈现出全方位、多层次、宽领域的互动格局，已经形成了“你中有我，我中有你”的局面。目前，中国已经成为澳大利亚第一大货物贸易伙伴、第一大货物出口目的地、第一大货物进口来源地、第一大服务贸易出口目的地、第一大旅游收入来源国，澳大利亚也是中国第八大贸易伙伴。今年是中澳建交40周年，对两国经贸关系进行宏观的述评，归纳和总结两国经贸关系发展的特点、成功的经验以及存在的问题，可以为将来的经贸合作机制的建立提供一个前瞻性的视角。

## 一、逐步成型阶段（1972—1978年）

中国和澳大利亚的经贸交往由来已久，早在18世纪就有商船往返于中国的广东省和澳大利亚的悉尼之间。1949年新中国建立后，澳大利亚出于自我利益的考虑，追随美国的外交政策，遏制中国。尽管如此，两国在民间贸易上还是取得了一定的成就：20世纪50年代，两国贸易额累计达1.57亿美元；60年代，中国从澳大利亚进口了300万吨的小麦，进口的羊毛数量达到几千吨至1万吨，价值3000多万美元；中国在澳大利亚的出口贸易中，一度占到6%的比重，为澳大利亚第五大商品输出国。澳大利亚出口到中国的小麦，最高时曾达到澳出口小麦的1/3。[1]但是，70年代随着澳大利亚支持美国出兵越南，严重威胁了中国的安全，中国减少了澳大利亚的羊毛和小麦的进口量，在与中国建交前，两国的贸易额仅维持在1亿美元。[2]1972年，澳大利亚的外交政策发生了重大的调整，两国经贸上的不稳定关系，随着1972年中澳正式外交关系的建立而告终，从此以后，两国的经济和贸易关系随之进入一个新的时期。

### （一）双边贸易向多元化方向发展

中澳建交后，两国贸易领域不断多元化，在传统产业的基础上，不断往外延伸，双边贸易从民间贸易为主上升到以政府贸易为主的阶段。澳大利亚向中国出口小麦、羊毛、糖、铁矿石、铝、有色金属，特别是小麦的出口，在1972年每年保持着大宗谷物出口。中国向澳大利亚出口纺织品、针织品、服装、鞋类、原油、化学制品、茶叶盒手工艺品等。两国贸易发展迅速。1972 年，两国间的贸易额仅为 8665 万美元，1973 年，两国的贸易额就达到 2.16 亿美元的新的高度，比 1972 年增长约 150%，并且还保持着稳定发展的趋势。建交后头 3 年，中澳贸易额不断高速增长，1978 年的进出口总额是建交前 1972 年的 10 倍。[3]

## （二）投资领域初具规模

在此阶段，两国投资主要集中于政府层面，在资金方面的合作主要有政府贷款、开发援助、合资经营（包括相互投资）等。1978 年澳大利亚同意中国享受澳大利亚对发展中国家的普惠制待遇；澳大利亚向中国提供 5000 万澳元贷款，用于购买澳方基础建设设备和支付有关服务费用。这也是当时澳大利亚向外国提供的最大一笔贷款。澳方也适当增加了对中国的投资，在某些具体的领域进行合作。

## （三）中澳两国经贸关系的发展

1973 年 5 月，澳大利亚联邦政府派出了由海外贸易部长凯恩斯率领的第一个贸易代表团对中国进行访问，并于 7 月签订了中澳贸易协定。根据协定，双方给予对方最惠国待遇地位；支持长期商品协议的原则，孤立技术交流，并规定每年举行会谈联合贸易洽谈；同时，组成中澳贸易联合委员会，由它负责定期商讨两国经济贸易事宜。同年，中澳还签订了中国从澳大利亚进口小麦、生铁、铁矿砂的三项长期协议。两国还达成食糖长期交易合同，规定按照国际市场价格，由澳按年向中国提供食糖。从此，双边贸易提升级别，从无组织的民间贸易上升到政府协议下的贸易往来，并为长期稳定发展双边贸易打下了基础。

### （四）中澳建交初期贸易发展特点

从总体上看，这一阶段中澳经贸关系的发展主要体现在双边贸易与投资两个方面。首先，在双边贸易方面，这一阶段两国经贸关系从发展传统贸易扩大到新的领域，双边贸易从民间贸易为主上升到以政府贸易为主阶段。其次，在相互投资方面，主要是以提供贷款方式完成的。但是两国的贸易也存在一定的问题，政治上的分歧严重影响双边贸易关系的发展，在70年代中期后，部分地受到中国国内政治的影响，两国的贸易经历了两年的徘徊局面。

### （五）中澳经贸关系发展的原因

中澳经贸关系的发展不仅有市场的作用和商品间的互补，还包括综合的政治因素，在此阶段尤为突出。

第一，政治与经济相互依存，经济决定政治，政治又反作用于经济。著名国际政治经济学家吉尔平认为：“民族政府仍对经济事务做出主要决策，而且能够动用相当大的权利来影响经济后果。”[4]中澳建交后，和平共处五项原则为两国的具体合作铺平了道路，解决了一些技术性的难题。政治上的稳定，两国人民不间断的交流，消除了分歧，也为经贸合作带来了稳定的外部环境。

第二，国际环境的变化促使两国经贸关系的发展。中美苏三角格局逐渐形成，美国也放弃了对中国的围追堵截政策，与中国发展友好的经贸关系，这对紧随美国外交政策的澳大利亚而言，可以搁置意识形态的分歧，实现两国贸易的正常化。

第三，对澳大利亚来说，在此之前澳贸易严重依赖英国和英联邦国家。在英联邦成立之前，其出口产品的70%输往英国，“二战”之前其比重仍占50%，在1951—1955年间虽有下降，但仍保持在36%。[5]1973年，英国加入欧洲经济共同体后，英联邦贸易特惠制不复存在，澳大利亚传统农牧业产品出口受到限制，迫使澳大利亚重新选择市场。

## 二、快速发展阶段（1979—1989年）

20世纪70年代末到80年代初，中国实行改革开放，澳大利亚也推进经济改革，两国都实现了长期持续发展。正是由于双方经济的强劲增长，彼此经济结构的高度互补，使两国经贸合作获得了内生动力，不断走向深入。中国的巨大市场给澳大利亚带来了稳定的需求，澳大利亚的产品出口也为中国经济增长做出了特有的贡献。1989年北京政治风波发生后，霍克总理和埃文斯外长对中国进行无端指责。7月，澳政府内阁会议发表了对华政策声明，系统地提出了对华政策的原则，单方面从政治、经济、军事、文化教育等方面采取一系列有损两国关系的行动和措施，中澳贸易又跌到了冰点。

### （一）双边贸易在规模、深度、内容上快速扩大

在此阶段，中澳贸易总体呈增长的趋势。根据中国海关的统计，1980年中国对澳大利亚的出口首次突破2亿美元，

中澳两国间的贸易额也达到近13亿美元，比1979年增长12.9%（见表1）。从产品结构来说，中国对澳大利亚的出口主要集中于初级产品，纺织品、服装和鞋类约占半数，轻工产品为14.8%，土畜产品为10.8%，工艺品为7%、化工产品占5.4%。[6]澳大利亚对中国的出口主要集中于羊毛、铝、铅、糖类等。纺织纤维是澳大利亚对中国出口的传统商品，其中羊毛出口占澳大利亚对华出口总额的30%左右。1987年澳大利亚向中国出口铅156万美元，铝1353万美元，成为中国最大的铅来源国和第二大铝来源国。1989年中国从澳大利亚进口铁矿砂超过千万吨，创历史新高。糖类在双边贸易中也占有重要位置，澳大利亚已成为仅次于古巴和泰国的中国糖类进口的第三大来源国。

**表1　中澳双边贸易变化**

| 年份（年） | 1980 | 1984 | 1985 | 1986 | 1987 | 1988 | 1989 |
|---|---|---|---|---|---|---|---|
| 贸易额（百万美元） | 1296.6 | 1179.8 | 1217.0 | 1610.0 | 1617.0 | 1470.0 | 1890.0 |
| 占中国外贸比重（%） | 3.4 | 2.2 | 1.9 | 2.2 | 2.0 | 1.4 | 1.7 |

资料来源：《中国统计年鉴》、《中国对外经济贸易年鉴》、《世界知识年鉴（1981—2000年）》。

## （二）投资方式日益呈现多样化

自1978年起，澳大利亚就一直坚持通过援助的方式直接投资。80年代通过其政府贷款，中国获得很多建设所需的资金，建设了一大批技术比较先进的项目，如1981年澳大利亚墨尔本享利·琼斯公司和中国南宁农工商联合公私合营南宁菠萝种植场。此后，在广州、深圳、天津、上海、哈尔滨、秦皇岛、鞍山等地也出现了大批中澳合资企业。除政府投资外，澳企业也积极参与中国的投资，1979年，澳建筑材料公司投资1000万美元在深圳与中国合作经营鸟石古石场。改革开放后，中国的经济体系逐渐成熟，慢慢形成了“引进来”与“走出去”相结合的道路。在吸引澳外资的同时，中国也积极向澳进行投资，将投资重点放在澳大利亚的资源工业上，如中国第一次参与澳的重大开发项目：1989年中国国际信托投资公司签订了一项协议，购买维多利亚波特兰炼铝合资企业10%的股票，价值约1.1亿澳元。到1986年，中澳达成的合资项目已超过20个，另外还有37个合营项目在审议中。

### （三）双边贸易关系逐渐稳定

1980年起，两国外交部建立了定期官员磋商，至1987年已经在北京举办了5次磋商；1981年10月中澳两国政府正式签署《中澳技术合作促进发展计划协定》，协定包括：澳准备在农业生产、农产品加工、林业、矿物的勘探和提炼、散装货装卸、交通运输、港口设施、城市发展、教育等方面给中国的一些项目提供财政支持；1985年堪培拉技术开发合作会议上，决定扩大1981年的协议内容，双方在地质开采、钢铁冶炼技术、煤炭工业方面的深化合作；1988年3月，中国政府和澳大利亚政府签署《中澳关于相互促进开发项目提供优惠贷款的谅解备忘录》。这一定程度上推动了澳大利亚技术与设备对中国的出口，为澳大利亚公司和企业带来了商业利益。澳企业也积极参与对华投资和建设中。此外，1984年的“中国行动计划”，[7] 1985年11月，中澳两国政府签署《避免双重征税协定》，1988年7月，中澳两国政府签署《相互鼓励和保护投资协定》，1986年，两国建立了部长级经济联合委员会以协调经济关系。

### （四）双边经贸关系的特征

这一阶段，中澳经贸关系的快速发展主要体现在双边贸易、投资以及经济技术合作三个方面。首先，从双边贸易来看，双边贸易在规模、深度、内容上快速扩大；其次，在相互投资方面，投资方式日益呈现多样化；最后，在双边经济技术合作方面，领域和规模在不断扩大。

### （五）该阶段发展的原因

总体而言，中国的改革开放是根本原因。1978年后，中国实行改革开放，积极吸引外资，调整经济体制中不健全的部分，为“引进来”和“走出去”做好了铺垫。从澳大利亚方面来说，主要是其在该阶段不断改革和调整国内经济制度和产业结构，逐步实行了贸易自由化政策。1983年起，澳大利亚推行重大的经济改革计划，转变其经济的封闭性和内向性，使之具有开放性和外向性。此外，亚太经济的迅速发展，促使澳重视发展“与整个亚洲太平洋地区以及与该地区内各个国家之间的外交和外贸关系。”[8] 在此阶段，东亚发展中国家和地区经济年增长达7.5%，大大高于同期发达国家经济年均2.9%和发展中国家经济年均3.0%的增长水平。特别是韩国、新加坡和中国台湾与香港地区经济持续高速增长，被誉为亚洲“四小龙”。欧洲一体化的深入发展，区域一体化趋势进一步明显，促使中澳加强合作，共同应对新一轮的挑战。

## 三、越加成熟的经贸关系（1990—1999年）

虽然1989年北京政治风波发生后中澳政治关系急转直下，但双方的经济贸易、文化与技术合作仍然在徘徊中前进。因为多年以来中澳双方交往日益紧密，尤其是经贸关系的加深，使双方都能够放下政治上的分歧，从经济上考虑双边关系。中国改革开放形成的巨大市场及其在亚太地区的重要地位，能够为澳大利亚带来巨大利益，而澳大利亚的技术和产品上的互补，能够为中国的发展带来动力。于是，自20世纪90年代初，中澳关系开始进入了理性务实的交往。1997年，澳大利亚政府发表了第一份《外交贸易白皮书》，指出澳大利亚四对重要伙伴为美国、日本、印尼、中国，并将中澳关系列为最重要对外关系之一。

### （一）贸易发展概况

1989—1990年，两国的经济始终在18亿美元左右徘徊，1991年2月，澳政府宣布取消对华制裁，最终在1991年突破了20亿美元的大关，从1991—1997年连续7年创历史纪录，从21亿美元上升到53亿美元，扩大了1.5倍。在1997/1998年度，中国为澳大利亚第五大贸易伙伴和第七大商品出口市场，澳大利亚是中国的第四大出口市场。[9] 1998

年由于东南亚金融危机稍有波折，中澳双边贸易下降为50亿美元。[10]在双方的贸易过程中，中国对澳大利亚进口主要为羊毛、铁矿石、谷物、氧化铝等。1997年，中国进口澳羊毛价值9.9万吨，价值4.7亿美元。1998年，中国进口澳羊毛价值3.77亿美元（见表2）。

**表2　1997—1998年中澳贸易额**

| 年份（年） | 1990 | 1991 | 1992 | 1993 | 1994 | 1995 | 1996 | 1997 | 1998 | 1999 |
|---|---|---|---|---|---|---|---|---|---|---|
| 贸易额（亿美元） | 18.0 | 21.1 | 23.3 | 30.1 | 39.3 | 42.1 | 51.1 | 53.0 | 50.4 | 63.1 |
| 增长率(%) | -0.5 | 12.3 | 10.4 | 29.1 | 30.8 | 6.8 | 21.3 | 3.8 | -5.2 | 25 |

资料来源：《中国对外经济贸易年鉴》、《世界知识年鉴（1991—1999年）》。

## （二）投资发展情况

在整个90年代，澳大利亚的对华投资主要包括对华援助和直接投资。至1998年底，中国利用澳援助已完成合作项目63个，正在执行的项目30个，澳方实际投入3.8亿澳元；中国利用澳政府混合贷款项目已经生效的项目有102个，协议总金额6亿美元，主要用于邮电、通讯、农林、原材料、环保等国民经济优先发展领域；1997年底，澳总理霍华德再次宣布将向中国提供2000万澳元无偿援助，用于中澳两国政府部分在社会保障等领域的交流和合作，该项目历时4年。到1998年，中国在澳设立的各种贸易性机构和生产性企业就达169家，中方协议投资额近4亿美元。

在直接投资方面，1990年初，澳大利亚在华投资项目55个，协议投资额为2.37亿美元。1997年，澳来华直接投资项目累计3128个，澳资实际投入14亿美元。[11]投资项目主要分布在农业、建材、纺织、电子等领域。1998年，中国累计批准澳在华直接投资项目3403个，澳方协议投资金额为50.6亿美元，实际投入15.1亿美元，主要分布在农业、建材纺织、电子等领域。

## （三）服务贸易的增长

双方的服务贸易主要集中于旅游业。从中国来看，90年代以来人民生活水平的提高，出国旅游人数不断增加，特别是1997年，中方批准将澳作为中国公民自费旅游的目的地之一，并于1998年4月批准澳康联保险公司在华开设营业性机构。1998年，中国出境总人数为843.26万人，其中赴澳人数达到了10万人以上，其中商务旅游和赴澳学习者占了大多数。随着交流的越加深入，澳来华人数也在不断增加。以1996—1999年为例，澳大利亚人来华旅游人数1996年为13.26万人；1997年为15.68万人，比上年增长18.12%；1998年为18.63万人，比上年增长18.81%；1999年则达到20.135万人，比上年增长9.2%。[12]到1999年底，中国已经成为澳大利亚第13大旅游市场。

## （四）中澳两国贸易关系的发展

1993年6月，基廷总理访华，强调澳将进一步调整对华政策，发展同中国和亚洲国家的关系。1999年4月22日，中澳代表在上海就中国公民自费赴澳旅游的具体实施办法正式签署换文。1999年9月，江泽民主席访澳期间，双方签署了《中华人民共和国发展计划委员会与澳大利亚工业、科学和资源部关于在矿业和能源领域贸易与投资合作的谅解备忘录》、《中华人民共和国国土资源部和澳大利亚工业、科学和资源部关于在矿业领域合作的谅解备忘录》、《中华人民共和国和澳大利亚领事协定》等合作文件。双边一致同意建立中澳面向21世纪长期稳定、健康发展的全面合作关系。1999年，江泽民主席对澳大利亚的访问是两国建交后中国国家元首对澳大利亚的首次访问，宣布建立两国高层的定期会晤制度，并将就共同构筑两国面向21世纪的长期稳定、健康发展的全面合作关系达成共识，对新世纪两国关系的发展具有重大意义。1999年10月，中澳双方签署《关于在信息产业领域合作谅解备忘录》。

### （五）两国经贸关系特点

中澳经贸关系的发展前景广阔，两国的经贸关系具有以下的特点：①澳大利亚对华出口多为原料和初级产品，约占对华出口总额的80%以上；从中国进口以纺织品、服装和轻工业产品为主。两国贸易中存在的主要问题是中国处于逆差地位，贸易发展不平衡。②两国经贸关系是互补型的，目前双方已从贸易发展到投资、联营、技术转让和补偿贸易等多层次多领域的经济合作。③澳大利亚对华经贸关系的发展是其对日、美经贸关系的补充，有助于维护西太平洋的经济与政治稳定，促进澳大利亚对外事务的多元化。

### （六）两国经贸关系成熟的原因

此时，澳大利亚的贸易重心也已经转向了东亚地区。同时，欧洲统一市场和北美自由贸易区的形成使澳大利亚更增强了与亚洲合作的紧迫感。中国的关税改革也是一个重要原因，关税率1992年为42.1%，随后逐年下调；还实行出口退税制，降低市场准入限制等开放政策。

## 四、步入21世纪的中澳经贸关系（2000—2012年）

自1999年江泽民访澳，达成建立中澳面向21世纪长期稳定、健康发展的全面合作关系后，中澳经贸关系的发展又上升到一个新台阶。截至2009年，澳大利亚成为中国第八大贸易伙伴，第七大进口来源地和第八大出口市场。中国已经成为澳大利亚第一大货物贸易伙伴、第一大货物出口目的地、第一大货物进口来源地、第一大服务贸易出口目的地、第一大旅游收入来源国。

### （一）双边贸易关系的发展

进入21世纪后，中国和澳大利亚两国经贸关系发展势头迅猛，前景广阔。仅2012年1—7月，澳对华货物贸易总额就达680.24亿澳元，同比增长12.79%。其中对华出口439.68亿澳元，同比增长15.91%，占其货物贸易出口总额29.30%。从中国进口240.56亿澳元，同比增长7.52%，占其货物贸易进口总额16.15%。实现贸易顺差199.12亿澳元。[13]根据澳大利亚统计局的数据显示，2011年1—11月，澳、中双向货物贸易总额1038.92亿澳元（合1083.25亿美元），同比增长17.85%，突破千亿澳元。[14] 2001—2009年中澳两国双边贸易具体情况如表3所示：

**表3　2001—2009年中澳双边贸易额**

| 年份（年） | 2001 | 2002 | 2003 | 2004 | 2005 | 2006 | 2007 | 2008 | 2009 |
|---|---|---|---|---|---|---|---|---|---|
| 贸易额（亿美元） | 89.97 | 104.36 | 135.6 | 203.9 | 272.5 | 329.45 | 438.7 | 596.6 | 600.8 |
| 增长率（%） | 6.5 | 16 | 30.5 | 50.3 | 33 | 20.9 | 33.1 | 36.1 | 0.7 |

数据来源：《世界知识年鉴》（2002—2010年各期）。

## （二）双向投资的发展

近年来中澳两国双向投资日趋活跃，发展势头总体良好，澳大利亚已成为我国重要的投资目的国之一。据中国商务部统计，截至2008年底，澳累计在华投资项目8954个，实际投资额58.2亿美元。2009年底，澳累计对华实际投资额62.1亿澳元。其中，2007年当年澳对华直接投资21.27亿澳元，比上年增长114.63%，占同期澳对外直接投资总额的1.70%。截至2009年底，中国累计在澳非金融类直接投资额为53.2亿美元。[15] 据澳外商投资审查委员会（FIRB）2012年的最新数据显示，中国连续3年在外商对澳投资中排名第三，获批的投资项目达5033个，总价值

149.76亿澳元。中澳双向投资发展迅速，近5年来澳累计批准中国投资近600亿澳元。

中澳两国于2005年5月正式开始双边自由贸易协定（FTA）谈判。2010年6月，两国在北京进行了15轮FTA谈判，尽管双方在多项领域中存在分歧，在技术层面上停滞不前，但关于农业问题双方已达成谅解。如若双方达成共识，双向投资将会进一步扩大。

### （三）两国服务贸易的发展

2010年，中国取代美国成为澳大利亚最大的服务出口市场。澳外交贸易部数据显示，2011年，澳大利亚服务贸易总额1090亿澳元，服务贸易出口501亿澳元，而中国仍然保持澳大利亚服务贸易第一大市场，达57亿澳元。澳洲统计局（ABS）的数据，自2002年以来，中国游客的数量增加了350%。仅2011年6月，中国游客数量就达到了53400人。2011—2012年的总人数则有59.4万人，同比增长18%，在澳洲600万外国游客中占比10%。在2012年公布的1—5月澳洲海外游客情况，中国游客增加了17%，人数突破5万人次。按这种趋势发展下去，预计今年中国游客数量将突破60万人次，而在2010年和2002年的数据分别是54.2万和15.8万。

### （四）两国经贸关系发展取得的重大成果

2003年10月，胡锦涛主席应邀对澳大利亚进行国事访问，就深化中澳全面合作关系与澳领导人达成共识。双方签署了《中澳贸易与经济框架》以及能源、教育、质检、食品安全、水利、卫生等一系列合作文件。2005年4月，霍华德总理和温家宝总理在北京启动双边自由贸易协定谈判是两国经济关系上的一个重要里程碑。一项全面的、高质量的自由贸易协定将建立在2003年胡锦涛主席访问堪培拉时签订的经贸框架上。该框架承诺将进一步促进贸易往来和贸易自由化；促进广泛的重要领域中的战略合作；增强高层对话和合作以及在经贸方面的互访。

2006年4月，温家宝总理正式访澳，与澳领导人就发展21世纪互利共赢的全面合作关系达成共识。双方签订了《中澳和平利用核能协定》、《核材料转让协定》，为澳大利亚向中国核能计划提供铀矿，以及中澳和平利用核能技术的合作奠定了基础。2007年9月，胡锦涛主席对澳进行国事访问，并出席悉尼亚太经合组织（APEC）领导人非正式会议，与澳领导人就进一步发展中澳互利共赢的全面合作关系达成重要共识。

### （五）中澳经济关系迅猛发展的原因

中澳经贸关系迅猛发展的原因众多，如人民币与澳元相对稳定的汇率、两国政府高层互访不断等，但更多的得益于双方经济有较强的互补性，这种互补性是发展双边经贸关系的坚实基础和有力推动力量。①经济结构方面的互补性。在产品结构上，中国主要集中于第二产业，而澳主要集中于第三产业；在贸易结构上，农产品出口占澳大利亚产品和服务出口总额的23%左右，是澳大利亚出口的重要组成部分和创汇的主要来源。②技术水平上的互补性。澳大利亚的优势产业是第一和第三产业。中国除某些产业具有高技术生产水平外，总体来说，技术水平仍较为落后。③在多边及区域经济合作中地位与作用的互补。双方都重视多边机制的建立，在APEC和“中国－东盟自由贸易区”中双方相互合作。

## 五、面向未来的中澳经贸关系

21世纪将成为太平洋的世纪，21世纪世界经济的中心将转移到亚太地区。中澳关系已经有了良好的基础，尽管两国由于政治制度以及文化和历史背景不同，对一些问题的看法存在分歧，但只要中澳两国政府严格按照和平共处五项原则处理相互关系，两国在21世纪继续发展互利合作的前景将是十分广阔的。由于经济全球一体化的冲击，中澳经济都在经历着迅速变化。两国经济各有优势，互补性强。澳中经济所具有的互补性和两国在风云变幻的亚太地区利益的相似性是两国关系不断发展的动力。[16]两国的经贸发展应当站在战略高度，以全球眼光规划中澳经贸关系的未来，以多维空间拓展双边务实合作，携手推动两国经贸关系向纵深发展。

### （一）双方经贸关系存在的隐患

虽然双方经贸关系取得了巨大的成就，但是也存在一些重大的隐患。主要表现在：

第一，中澳贸易存在不对称依赖的关系。

一国对另一国贸易的重要性，不仅取决于贸易量的增长速度，更重要的是双方贸易关系的不对称依赖程度，特别是不对称的脆弱程度。衡量贸易不对称关系脆弱性的指标主要是一国对另一国进出口商品的市场替代性。替代性越强，脆弱性依赖较小的一方在贸易谈判中往往拥有更多的定价权，它同时在双边经济合作关系中具有更多的主导权。中国对澳大利亚的矿产品贸易依赖性很强，特别是铁矿石的进口。中国在澳大利亚的核心经济利益也集中在铁矿石贸易上。据中国海关统计，铁矿石是中国第四大进口商品，澳大利亚是中国最大的铁矿石进口来源地。因此，中国对澳大利亚贸易的依赖程度之高是不言而喻的。因此，澳大利亚对中国出口的矿产品替代性很小，从而造成澳大利亚在贸易谈判中往往拥有更多的定价权和主导性。亚洲很多国家如今都处于经济高速发展时期，它们也构成澳大利亚铁矿石的潜在出口市场。铁矿石的消费与经济关系直接挂钩，而且目前新兴市场国家普遍采用长流程工艺生产钢材，这使得铁矿石对一国的经济发展来说是一种很强的刚性消费品。

第二，中澳产品结构不对称。

中国出口澳大利亚的产品技术含量不高，市场替代性强，消费刚性比较小，在澳市场上的竞争十分激烈。美国、日本、意大利、韩国、新加坡、新西兰等国家在此类商品的制造和出口方面具有较强的竞争能力，在澳大利亚的高端市场占据一席之地；印度尼西亚、马来西亚、越南等周边发展中国家同样依靠成本优势，在澳大利亚此类商品市场上显示出较强的竞争潜力。对澳大利亚而言，从中国进口的几类主要制成品在上述市场上具有进口替代性。

第三，中澳经贸关系的发展还受到诸如美国、人权、中国台湾问题等非经济因素的影响。

“二战”后，澳大利亚成为美国在南太平洋的重要军事盟友，是美国亚太战略的核心支柱，和日本分别构成了美国亚太战略的"南北双锚"。作为美国在太平洋上的"南锚"，澳大利亚的战略地位不言而喻。澳美的这种特殊关系在一定程度上影响着澳的外交政策和战略思维，包括对华关系的发展。近年来，澳美联盟的走向特别是澳积极支持美国的导弹防御计划。"9·11"后澳急于反恐而效仿美国的"先发制人"战略也在一定程度上影响着中澳政治关系。尽管近几年澳大利亚在对局部政策方面包括台湾问题上发出与美国不同的声音，如称台海有战事不会自动站在美国一边，但是考虑其国家政策的独立性、完整性、严密性、可行性的相对欠缺，这就为未来中澳经贸关系的持久快速发展带来了不确定因素。

### （二）推动双边经贸关系的具体措施

为了达成共同发展的目的，双方应推进两国经贸关系不断发展的途径：

第一，发挥比较优势，稳步推进中澳自由贸易区建设进程。

中国与澳大利亚经济和产业结构具有明显的互补性，中国在鞋类、帽类产品、文教体育用品、纺织产品、家具、金属制品、茶叶等饮料、非金属矿物制品、机械设备和交通运输设备等产品上竞争性明显，而澳大利亚在矿物产品、粮食、畜产业、植物和饲料、有色金属冶炼加工品、矿物燃料、动植物油脂及其产品和纺织原料方面的优势较大。中国经过30几年的改革开放，国民经济高速发展，国内需求不断扩大，需要澳方发挥产品结构优势，实现互补。另一方面，澳拥有丰富的农业资源、矿产和能源资源，其铁矿石、铀、煤、矿砂和氧化铝等17种矿物资源的产量名列世界前6位，同时还是世界第五大液化天然气出口国。澳2004年对中国的矿物出口量约占对中国出口产品总量的60%，对中国矿物出口近10年内实现几乎500%的增长。

对澳大利亚而言，其国内市场狭小，对国际市场依赖性强。中澳两国经济具有较强的互补性，双方已互为非常重要的投资伙伴。建立自由贸易区不仅能提高双方这些优势产业的产出，整体上促进双方GDP的增长，提高双方和世界的总体贸易水平，还可以营造一个更加公平、更加稳定的投资与商贸环境。中澳经贸关系的合作和进一步发展，也有利于双方在周边事务中扮演更加重要的角色。同时，加强与澳大利亚的合作，有利于提高农产品、能源和资源供应方面的保障。此外，澳大利亚还有些技术，如电讯、导航、交通控制、港口建设、采矿、粮食储运等方面处于国际领先地位，也是当前中国经济建设时所需要的科学技术。

第二，进一步增进互信，加强机制建设，提升中澳合作层次。

40年来，经贸合作始终是中澳关系长期健康稳定发展的基石和推动力。政治和经济密不可分，经济的发展推动了双边政治关系的发展；反过来，政治的发展也会推动双边关系的深化。两国特别是澳工商界可以为增进中澳互信发挥积极而重要的作用，为推动构建全面、稳定、成熟、健康的中澳战略合作伙伴关系做出重要贡献。两国应淡化意识形态上的分歧，以经济利益为主要考量对象，求同存异，形成稳定的双边关系。中澳双方应在相互交流和合作中，努力构建稳定的合作机制。建立和完善双边协商和移交机制，采取建立知识产权小组等方式加强在政策和法律方面的协商。在监督机制上也应寻求进一步的突破。

除继续发展稳定的经济机制外，双边的政治机制也应进一步增强。加强在联合国中的政治合作，共同应对国际社会中发生的一些影响较大的国际和地区性问题；保持在亚太经合组织中的高层合作，通过 APEC 领导人非正式会议，针对热点问题交流看法；努力在太平洋论坛、东盟倡导的“10 + 3”等机制中相互交流，增进互信。

## [注释]

[1] 林珏主编：《涉外经贸关系——中国与主要贸易伙伴》，上海：上海财经大学出版社，2006 年，第 330 页。

[2] 同上，第 331 页。

[3] 冯承柏主编，宫占奎副主编，《亚太地区经济关系与中国》，天津：南开大学出版社，1992 年，第 249 页。

[4] 罗伯特 · 吉尔平：《全球政治经济学——解读国际经济秩序》，上海世纪出版集团，2006 年版，第 13 页。

[5] 澳大利亚统计局：《海外贸易》（Australian Bureau of Statistics, Overseas Trade）有关各期。

[6] 林钰主编：《涉外经贸关系——中国与主要贸易伙伴》，上海：上海财经大学，2006 年版，第 335 页。

[7] “中国行动计划”，其主要内容为：促进和支持澳大利亚企业向中国的出口；支持澳大利亚商户参与在中国的商业合作；协助中国加强在非敏感的澳大利亚进口市场的地位等，目标是三五年内将贸易增加一倍。

[8] 王惠珍主编：《面向 21 世纪的选择》，上海：上海社会科学出版社，1991 年版，第 23 页。

[9]《世界知识年鉴》1999/2000，第999页。
[10] 黄梅波等著：《澳大利亚经济》，北京：经济科学出版社，2011年版，第383页。
[11]《世界知识年鉴》，1998/1999年，第904页。
[12]《中国旅游报》，2000年5月29日
[13] 中华人民共和国驻澳大利亚使馆网站：http：//au. mofcom. gov. cn/tjsj/6/dyncolumn. html
[14] 澳大利亚统计局：http：//www. abs. gov. au/
[15] 中华人民共和国商务部网站：http：//www. mofcom. gov. cn/
[16] 王惠珍、段锡平主编：《面向二十一世纪——中澳经济合作与发展》，上海社会科学院，1991年，第2页。

## 作者简介

**蒋启良**，江苏师范大学澳大利亚研究中心成员，南京大学国际关系专业研究生

**张秋生**，教授，现任江苏师范大学澳大利亚研究中心主任、中国澳大利亚研究会副会长。主要研究方向：澳大利亚史、亚太国际关系史、华侨华人。（Email：qiushengzhang2004@126. com）

# 4

# 中澳天然气合作研究

侯敏跃

中国一定规模的天然气进口始于2006年5月澳大利亚液化天然气（LNG）抵达广东大鹏液化天然气公司。迄今为止，澳大利亚供应了我国约50%的进口LNG，未来，它也将是我国主要LNG供应方。多年来，中澳燃气业合作，发挥了积极有益的经济和社会效益，有助于我国完善一次能源消费结构、保障能源供应安全和改善环境质量，但合作中也出现了一些应予重视和解决的问题。本文旨在剖析中澳燃气合作的历程、意义和前景，探索解决问题之思路。

## 一、天然气：中澳能源互补领域之一

我国能源禀赋特点之一是“富煤、少油、缺气”。中华人民共和国成立后数十年间，对天然气的作用和重要性认识有限，其结果是天然气在我国一次性能耗中的比例长期在2%上下徘徊，大大低于全球平均24%的水平。进入21世纪后，我国逐渐重视完善一次能耗结构，采取诸多举措降低煤炭在一次能耗中的占比，推动更为清洁的天然气的产销和进口。我国制定的目标是，至2015年燃气要占总能耗的8%，2020年升到10%。由于中国能耗急速攀升，燃气占比的提速步履蹒跚，目前约为4%（见图1）。[1]

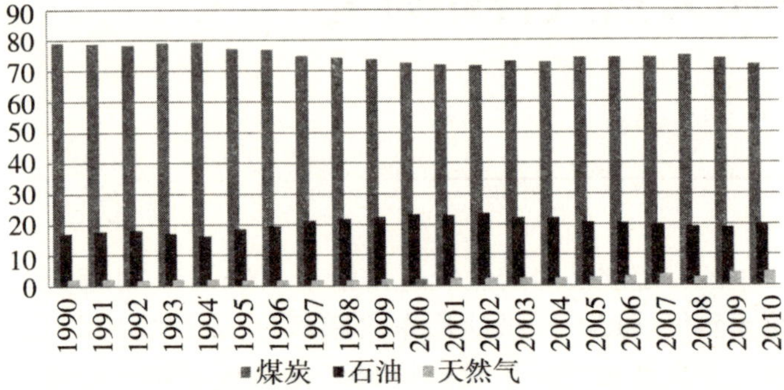


图1　中国煤炭、石油、天然气在一次能耗中占比（1990—2010年）

然而，即便天然气在我国能耗结构中比例低下，近年来我国许多地区的“气荒”仍时有发生，经济发展面临天然气短缺的制约。日益增长的供需缺口以及产量增长落后于需求增速的局面，使得加快进口势在必行。这为中澳合作提供了新领域。澳大利亚是重要的能源生产与出口国。截至2011年底其已探明的天然气储量为3.8万亿立方米，占世界探明储量的1.8%。此外，澳大利亚非常规天然气资源相当丰富，包括煤层气、致密气和页岩气。虽然澳天然气储量不算高，但其人口和国内市场规模相较其储产量小很多，所以产出的很大部分用于出口。由于澳四周濒海，无陆地接壤国，其天然气只能以适于船运的液化天然气（LNG）形式输出，多年来为亚太第三、全球第四液化天然气出口国，主要输出对象为日本、中国等亚太经济体。近年来，澳大利亚国内掀起了方兴未艾的 LNG 增产热潮（见表 1）。[2]

**表 1 截至 2012 年 6 月全球和澳大利亚 LNG 工厂数对比**

| | 全球 | 澳大利亚 |
|---|---|---|
| 运行工厂 | 31 | 3 |
| 在建工厂 | 10 | 7 |
| 规划工厂 | 15 | 6 |

据乐观的预测，若澳大利亚 LNG 增产计划进展顺利，其年产能 3 年内将自 2000 多万吨增至约 8000 万吨，2018 年时可逾 1.2 亿吨，若有市场需求，2020 年后的远期规划可突破 2 亿吨。澳大利亚将挑战卡塔尔全球第一 LNG 出口国的地位，其对中国的供应能力将有极大提高，中澳天然气互补、互惠合作可望迎来巨大提升。

## 二、大鹏 LNG 项目：引领中澳天然气合作

由澳大利亚西北大陆架公司提供 LNG 的深圳大鹏液化天然气公司，是我国首个引进 LNG 项目，已成为中澳天然气合作范例。自 2006 年 5 月项目投产至 2011 年，澳方累计向我供应廉价 LNG 228.7 亿立方米，占 6 年间我国进口 LNG 总量的 49.4%（见表 2）。[3]

**表2　中国LNG进口量（2006—2011年）**

（单位：亿立方米）

| 年份（年） | 进口总量 | 从澳进口量 |
|---|---|---|
| 2006 | 10 | 10 |
| 2007 | 38.7 | 33 |
| 2008 | 44.4 | 36.1 |
| 2009 | 76.3 | 47.5 |
| 2010 | 128.0 | 52.1 |
| 2011 | 166 | 50.0 |
| 6年累计 | 463.4 | 228.7 |

早在1988年，澳就派人对中国能源部门进行考察，在随后出台的报告中，澳方提出，“中国的能源供应中，天然气的用量显然太低”，并提示我们，使用天然气有助于改变对煤和原油的依赖，减少环境污染。[4]我国也逐渐意识到，靠大规模提升国内原油产量来满足内需已难以实现，煤炭消费的猛增带来极大的环境压力，不可持续，天然气、核能、风能、太阳能等的作用应予加强。1990年代中，广东、福建、上海陆续筹划LNG项目。但中央对何时开启项目建设和接受国外LNG，一度难以决断，因为政府对中国燃气市场未来是否大到必须进口燃气才能满足需要暂时把握不定[5]，而且，LNG供应合同一般为期20年左右，一旦供大于求，难免造成巨大浪费。因此，我国最初在LNG产业实施有限的试验。

1997年，朱镕基副总理访澳和澳总理霍华德访华期间，两国重申要加强和扩大能源、矿产资源互补合作。同年10月，西北大陆架公司所在的西澳州总理理查德·考特来华推动对华天然气销售，受到朱镕基的接见。年底，澳方向中方递呈了气电与煤电比较报告，结论是LNG更有竞争力。1998年10月，考特再度访华，与朱镕基总理再次商讨了LNG项目。10月28日，朱总理批示："可考虑引进LNG的试点，先在广东试点。"[6]这表明中国首个进口LNG项目获国家正式批准和立项，并落户广东，也意味着澳大利亚的支持、鼓励、协作对我国发展LNG产业决策有积极意义。

广东大鹏项目立项后，引来多国公司竞争，包括澳大利亚西北大陆架公司和卡塔尔、印尼的公司。三国中，印尼距中国最近，澳出价最高，澳何以赢得大鹏项目？首先，澳突出本国资源充沛，政局稳定，无动荡之忧，能保证供应的长期稳定。当时，印尼正遭受亚齐分离运动之痛，而供应的安全和稳定正是我们选择澳大利亚的考虑因素之一[7]。其次，澳强调本国法制完备，商业信誉良好，自1989年向日本等国出售LNG以来，保质保量按时交货，从未出错。最后，澳方满足我上游参股等要求，并推出由澳方出资2500万澳元、旨在帮助中国LNG产业发展的"中澳天然气技术伙伴关系基金"，增强了吸引力。此外，澳联邦和州两级政府在政策上对企业的扶持和积极的对华外交也发挥了不可或缺的作用。如揭标前夕的2002年5月，澳总理霍华德亲率代表团来华游说，拒见窜访澳大利亚的达赖喇嘛，为澳公司最后胜出创造了有利的政治氛围。8月，中国做出最终决定，把年购300多万吨LNG、期限25年、总值250亿澳元的大单给了西北大陆架公司。这个合同具有里程碑意义，标志着中澳能源合作时代的诞生，将与中澳矿产资源合作形成两轮驱动，把两国资源合作推向新的高峰。

中国能源安全包括能源供应的稳定、可持续、多元化，能源种类的多样化，所获能源为环境和市场可承受，能源运输的安全、畅通和多渠道等；澳能源安全的要素之一，则是能源销售市场的多元化。我国80%的进口石油要途经马六甲海峡这个狭窄的运输渠道，线路较为单一，安全风险相对较大。经海运进口的澳LNG，风险相对较小，可直达我国东部沿海主要能耗区，不必转运，既节省成本，又避免了管输可能造成的沿途环境问题、损耗和对管道安全的担忧。对澳而言，实现向华输气，缓解了其能源出口对日本的过度依赖，利于销售安全。

大鹏项目投产给我国带来了可观的经济价值和积极的社会效益。2002年中澳签约时，天然气处于买方市场，几年后国际燃气价步入上行通道，2008年飚涨的国际油价更带动气价迅猛上冲，日本市场价自2002年的4.27美元/百万英热单位，升至2008年的12.55美元/百万英热单位[8]。但中澳签订的是25年“照付不议”合约，与15～25美元/桶国际原油定价区间挂钩，即澳方售予大鹏的LNG价格最高不得超过国际油价25美元时相应的LNG价。其结果是，在2008年国际气价高峰时刻，大鹏公司供应的合同气价仅为1.6元/立方米，较国际气价低2.4～4.7元/立方米[9]；在近年全国上调天然气零售价的背景下，来自澳大利亚的深圳燃气不涨价；2011年上半年，广东整体上调火电上网价0.8分/度，使用澳气发的电却能下调3.8分/度，而其盈利水平仍远高于火电行业平均每度电盈利0.01元的水平[10]。大鹏项目的经济和社会效益之高得以充分体现，为缓解广东的电荒、气荒做出了突出的贡献。

大鹏项目对我国 LNG 产业发展的意义绝不限于采购到廉价的 LNG、缓解气荒和电荒。根据合约，中海油公司可收购西北大陆架天然气项目 5.3% 的权益，以及获得西北大陆架公司架构下专设的负责对华供气的中国液化天然气合资公司 25% 的股份，这意味着我国进入了澳 LNG 产业链上游，可参与勘探、生产、租赁等。依照合约，上海的沪东船厂承接了建造高技术、高造价、高收益的 LNG 运输船任务，这为中国船企在该领域实现零的突破，打破日、韩同行的垄断，并为我国船企拓展国际市场积累了宝贵的经验（见表3）。[11]

**表3　中国最先制造的 3 艘液化天然气船情况**

| 船名 | 航线 | 建造公司 | 交付日期 | 储罐数 | 容量（立方米） | 气源 |
|---|---|---|---|---|---|---|
| 大鹏昊 | 澳—中 | 上海沪东中华造船集团有限公司 | 2008.4 | 4 | 147000 | 澳大利亚西北大陆架气田 |
| 大鹏月 | | | 2008.7 | 4 | 147000 | |
| 闽榕 | | | 2009.2 | 4 | 147000 | |

而大鹏项目下的“中澳天然气技术伙伴关系基金”，自 2004 年启动以来，支持了双方诸多相关研究项目，培训了数以千计的中国燃气业人员，为大鹏项目的顺利投产和运作、为我国 LNG 人才培养和产业发展发挥了独特的作用。

## 三、长期协议不断涌现：中澳合作势头迅猛

大鹏项目立项后，东部沿海省市对建设LNG接收终端项目热情高涨，省与省以及省内部各地之间展开了立项竞争，有的省推出了多个计划。经中央控制和协调，目前，国家发改委在沿海布点的14个已投产、在建或拟建的LNG接收站如表4所示。[12]

**表4　中国已建、在建、拟建的液化天然气接收站（截至2011年12月）**

| 项目名称 | 一期规模（万吨/年） | 一期投产日期 | 二、三期扩建后规模（万吨/年） |
|---|---|---|---|
| 广东大鹏 | 370 | 2006.5 | 700 |
| 福建莆田 | 260 | 2009.7 | 600 |
| 上海洋山 | 300 | 2009.9 | 600 |
| 江苏如东 | 350 | 2011.5 | 650 |
| 辽宁大连 | 300 | 2011.7 | 600～780 |
| 浙江宁波 | 300 | 2012 | 600 |
| 广东珠海 | 300 | 2013 | 1000 |
| 山东青岛 | 300 | 2013 | 500 |
| 河北唐山 | 350 | 2013 | 650 |
| 广西北海 | 300 | 2014 | 500 |
| 广东粤东 | 200 | 2013 | 400 |

（续上表）

| 项目名称 | 一期规模（万吨/年） | 一期投产日期 | 二、三期扩建后规模（万吨/年） |
|---|---|---|---|
| 广东粤西 | 200 | 2014 | 300 |
| 广东深圳 | 200 | 2013 | 400 |
| 海南洋浦 | 200 | 2014 | 300 |

表4所列14个项目一期工程2014年全部竣工投产后，总计每年需要3930万吨液化天然气（合530.5亿立方米天然气），若后期扩展计划均顺利于2020年前建成投产，则年度需求量为7800～7980万吨（合1050～1070亿方天然气）。此外，在天津、河北、浙江、辽宁、江苏等地尚有诸多初步获批、待批或计划中的液化天然气接收站建设项目10余个，若投产另需数千万吨一年的液化天然气。目前看来，较能确定的是，2014年，我国年度液化天然气进口量须达到3930万吨，方能基本满足终端站接收能力需要，2020年时需求会有更大攀升，尽管具体增量目前尚难以确定。

如此巨大的需求必须有长期和充足的气源保障，不然所建的接收站将成空巢，造成国家投资的浪费，加剧我国能源供应紧张，威胁我国能源安全。几年来，中海油、中石油、中石化三巨头加快与LNG产地接洽，已签订诸多长期供应协议。鉴于澳大利亚是全球未来LNG增量最大的国家，印尼和马来西亚的增能有限，卡塔尔距我国相对较远，俄罗斯未来向我国提供的主要是管道天然气，对我国而言，澳在地缘、生产潜力、供应能力等方面拥有优势，加之大鹏项目的示范效应，至2011年末，澳是与我国签订LNG长期供货合约最多的国家（见表5）。[13]

**表5　中外主要液化天然气长期购销协议（截至2011年底）**

| 签约时间 | 供货时间 | 合约期限（年） | 年供量（万吨） | 签约公司 | 气源地 |
|---|---|---|---|---|---|
| 2002.10 | 2006.5 | 25 | 330～370 | 中海油、澳西北大陆架 | 澳大利亚 |
| 2004.7 | 2009.7 | 25 | 260 | 中海油、印尼东固气田 | 印尼 |
| 2006.10 | 2009.9 | 25 | 303 | 上海液化天然气、马来西亚液化天然气 | 马来西亚 |
| 2008.4 | 2011.5 | 25 | 300 | 中石油、卡塔尔天然气、壳牌 | 卡塔尔 |
| 2008.11 | 2014 | 20 | 200 | 中石油、壳牌 | 澳大利亚 |
| 2009.8 | 2015 | 20 | 225 | 中石油、美孚澳大利亚 | 澳大利亚 |
| 2009.11 | 2014 | 20 | 200 | 中石化、埃克森美孚 | 巴布亚新几内亚 |
| 2010.3 | 2014 | 20 | 360 | 中海油、英国天然气 | 澳大利亚 |

（续上表）

| 签约时间 | 供货时间 | 合约期限（年） | 年供量（万吨） | 签约公司 | 气源地 |
|---|---|---|---|---|---|
| 2011.4<br>2011.12 | 2015 | 20 | 430（2011年4月签约量）、330（2011年12月签约增量） | 中石化、澳太平洋液化天然气 | 澳大利亚 |

表5所列为公开报道的三大石油公司所签重要长期合约，这些协议锁定的年度最大供应量为2978万吨液化天然气，其中约64%（1915万吨）来自澳大利亚。液化天然气产业的上下游呈齿轮般紧密结合关系，一旦签署买卖合约，在合约期内双方谁也离不开谁。有鉴于此，国内外业界普遍认为，在液化天然气领域，中澳已显示出较大的相互依赖，液化天然气合作将成为中澳能源合作的新亮点，以及增进和提高两国互信的新渠道。

中澳LNG协议具有多重意义。如2010年3月和2011年4月、12月签订的合同，不仅是供应量和金额巨大的两个合约，对两国更具深层意义。长期以来，澳LNG出口地主要是西部的西澳州，东部昆士兰州的燃气业以满足国内市场为主，与国际市场联系有限。但该州富有煤层气，昆士兰提出的宏大的LNG产业规划即以煤层气转产LNG为基础，未来向中国出口的LNG也是煤层气转化而来。澳国内对煤层气转LNG产业前景存在争议，中海油和中石化签订的大单，无疑显示了国际市场看好煤层气转LNG的前景，对澳是支持和鼓励，将有助于澳成为煤层气转LNG的领先国家，促进澳东部出现新兴的LNG生产和出口基地，使澳LNG产业形成东西联动发展的局面，扩大和延续资源景气。

我国是全球煤层气第三大储量国，煤层气是我国发展清洁能源的重点之一，“十一五”规划要求2010年时新增煤层气探明储量3000亿立方米，煤层气产量100亿立方米。[14]最后由于开发困难、机制欠妥等原因，我国未能完成“十一五”确定的煤层气发展目标。中国公司参与澳煤层气转LNG产业发展，是具有战略智慧和意义、达到双赢或多赢的明智举措。以中海油和英国天然气公司所签协议为例，昆士兰规划开发全球第一个大规模的以煤层气为原料生产液化天然气的柯蒂斯LNG项目，为分解风险，它不仅需要英国的LNG技术和全球网络的支持，也需要中国公司能带来的未来的市场保障和一定的资金投入。因此，那份协议不是简单的360万吨LNG一年的购销协议，而是一份涉及煤层气开发及其液化处理、造船、运输等LNG整个产业链的全方位合作协议。根据协议，中海油获准购买英国天然气集团在昆士兰的煤层气储量权益的5%，可获两条液化天然气生产线中第一条10%的股权，双方共同组建船运公司在华建造2艘LNG运输船。通过合作，中英澳三方可实现各自目的，达到多赢。对此，国家能源局予以充分肯定，认为该合作项目将对我国提高煤层气利用提供有益借鉴。

2011年4月，与中石化签订年供430万吨LNG大单的澳太平洋液化天然气公司，也以昆士兰的煤层气为原料炼制LNG。双方除签订LNG购销协议外，还签署了股份认购书，规定中石化将出资15亿美元认购太平洋液化天然气公司15%的股份，使得公司演变为包括中石化的三方合资企业。同年12月，双方增签协议，规定中石化增加采购330万吨/年的液化天然气，累计采购760万吨/年，2015年供气，为期20年；协议还规定中石化认购的股权自15%增至25%。协议金额未披露，但显然刷新了澳大利亚单一出口合同金额最高、售气量最大的记录。这意味着澳大利亚太平洋液化天然气公司规划中的两条液化天然气生产线的产量销售得到了全面保障，并吸收到了中方更多的资金投入，而中石化则锁定了长期资源供应，而且价格相对固定、便宜，并获得项目的部分权益。这种以贸易促投资、借投资进入澳大利亚天然气上游勘探、生产和管理，学习先进技术和经验，同时有助于保障供给平稳的中国企业走出去的方法，不失为中企投资海外的有效方法之一，对实现我国能源发展战略具有积极的现实意义。

表5所列以澳大利亚为气源地的5份LNG长期购销协议中，3个协议实现了我方期盼的上游参股和全产业链合作。另一案例也显示中澳燃气业战略合作的成功。2010年3月，中石油联合壳牌，出资35亿澳元全面收购拥有昆士兰丰富煤层气资源的澳大利亚箭牌能源公司，三方将携手推动昆士兰的煤层气和煤层气转LNG产业发展。项目投产后，不仅可扩大对澳国内的燃气供应，每年还可出口700～800万吨LNG，约一半将运往中国。中石油也将获得宝贵的煤层气生产、管理和煤层气转LNG的经验，有利于推动中国的煤层气产业发展。

概而言之，澳大利亚正经历本国史无前例的LNG大开发，会迎来极大的产能增长，中国正全力以赴发展天然气产业，会有大规模的市场扩增，中澳在LNG领域有着互补的基础、相互依赖和互利合作的刚性需求。

## 四、挑战和影响因素

毋庸置疑，中澳合作过程中也出现了一些矛盾、困难和问题，值得双方重视并加强沟通和协调，予以妥善应对或解决。关键是价格问题。21世纪初，油价处于低区，签订大鹏项目协议时，即便我们选择了出价最高的澳大利亚LNG，也依然是价格史上的低位。此后，国际油价趋涨，带动LNG价格上扬。2008年，油价升到峰值，我国购买的LNG现货价一度骤升至20美元/百万英热单位。2010年，我国进口的LNG均价为6.41美元/百万英热单位，澳大利亚气价为4.66美元/百万英热单位，较最高的卡塔尔气价12.69美元低8.03美元。[15]由此，澳认为，大鹏项目合约规定的25年“照付不议”价格给澳造成了巨大经济损失。澳方有调价的欲望，可由于合约中25年价格不变的约束，又显得无奈，但怨气却在积累。[16]这表明合约期内几十年价格不变的照付不议原则，随着价格的起伏必然给买方或卖方带来利益损害，引起不满或怨恨，可能影响双方合作顺利。

大鹏协议签署后，多年间中澳LNG贸易谈判不顺，较大程度上为价格使然。2003年10月，中海油与澳高庚LNG项目签订初步协议，规定中海油购买高庚项目12.5%股权，参股项目的上游开发，购买总额达300亿澳元的高庚LNG。此后双方进入商业谈判。该项目受到两国最高层领导支持，双方都抱着极大的期望，预计 2004 年结束谈判，首船 LNG 于 2008 年运抵中国。可最后由于价格原因中海油失去合同。2003 年双方初步约定的交易价是 4 美元/百万英热单位，但 2005 年，日本和欧美市场燃气均价已达 7.47 美元/百万英热单位[17]，现货价更达到 12 美元。谈判中双方在价格上的分歧由此产生，此时日本出价 7 美元，高庚项目作业者雪佛龙公司最后选择了日本。

大鹏项目的成功和高庚合同的丢失颇有启迪。其一，LNG 交易中遵循市场竞争原则极为重要，良好乐观的愿望、领导人的高调支持代替不了公司的商业诉求；其二，合同期内价格予以固定的照付不议原则，难以保证合约期数十年内的双赢效果，这样的 LNG 合约价格有缺陷，应有价格复议的安排，或需买卖双方考虑合理、灵活、平衡的解决方案；其三，彼时成功方法，此时不一定管用，囿于前期成功买卖的经验而忽视变化了的市场条件，无助于争取更多、更稳定的资源供应。

双方面临的另一挑战是变幻莫测的国际市场及其带来的前景不确定性。随着节能减排、环境保护、可持续发展日益受重视，作为清洁、高效能源之一的天然气愈发受青睐，燃气价趋涨，由 21 世纪初的买方市场进入几年后的卖方市场。国际观察家们异口同声地唱好燃气市场前景，各国纷纷推出天然气液化厂或再气化工程。但 2008 年的金融危机重挫了燃气市场提升势头，压制了欧美需求的提高。自那时以来，业界对燃气市场的走势莫衷一是。有人认为，危机影响了燃气需求的增长，美、欧、日、韩等国的燃气需求缩减，或增幅极小，加之美国页岩气和煤层气开采取得有效进展，拉低了燃气输入增长，而前几年包括澳在内的各国生产商上马了许多新的生产项目，这意味着燃气市场将供过于求，进入买方市场。[18]

另有意见认为，由于成本提高和金融危机的打击，全球上游天然气液化产能发展已大受影响，投资严重短缺，开发项目遭推迟或减少，但是下游再气化产能增长的影响却不大。其结果是，2008—2012年的全球天然气液化产能增长率将自原计划的17.06%降至14.61%，减少LNG增量7093万吨；同期，全球再气化产能的预期增长几乎不变。[19]2012年后，全球LNG供应会有不足，亚太市场缺口更大。尤其是2013年后LNG新的巨大增量能否出现尚不明朗，因此，2015年后，供应短缺状况将逾趋严重。[20]2011年的日本核泄漏危机正进一步引发全球能源变局，各国均重新审视核能产业，诸多国家面临国内"去核电"或"减核电"的巨大社会压力，势必加大天然气和煤炭进口用于发电，以弥补核电缺口。这加剧了人们对未来全球尤其是亚太LNG供应可能趋紧的担忧。

两种针锋相对的预测，揭示了未来数年国际LNG市场欠明朗的前景。这对中澳两国燃气业的规划、发展形成挑战。澳面临的挑战是，未来市场能否全部消化其大规模投入带来的巨大增产。澳方已意识到该问题的严重性，并采取了一些举措，平衡本国产能增长和国际需求增速之间的关系。因此，澳大利亚并非所有项目同时施工建设，一个项目从提出计划到做出最终投资决定，会经过漫长的可行性评估，以及须与一些买家签订LNG长期购销协议，提前锁定部分增长产能的市场。因而，澳表现出的特征之一是，项目评估审核费时、复杂，最终投资决定谨慎，项目建设速度慢。如年产能1500万吨、投资额高达500亿澳元的高庚项目，原预计2008年投产，后推迟，至本文截稿时仍在建中。但截至2009年8月，高庚项目已签售1020万吨LNG[21]，其中包括中石油已签两合约的425万吨，基本解除了销售的后顾之忧，保障了项目能建成投产。

而中国签署从昆士兰购买高达1120万吨以煤层气为原料的液化天然气的长期协议，对促进当地柯蒂斯液化天然气项目、澳大利亚太平洋液化天然气项目的投资决策和建设进度也发挥了积极有益的作用。这证明了液化天然气领域中澳的相互依赖和利益共存。良好、健康的中澳燃气合作，有利于双方成功应对市场变化的复杂性和欠明朗性，有助于促进双方经济发展。

面对难以捉摸的市场前景，中国须关注两点。其一，国内LNG接收站建设不应一哄而上，缺乏统一规划和循序渐进，造成LNG开发商对需求的过度强烈预期，从而没有节制地抬高售价，损害我国经济利益。我国铁矿石贸易多年来受高价的折磨，LNG不可步铁矿石后尘。其二，必须保证每个接收站投产后有长期、稳定、足量的LNG供应，发挥预期的经济和社会效益，避免投资浪费。

实现第一点，靠国内的调控和协调；兑现第二点，则须加强与包括澳在内的LNG供应国的合作。由于未来LNG最大需求增量源自亚太地区，该地区的市场竞争最为激烈，澳则是全球LNG产能增量最大的国家和我国第一LNG供应国，无论将来是买方还是卖方市场，中澳都得合作。双方应该多考虑如何保障长期互利、双赢才有利于合作的健康、稳定发展，任何一方片面考虑和追求己方利益，最终都将令贸易和经济合作难以持续，中澳双方应该发挥足够的智慧，使两国关系避免再受到类似铁矿石价格纠纷的冲击。

中澳 LNG 贸易还面临供需多方博弈。长期以来，国内对引进俄罗斯燃气热情不减。中俄规划通过两条管线，每年向华输送 700 亿立方米俄气，若顺利实施，无疑会对中国从其他国家进口燃气产生影响。虽经中俄双方多年努力，两国天然气合作至今依然未能逾越价格这道坎。导致这一现象的一大原因，是双方都有其他选择，远未到离开对方、另一方就难以生存的程度。俄罗斯燃气主要面向欧洲市场，且可卖高价；中国则以成功从澳大利亚、印尼、卡塔尔等国的燃气进口，以及已锁定更多非俄罗斯气源，不但缓解了进口俄气的压力，反而使俄方感受到了销售竞争。此外，尽管中澳互为重要贸易伙伴，各自也都奉行着多元化战略，有着其他伙伴。这种多方供需间的博弈和多元化的追求，将始终左右中澳 LNG 合作的规模和走势。

## [注释]

[1] 国家统计局能源统计司：《中国能源统计年鉴 2011》。北京：中国统计出版社，2012 年。表 4－1。

[2] Global LNG, World's LNG liquefaction plants and regasification terminals, June, 2012, http://www.globallnginfo.com/World%20LNG%20Plants%20&%20Terminals.pdf

[3] 根据历年 *BP Statistical Review of World Energy* 的数据整理而成。(BP, 2011, *BP Statistical Review of World Energy June* 2011)

[4] 鲁华：澳大利亚专家谈中国能源问题，《能源政策研究通讯》，1989 年第 6 期，第 10－14 页。

[5] Mehmet Ögütçü, , China's energy future and global implications, in Werner Draguhn, Robert Ash (eds.), *China's Economic Security*, Richmond, Surrey: Curzon Press, 1999, pp84 - 141.

[6] 中国液化天然气网，积极推动广东 LNG 项目的实施和发展，2010 年 1 月 3 日，http://www.cnlng.com/bencandy.php?fid=65&id=12462

[7] 许芙：中澳能源合作：另一种思路，《中国石油石化》，2006 年第 8 期，第 26 - 27 页。

[8] BP, *BP Statistical Review of World Energy June* 2011, 2011, p27.

[9] 中国燃气网，广东天然气电厂气源全线告急，2008 年 3 月 17 日，http://www.chinagas.org.cn/hangyexinxi/veiw_gnrq.asp?id=2171

[10] 一涨一降 广东省逆势下调天然气电厂上网电价，《21 世纪经济报道》，2011 年 5 月 5 日，http://stock.jrj.com.cn/2011/05/0501479890330.shtml

[11] 庞名立：2010 年驶向中国的液化天然气船状况，2010 年 10 月 28 日，http://www.cngascn.com/html/news/show_news_w1_1_5039.html

[12] 根据中国能源讯息网 2011 年 5 月 27 日报道"中国 LNG 产业现状"和网络及报纸公布的其他信息整理所得。

[13] 资料来源：根据网上和报纸公布的信息整理所得。

[14] 中国燃气网，我国煤层气开发利用规划出台，2006 年 7 月 21 日，http://www.chinagas.org.cn/hangyexinxi/veiw_gnrq.asp?id=1886

[15] 中国天然气全景网，中国 2010 年 1 - 12 月液化天然气进出口分项数据，2011 年 3 月 10 日，http://www.cngascn.com/html/news/show_news_w1_1_6985.html

[16] Wyatt, Stephen & Ryan, Colleen, China signs up for $50bn gas deal, *The Australian Financial Review*, 19 August, 2009, pp. 1, 10.

[17] BP, *BP Statistical Review of World Energy June* 2011, 2011, p27.
[18] Energy Global, Oversupply of gas expected on the market for next five years, 22 June, 2010, http://www.energyglobal.com/sectors/liquid-natural-gas/articles/Oversupply_of_gas_expected_on_the_market_for_next_five_years.aspx
[19] Energy Global, Global LNG industry set to regain momentum after 2012, 19 October, 2009, http://www.energyglobal.com/sectors/liquid-natural-gas/articles/global_lng_industry_set_to_regain_momentum_after_2012.aspx
[20] Global LNG, Further & fundamental developments-Some key points, 28 August, 2010, http://www.globallnginfo.com/futher%20and%20fundamental.htm
[21] Andrew Burrell, Gorgon misgivings laid to rest, *The Australian Financial Review*, 19 August, 2009, p10.

## 作者简介

**侯敏跃**，博士、教授，现任华东师范大学澳大利亚研究中心副主任。主要研究方向：中澳关系、澳大利亚外交和社会文化、亚太研究、中外关系研究、文化研究、新西兰研究。（Email：myhou@english.ecnu.edu.cn）

# 5

# 澳大利亚能源新战略评析*

唐小松　许　嬉

充足的能源资源是国家发展经济、维持繁荣的重要保障，谁控制了能源，谁就控制了经济增长。[1]因此，能源安全一直受到各国高度重视。澳大利亚作为天然的能源大国，近期通过发布《国家能源安全评估 2009》和《白皮书战略指针》等相关文件，重新对其自身的能源结构进行了评估和战略调整，以应对当前国际形势新变化。这无论是对于澳大利亚自身的发展，还是周边国家和地区的战略调整来说，都值得引起高度重视。

## 一、澳大利亚能源新战略的内涵

澳大利亚最新公布的《国家能源安全评估 2009》文件将“能源安全”界定为：能源得以充足、可靠、可承受的供应，以支持国家经济运行和社会发展。[2]作为制定澳大利亚国家能源安全政策的第一步，该文件对液化燃料、天然气

* 本文原载于《国际观察》2010 年第 3 期。

和电力三个部门在当前以及未来5年、10年、15年的能源安全进行了整体评估，为未来的能源评估建立了一套评估标准，同时也为《能源白皮书》的出台奠定了基础。自2008年9月开始，澳大利亚《能源白皮书》的起草工作在政府的支持下展开，确定了一个将延续到2030年之后的全方位、灵活性的政策性框架。该文件建立在与澳大利亚政府低碳政策框架相一致的基础上，通过对当前国际形势和澳大利亚自身能源结构进行分析与评估，为下一步的政策行动指明方向。从这两个标志性文件可以看出，澳大利亚能源战略的新调整主要体现在以下几个方面：

一是加大能源资源基础设施建设，促进能源市场的发展和能源使用多样化。

澳大利亚政府通过对其能源结构进行科学详细的评估，让自身和世界都看见了其能源潜力，为进一步促进能源市场的发展打下基础。澳大利亚拥有丰富的能源资源，虽然石油、煤、天然气等传统能源在一定时期内仍占主导，但近几年非传统能源的进一步发展，促成了能源使用的多样化，这为澳大利亚在维持竞争力以及在低碳时代确保能源安全方面提供了更多选择。[3]同时，澳大利亚政府认为，发展多样化能源资源有助于新兴技术和服务的成熟，应创造机会将其投入市场，一方面可推动整体经济发展，另一方面也有助于其他相关部门的发展。可见，高效的能源市场促进了能源和技术的多样化，形成了更强大的供应链，有助于澳大利亚确保区域能源安全。

澳大利亚政府认为，能源资源基础设施包括供应链基础设施、社区基础设施和服务基础设施。由于澳大利亚远离其国际进出口市场，即使是满足其国内需求的能源资源也远离人流中心和其他能源负荷中心，澳大利亚的繁荣很大程度上取决于满足国内外客户需求的能源运输和转化系统。[4]澳大利亚政府还把基础设施作为吸引外来投资的工具，2006 年签署了《竞争和基础设施改造协议》；最近，又建立了基础设施部门，为其未来的基础设施建设描绘战略蓝图，不仅就那些阻碍经济发展的基础设施缺口和瓶颈为各级政府提出建议，还将确定投资重点和政策调整改革。[5]此外，在 2008—2009 年财政预算中，政府宣布建立澳大利亚建设基金，基金的分配将以国家基础设施审计和基础设施重点列表为依据。[6]

二是强调能源技术革新和可再生能源的使用。

国际能源署在《世界能源展望 2008》中指出，世界能源系统随着当前能源供应和消费趋势已经走到了十字路口，这无论是在环境、经济还是社会方面，都是难以承受的。我们急需进行一次能源革命，以此解决当前面临的两大主要的能源挑战：确保可靠的和可承受的能源供应；快速实现向低碳、高效和对环境负责的供应体系的转变。[7]随着澳大利亚人口数量的增加和对能源的需求不断加强，温室气体的排放将大大增加。能源技术上的创新可以为澳大利亚提供更多的选择，从而以负责任和更有效的姿态去应对能源压力。如为实现2050 年时的温室气体排放量比2000 年减少60%，以及在 2020 年底减少 5%～15% 温室气体排放的中期目标[8]，澳大利亚政府承诺在 2010 年引进碳污染减量方案，并增加补充措施，包括加快碳捕获、注射和储存，以及可再生能源技术和能源有效投资等方面的发展。对于重要的排放密集型贸易行业，澳大利亚政府承诺将提供大量援助，以帮助这些企业向低碳经济转变。此外，澳大利亚政府也采取了一系列政策支持可再生能源的发展，如执行《可再生能源目标》（RET）方案，鼓励可再生能源的研究、示范和商业化，拨出500万美元可再生能源基金、150万美元研究太阳能和洁净能源、超过500万美元打造太阳能城市等[9]，并要求20%的电力产生于可再生能源。

三是继续参与国际多边、双边能源协议，有针对性地加强国际能源合作。

澳大利亚参与的多边、双边协定多种多样，并涵盖了所有影响其国家利益的能源政策问题。作为一个中等强国，多边协定的全球性为其追求更全面的政策目标提供了有效工具。[10]而双边协议则是澳大利亚具体的有针对性的促进能源贸易和投资利益的有效手段。事实上，由于全球化将各国的利益联系在一起，很多问题都需要各国共同参与、共同承担才能实现共同获利。澳大利亚根据自身的实力和准确客观的定位，从以下几个方面来保证其能源战略在国际参与中得到实现：一是促进高效、透明和有竞争力的地方、区域及全球能源市场的发展，以最少的成本解决经济、安全、可持续发展上面临的挑战；二是追求更有效地参与主要能源消费，包括作为最主要的消费者、投资者的中印两国和出口原油的关键区域；三是有效促进国际能源机构在其框架内参与国际合作；四是促进澳大利亚的铀能源出口沿着核不扩散目标展开；五是促进能源政策的实施，以最小的成本解决化石燃料对环境的影响，同时减少碳排放和能源消耗时最小化对经济的冲击。[11]

## 二、澳大利亚能源战略调整的原因

澳大利亚重视能源安全、进行能源战略调整，是出于对本国和国际综合环境的评估，自然也是多种因素相互作用的结果。经济危机对国际能源市场的冲击，加上澳大利亚对能源过分依赖的经济发展模式，让确保能源市场多样化发展以及保证能源供应成为其重点考虑的问题；全球气候问题的日益严重，对传统能源利用率和新能源开发提出了更高的要求；外交与能源安全无孔不入的结合，也使得澳大利亚开始综合考量能源政策的新走向。

首先，经济危机导致全球能源市场面临困境，澳大利亚经济上对能源的过分依赖凸显了确保能源供应链可靠运行的重要性。

经济危机之际，面对严峻的融资环境、疲软的能源需求和较低的现金流，世界范围内的能源投资大幅度下降。能源公司减少了在能源基础设施上的投资，在石油和天然气行业，大多数公司因为现金流减少宣布要缩减资本支出，延期或取消一些项目。2009 年全球石油和天然气投资预算缩减了 19%，超过 900 亿美元。因为融资困难以及电力需求下降，电力行业的投资也严重受损。可再生能源的投资更是大幅度下降，如果没有政府的投资，下降程度将会达到 30% 左右。[12]可见，经济危机在世界范围内蔓延，对能源市场普遍造成了严重的影响。然而，在 75 年来全球最严重的经济危机面前，与全球主要先进国家相比，澳大利亚却有着最快的增长，最低的借贷、赤字以及全球第二低的失业率。[13]这主要归功于澳大利亚自身的资源禀赋和政府有力的应对措施，特别是后者起着关键性的作用。澳大利亚是一个重要的能源净出口国和地区能源供应国，它不仅是世界第二大动力煤出口国，约占世界份额的20%，也是世界第二大铀和重要的液化天然气出口国。[14]澳大利亚能源部门收入在2007—2008年间占澳大利亚GDP的8%以上，能源出口在2008—2009年间更是预计达到750亿美元左右，比上一年增长了72%。[15]澳大利亚产出的能源中，用于出口的占66%，用于国内的占34%。[16]丰富的能源资源为其出口经济做出了重要贡献，但同时也带来了经济过度依赖导致的脆弱性，“其他国家处理能源安全的方式将对澳大利亚的利益造成重大影响”，[17]这不仅仅是一个经济问题，更是战略问题。如今各国已意识到能源安全的重要性，尤其是依靠进口能源快速发展的国家，如欧洲国家越来越依赖俄罗斯的能源供应，波斯湾更多的石油和天然气流向了中国和印度[18]。这些国家通过发展战略性的石油储备、扩大核能的使用、提高能源使用率和在外国投资更多的能源股权等方式来减少本国能源安全的脆弱性，拓宽获取途径，减少能源供应中断的可能性。这必将对澳大利亚造成一定影响。为持续经济危机中的良好表现，澳大利亚政府不得不长远考虑，相应重新调整其能源战略，进一步刺激国内市场运行，加大对能源基础设施的投资，提供公平、开发、透明的投资环境吸引外资，确保在下一轮的经济复苏前能源市场的有效运行。

其次，气候问题日益严重，国际社会的减排呼声愈加强烈，澳大利亚在能源政策方面也不得不顺应低碳趋势做出调整。

1992年《联合国气候框架公约》在里约热内卢通过，呼吁各方共同努力，为实现未来的可持续发展，稳定温室气体的排放，承认共同的原则但承担不同的责任。[19]然而，大部分国家出于自身利益考虑，在这种宽松、不受约束的框架下，并未承担相应责任。如果任其发展下去，后果是惊人的——根据《世界能源展望2008》预测，到本世纪末，温室气体排放将使其在大气中的浓度增加1倍，最终导致全球的平均温度上升6℃；全球与能源相关的二氧化碳排放将从2006年的280亿吨增长到2030年的410亿吨，增长45%。[20]采取有力行动控制温室气体排放和由此引发的全球气温上升已迫在眉睫。经过18年的气候谈判，国际社会在气候政策上仍未达成一致，2009年底的哥本哈根会议也未达成实质性协议，各国仅独立做出了减排承诺。然而，国际能源系统的低碳化趋势已不可阻挡。澳大利亚作为少数履行《京都议定书》承诺的能源大国，积极采取有效而有力的措施减少国内温室气体排放量，提高能源利用率，增加低碳排放技术的部署和研发，这不仅能从更大程度上确保其能源安全，而且有利于增强澳大利亚负责任的国际形象。此外，减排压力也推动了新能源的开发和新技术的研发，这也有利于澳大利亚向外提供先进的能源、技术服务，得到可观的经济收益。

最后，新形势下澳大利亚政府对其能源外交的再定位，也在很大程度上推动了其能源战略的调整。

尽管金融危机带来了经济的衰退，但能源需求仍将继续增长。《世界能源展望2008》预计，到2030年国际上对能源资源的需求将增加45%。因此，澳大利亚若充分运用自身的能源潜力，不仅能有效扩大其能源市场，带来可观的经济利益，还能提升其在亚太地区的地位。传统意义上来说，澳大利亚的能源安全利益主要表现在以下两方面：一是继续从公开且充满竞争的国际市场里获得原油和石油产品，特别是在其自给自足能力逐渐下降的情势下；二是作为煤炭、铀和天然气的主要出口国的地位，促使澳大利亚成为一个稳定、可靠的能源供应国。如今，澳大利亚还谋求“在未来的可能范围内运用能源潜力在国际讨论和与亚太地区的贸易合作中谋求更大的影响力。”[21]因此，澳大利亚需要一个更有效的能源政策让其更充分地展现自身实力，并以此增强它在全球能源政策方向上的影响力。不得不指出的是，澳大利亚政府已经意识到，作为一个中等国家，其大部分的政策优势都需要在与其他国家的合作中得到最大实现。[22]如今澳大利亚参与的有关能源问题的多边论坛包括国际能源署、亚太清洁发展和气候新伙伴计划、G8在气候变化和可持续发展上的对话、亚太经济组织能源合作等。此外，澳大利亚还进行了一系列双边能源协定，特别是在能源交易和投资利益方面，以实现其特定的、有针对性的国家目标。澳大利亚希望通过这些国际合作，找到自身的最佳位置，以实现利益的最大化。

## 三、澳大利亚能源新战略对中国的启示

在全球经济危机影响犹存、国际社会减排呼声四起的形势下，澳大利亚能源战略的一系列调整，既给出了有益的提醒，又暴露了值得考虑的警示，对同为亚太事务重要参与者

的中国来说，既是机遇又有挑战，带来了许多有益的启示。

第一，中澳两国可以进一步加强清洁能源和技术方面的合作。

澳大利亚拥有丰富的自然资源，大量的煤、天然气、铀等能源和太阳能、地热、风能、波浪能等可再生资源。中澳作为世界上最大的煤炭买卖方，在清洁能源技术合作方面有巨大潜力。特别是在气候问题备受关注的今天，进一步加强开发洁净能源、减少碳排放不仅是挑战，更是责任。目前中澳能源合作项目有两个，一个是哈尔滨电力设备制造公司和维多利亚州 HRL 公司的合作，另一个是香港 China lingt Power 公司投资了 2.9 亿澳元的太阳能发电项目。2008 年 4 月 10 日，中澳两国政府发表了关于进一步密切在气候变化方面合作的联合声明。[23] 2009 年 12 月，中国在哥本哈根大会上承诺将在 2020 年前把单位 GDP 碳排放比 2005 年下降 40% 至 45%，[24] 开发新能源也成了当务之急。中国目前是拥有核电机组最多的国家，澳大利亚拥有丰富的铀资源，双方可以进行能源贸易或共同开发铀资源，促进清洁能源的使用。由此可见，中澳两国在未来将进一步加强清洁能源和技术方面的合作，将带来双赢的效果。

第二，要进一步开拓澳大利亚能源市场，加强两国能源贸易，但对澳能源投资需谨慎。

双赢毕竟是需要建立在彼此的实力基础之上，否则合作既可能带来利益扩大，也可能是危机四伏。中澳目前的合作既有能源贸易，又有能源投资。在 2008 年经济危机爆发之前，澳大利亚作为一个能源净出口国，强势的经济增长主要来自于中国和印度能源需求的推动。中印两国 GDP 目前占全球的15%，无论是作为买方还是投资者，对澳大利亚都具有重大意义。如今经济衰退导致全球投资锐减，澳大利亚政府已经意识到，要想确保能源安全和经济发展，就要吸引其主要能源市场国的有效参与。因此，中国可以充分利用当前形势进一步加强两国能源贸易，确保能源供应满足国内经济的增长。近年来中澳能源交易不断扩大，2009年8月18日，埃克森美孚与中石油签订协议，从所持澳大利亚Gorgon液化天然气（LNG）项目份额向中石油出售天然气，交易价值约为500亿澳元（约合412.9亿美元），是澳中两国最大的一笔贸易交易。[25]澳大利亚贸易委员会表示，2010年，澳大利亚同中国的双边贸易额可能增加到1000亿澳元（约合910亿美元）。中国已成为澳大利亚第一大贸易伙伴。[26]可以看出，中澳两国不断加强能源合作是出于双方的共同需要。虽然去年的“力拓事件”让中澳两国关系蒙上了阴影，但如今中澳已恢复自由贸易谈判，两国关系恢复正常。[27]但不得不指出的是，在资本投资方面中国仍需谨慎对待，经济衰退加大了投资项目的不确定性和能源价格的不稳定性，而且澳大利亚目前急需外部资金投资其能源开采或基础设施建设等，中国投资之前更需考虑清楚。

第三，要警惕澳大利亚在能源市场上实施的平衡战略。

能源不仅与经济发展联系紧密，在全球化的背景下，它还可以成为一国有力的外交工具。中国和印度都是澳大利亚最重要的能源出口国，对澳大利亚经济发展和能源安全都有重要意义。近年来，澳大利亚政府决定进一步加强与印度的能源技术合作，将两国能源合作上升到国家战略的高度。澳大利亚外交部长最近承认，几十年以来，澳大利亚政府低估了印度，其潜力和未来的重要性，不光是在本区域范围，还是对世界而言的。[28]目前与澳印有关的能源双边、多边合作协定有：澳印能源、矿产联合工作组（JWG），全球碳捕获和存储计划（CCS），亚太清洁发展和气候新伙伴计划（APP）和东亚峰会（EAS），[29]澳印能源合作必定会随着其能源战略的推行而越来越紧密。同时，澳大利亚政府认为澳印之间具有共同应对经济危机影响的共同利益，并期望与印度在国际组织中进一步合作。此外，印度作为五大能源消费国之一，其与澳大利亚的经济互补性也为两国合作创造了可能性。澳大利亚对印度态度上的转变，越来越被认为是为了平衡中国在亚太地区的影响力。澳大利亚希望借助一个不断强大的印度，防止中国在亚太地区的崛起。2009 年 5 月澳大利亚公布的《澳大利亚国防白皮书》认为中国是未来亚太地区可能的危机爆发点。因此，中国不能不重视澳大利亚战略调整，无论是能源还是其他方面。澳大利亚作为中国巨大的能源供应国，其战略转向对中国能源安全将是潜在的危机。同时，在澳大利亚的能源战略推动下，中印两国将来不可避免会遇到能源资源和投资项目上的合作或争夺。合作上利益分配不均或者是竞争的关系可能会造成两国关系紧张，甚至损害地区稳定。因此，如何处理好与周边国家在能源上的竞争关系，对中国来说将是另一种挑战。

第四，要提防澳大利亚联合其他国家向中国施压。

中国作为世界上第二大与能源有关的二氧化碳排放国，其高能耗、高污染、高排放的增长特点一直备受国际关注和指责。随着中国经济的发展和国际地位的提高，中国必然要以负责任的大国姿态履行自己做出的承诺。然而，由于工业生产和经济模式具有一定惯性，原有的设备和技术在短时间内难以更新并投入使用，因此在向低碳经济转型的过程中必定困难重重。在目前这种大环境下，外部要求减排的压力不断涌向主要排放国，中国应该提防外部力量联合起来向中国施压，要求中国承担过多的责任。澳大利亚作为少数履行《京都议定书》的减排先锋国之一，一直将中国蓬勃发展的经济看做是温室气体争论的罪魁祸首，认为其为减排做出的努力将被中国高速增长的经济所淹没。因此，在未来的气候谈判中，澳大利亚政府仍有可能有针对性的联合其他国家向中国施压，要求中国进一步减少温室气体排放。在这种困境面前，中国可以通过与其他主要排放大国如印度等国相互声援和合作，或者是在多边组织中寻求途径分担这些国际压力，以维护本国的最大利益，在承担一定责任的前提下，防止中国经济成为全球减排的牺牲品。

## [注释]

[1] Martin Ferguson, Energy Security: The New Cold War, http://www.energysecurity.org.au/uploads/06_Martin_Ferguson_speech.pdf.

[2] *National Energy Security Assessment* 2009, p.5, http://www.ret.gov.au/energy/Documents/Energy%20Security/National-Energy-Security-Assessment-2009.pdf.

[3] *Strategic Directions for Energy White Paper*, March 2009, p.8, http://www.ret.gov.au/energy/Documents/Energy%20Security/Strategic%20Directions%20for%20Energy%20White%20Paper%20March%202009.pdf.

[4] *Strategic Directions for Energy White Paper*, March 2009", p.6, http://www.ret.gov.au/energy/Documents/Energy%20Security/Stra-

tegic% 20Directions% 20for% 20Energy% 20White% 20Paper% 20March% 202009. pdf.

[5] Discussion Paper – Investment, Competitive Markets and Structural Reform, April 2009, p. 16, http://www.ret.gov.au/energy/Documents/facts% 20statistics% 20publications/Discussion% 20Paper% 20 –% 20Investment% 20competitive% 20markets% 20APRIL% 202009. pdf.

[6] 参见 http://www.infrastructureaustralia.gov.au/

[7] *Strategic Directions for Energy White Paper*, March 2009", p. 4, http://www.ret.gov.au/energy/Documents/Energy% 20Security/Strategic% 20Directions% 20for% 20Energy% 20White% 20Paper% 20March% 202009. pdf.

[8] 同上，p. 6。

[9] 同上。

[10] Discussion Paper-International Energy, April 2009, p15, http://www.ret.gov.au/energy/Documents/facts% 20statistics% 20publications/Discussion% 20Paper% 20 –% 20International% 20Energy% 20APRIL% 202009. pdf.

[11] 同上，p16 – 17。

[12] World Energy Outlook, 2009 Executive summary, p5, http://www.worldenergyoutlook.org/docs/weo2009/ WEO2009_ es_ english. pdf.

[13] Kevin Rudd, Building Australia's future: Tackling Australia's long-term challenges, http://www.pm.gov.au/ node/6436.

[14] *Strategic Directions for Energy White Paper*, March 2009, p5, http://www.ret.gov.au/energy/Documents/Energy% 20Security/Strategic% 20Directions% 20for% 20Energy% 20White% 20Paper% 20March% 202009. pdf.

[15] Discussion Paper-Realising Australia's Energy Resource Potential, April 2009, p10, http://www.ret.gov . au/energy/Documents/

facts% 20statistics% 20publications/Discussion% 20Paper% 20 - % 20Realising% 20Australia% 27s% 20Energy% 20Resource% 20Potential% 20APRIL% 202009. pdf.

[16] *Energy in Australia* 2009, p1, http://www. abareconomics. com/publications_ html/energy/energy_ 09/au Energy09. pdf.

[17] Alexander Downer, The Impact of Energy Security on Australia's International Relations, http://www. energysecurity. org. au/ uploads/06_ Downer_ speech. pdf.

[18] 同上。

[19] Robert Pritchard, Energy Policy and Climate Policy must be integrated, http://www. ret. gov. au/energy /Documents/ewp/pdf/EWP% 200119% 20DP% 20Submission% 20 - % 20EnergyAlliance2. pdf.

[20] *World Energy Outlook* 2008 *Executive summary*, p11, http://www. worldenergyoutlook. org/docs/weo 2008/WEO2008_ es_ english. pdf.

[21] *Strategic Directions for Energy White Paper* March 2009, p7, http://www. ret. gov. au/energy/Documents/Energy% 20Security/Strategic% 20Directions% 20for% 20Energy% 20White% 20Paper% 20March% 202009. pdf.

[22] Discussion Paper-International Energy, April 2009 , p16, http://www. ret. gov. au/energy/Documents/facts% 20statistics% 20publications/Discussion% 20Paper% 20 - % 20International% 20Energy% 20APRIL% 202009. pdf.

[23] 中澳关于进一步密切在气候变化方面合作联合声明", http://www. gov. cn/jrzg/2008 - 04/10/content _ 941808. htm.

[24] 国务院：2020 年单位 GDP 二氧化碳排放降 40% 至 45%, http://finance. people. com. cn/GB/10461522. html.

[25] 中石油逾 410 亿美元向埃克森美孚购买液化天然气，http://news. china. com/zh _ cn/finance/11009723/20090818/15605470.

html.

[26] 中澳贸易额2010年有望增加到910亿美元 http：//world. huanqiu. com/roll/2010-02/723333. html.

[27] 澳大利亚恢复与中国的自由贸易谈判，http：//world. huanqiu. com/roll/2010-02/725940. html.

[28] Stephen Smith，"Australia and India：A Convergence of Interests"，http：//www. foreignminister. gov. au/ speeches/ 2009/091015 _ asia_ society. html.

[29] http：//www. iea. org/papers/roundtable_ slt/australia2_ mar09. pdf.

## 作者简介

**唐小松**，博士，现任广东外语外贸大学外交学系教授，广东国际战略研究院首席研究员。主要从事公共外交、网络外交和美国研究。(Email：xstang2006@163. com)

**许嫱**，广东外语外贸大学外交学系硕士研究生。

# 6

# 试论澳大利亚海洋安全战略与中澳关系*

甘振军　李家山

海洋安全是澳大利亚国家安全的重要组成部分，海洋安全战略作为一个较为复杂的综合性概念，涵盖政治、经济、外交、文化、军事等诸因素。尽管海军是达成澳大利亚海洋安全的关键力量，但实现澳大利亚海洋安全战略目标，还必须依托更为广泛的海上综合力量。

## 一、澳大利亚海洋安全战略的历史演变

### （一）联邦成立前后的海上防务政策

当澳大利亚还是殖民地的时候，各个殖民区就已经重视海洋安全问题，突出表现在海上防务政策上。如何处理与新赫布里底群岛的关系和力主建立属于澳自身的海军问题，是

* 本文原载于《世界经济与政治论坛》2011 年第 4 期，收入本文集前甘振军对材料进行了更新并对论文做了适度修改。

其海上防务政策的集中体现。

**1. 新赫布里底群岛问题**

新赫布里底群岛位于1853年被法国吞并的新卡莱多尼亚东北部600～700公里处。就地理位置而言，该群岛与澳东北部存在重要的战略联系，澳大利亚从来就没有放弃占有这些岛屿的希望。[1]当时澳力主推动英国吞并了新几内亚。其外交目标就是防止该群岛被法国作为基地攻击澳的军事基地。由于英法联合海军委员会作用不大，澳不断向英帝国政府呼吁并施加压力，要求吞并该群岛，并对英国殖民当局在解决此争端问题上的拖拉作风以及对澳大利亚海洋安全利益的漠视而甚感不悦。殖民当局则埋怨澳大利亚纠缠不休以及未能对谈判形势做出充分的估计。[2]澳与法国单独谈判也未成。虽然没能合并该岛，但若没有长期坚决的干预，最终该岛可能会落到法国人手中。

**2. 建立皇家海军的努力**

首先是澳大利亚殖民时期外部海洋安全环境促使其海防不得不依靠英帝国。19世纪中叶以后，随着淘金热的出现，海上人员往来和远洋贸易运输日益增多，保证海上贸易安全对殖民区各政府变得尤为重要，同时其他欧洲列强先后加强在太平洋岛屿上的开发、抢占殖民地的热潮风起云涌，各殖民区自治政府不得不认真考虑海上安全，英国却要求各殖民区加强自身海上防务能力。各殖民区都建立了各自的"海军舰队"，但力量相当弱小。海军只能够在沿海担任巡逻警戒和为近岸民用船只护航的任务，根本没有抗击海上强敌入侵的实力。由于各殖民区相距遥远又各自为政，"海军"根本无法成为一支"真正意义上的"联合海军。

直到联邦政府的成立，外部海上安全形势日益严峻。德国势力已经占据了俾斯麦群岛的北新几内亚；日本摧垮了俄国的海军。这增强了澳的不安全感，但是海军防务问题引发了复杂的帝国关系。英国对待殖民地海军政策模糊。1906年澳政府宣布不再继续每年为英国海军提供20万英镑的防务补贴。1909年澳英就建立海军舰队达成了新协议。次年政府通过了《海军防务法》，开始设立海军部，着手建立海军。联邦议会还通过《海军借款法案》，向英国贷款建造海军。

德国宣布到1912年将有13艘无畏舰下水，这直接推动了英国海军部最终同意澳组建海军舰队的计划。到“一战”爆发前，海军已初具规模。拥有1艘巡洋战舰、6艘轻型巡洋舰、6艘驱逐舰、2艘潜水艇和一定数目的轻型支援和辅助舰船。[3]澳大利亚终于迈出了国家海上安全战略的第一步。

### （二）“依附式”的海洋安全战略

一些评论家认为，“一战”前甚至到“二战”爆发时，澳大利亚没有外交，较大程度上体现为依附于宗主国英国的外交。其实，“依附外交”不过是一种很特殊的外交表现形式。这是和它的历史文化、国内外政治经济因素以及和防务安全等联系在一起的。[4]同样，澳大利亚的海洋安全战略也呈现出较明显的“依附式”，即将本土安全特别是海上安全委托于某一个大国。具体而言，就是在20世纪前半期将自身的海防安全主要交付给英帝国，“二战”后又转而采取所谓澳新美同盟的形式交付给美国，同时想方设法筹划地区安全联防。

**1. 建国后至“二战”时期依附大英帝国**

海军是国家海防的重要力量。澳在“一战”爆发前终于建立了海军，但是其指挥和调度权由英国掌握。但“一战”结束后，远东和太平洋地区的国际形势发生了变化。

作为战后凡尔赛华盛顿体系的一部分，在远东太平洋地区，澳也参加了华盛顿军备限制会议。在对英关系上，整个20年代，澳支持英国将新加坡修建为巨大的海军基地的拟议，赞成签订太平洋公约。[5]澳还希望国联能够真正实现集体安全。然而“九一八事变”宣告了“一战”后国际关系体系的破产，国联裁军会议失败，使其不安全感增强。澳也抱怨英国政府对澳海上安全利益重视不够。然而，澳并不能独立地承担本国海上安全。“一战”后，澳忽视了自身的海防建设，把安全完全托付给大英帝国。世界经济危机使澳国防经费最先削减，国防建设濒于停顿，国防能力已经降到了“一战”以来的最低程度。

在这一时期，澳因与英国在安全上的传统特殊关系，并未形成清晰明确的海洋安全战略，其海防政策完全“绑在英国海军的战车上”，海军的建设也不可避免地与英国一起，某种程度上受到国际裁军协定的制约。

**2. “二战”对澳大利亚海防战略的影响和调整**

“二战”是澳大利亚外交的转折点，包括海防在内的澳国防安全随着发生改变。澳逐渐认为“不能依靠英国在太平洋地区的海军来保卫澳大利亚。其原因主要是两国在太平洋地区利益不同，同时，英国海军不再像以前那样在太平洋地区所向无敌。”[6]太平洋战争爆发，英国远东舰队遭到了歼灭性的打击，太平洋失去了赖以寄托的海上保护。仅新加坡一地，15000名澳军全军覆没。日军还两次空袭北部门户达尔文港。浓厚的英国情结再也代替不了国防和生存的现实需要，澳大利亚在国防和外交上终于做出了正确的选择。

澳大利亚外交政策开始调整，将重心从大西洋转到太平洋，决定和美国结成同盟。这成为澳大利亚对外关系的基石。为了加强澳美关系，柯廷总理还向罗斯福提议将西南太平洋战区盟军司令部设在澳大利亚。双方决定建立美澳联合司令部，总部在墨尔本。[7]澳美军事联盟初步建立起来了。日本海军不得不修改作战方针，努力切断美澳太平洋交通线。澳美联合作战不仅保卫了澳洲本土的安全并且为战后澳新美同盟的缔结作了铺垫。安全和外交政策的转变，为澳大利亚国防和海洋安全日后逐渐依附于美国埋下了伏笔。

**3. 战后依附美国的基本战略基石**

“二战”结束后，世界进入两极格局。出于遏制共产主义在远东“扩张”的考虑，澳大利亚屈从美国签订对日和约[8]，实现“软和平”，将中国视为最主要的威胁。《澳新美同盟条约》从根本上来讲，是美国太平洋战略同盟体系中的组成部分，但对澳而言，这是其历史上与首个非英国的外国签订的防务条约，在外交防务史上具有标志性意义，“象征着澳大利亚外交和防务开始进入一个以太平洋地区为焦点的新时代”[9]。从此，对美结盟也就成为澳对外政策和国家安全的重要基石。

在“前沿防御政策”和多米诺骨牌理论的影响下，澳重点将其海军力量配置在本土以北的地区，防范“共产主义”来自海上的“扩张”。这构成了战后特别是“冷战”前期澳海洋安全战略的主要内容。海军的主要使命就是要提供一支有效的力量来配合盟国的行动，一则可以抵御来自东南亚方向和中国的可能“入侵”，保护其海洋贸易通道的安全，更重要的是可以在南太平洋和东南亚海域同美国一道，对抗苏联在这一范围内的海洋扩张。

“前沿防御战略”思想和依附美国的战略基石，使得澳可以用较少的资金维持小规模的海军力量就可以保证其海上安全，可以充分关注国内经济事务；然而长期“副作用”也是明显的，安全上完全依赖于美国，阻碍了政府独立自主地提出自身的海洋安全战略思想，使国防力量特别是海军布局结构畸形发展。正如曾担任国防军总司令的皮特·格拉顿所言，“前沿防御战略”从纯军事角度上讲至少给澳防务建设带来三个不利因素：首先，澳军首脑只重视如何对抗“国际性威胁”，而在如何对抗“对本国威胁”上不知所措；其次，澳三军只知本军种如何配合盟国同军种联合作战，而对澳三军如何协同则几乎毫无所知；最后，长期把军队派往海外作战使澳本土防卫设施极为不合理，大多集中在东南一隅，而在对澳安全同等重要的西部和北部则毫无建树。[10]可谓切中了澳大利亚自身海洋安全的命脉。

## （三）逐步走向相对独立自主的海洋安全战略

### 1. 20世纪70年代至“冷战”结束时期防务安全的调整

这一时期国际关系格局处于深刻的变革和调整之中，英美势力要相继从东南亚逐步撤出，而让海上军事实力较弱的澳大利亚继续留在“前沿防御”的最前沿，使澳不得不认真反思。澳政府认为，应当放弃沿袭几十年的“前沿防御思想”为核心的国防政策，奉行“睦邻友好”和“地区合作”，改善周边的国际关系环境。澳海洋安全战略呈现出相对独立的倾向。

与此相适应，国防白皮书也强调东南亚地区和西南太平洋对于自身安全的重要意义，主张本土防御，通过打击和阻止来自海空的外来侵略来维护自身的海洋安全。1976年公布的国防白皮书尽管还没有详细地阐述对自身海防力量建设的战略规划和目标，但在首次提出“自主防御”的安全指导原则具有标志性意义。

1986年，澳大利亚国际安全问题学者兼政府政策顾问保罗·迪比（Paul Dibb）向国会提交了《保罗·迪比报告》，认为澳在当时的形势下没有直接的军事威胁，应当依靠加强自身的防御力量来应对极有可能发生的低水平的武装军事冲突。与此同时，随着《联合国海洋法公约》的正式生效，政府和海军部更是加强了其在海洋专属经济区的经济利益和安全利益。政府和军方都认识到要维护好“良好的公海秩序”，即保证海上运输安全，保护海洋资源，保卫海洋主权，保护海洋环境。澳大利亚的海洋安全问题在新的历史条件下，其重要性日渐突出，内涵也日益丰富，多层次的功能也需要充分发挥，相应的战略构想也开始形成。

澳政府的基本主张是：①继续巩固和加强澳美同盟关系，作为自身对外关系和国家安全的战略基石，借助盟国军事力量减少潜在威胁国家通过澳海域入侵的可能性；②继续加强自身独立的海上军事力量，增强海军应对低水平武装冲突的能力；③通过高层互访、战略对话、军事演习和海军出访，建立有效的海上安全合作机制等多种手段，促进自身周边海上安全环境（主要是东南亚、东印度洋海域和西南太平洋海域）的稳定。澳海军功能也发挥了不同层次的作用，特别是在执行情报搜集、海上侦察、海上巡逻、保护海上交通线和海洋资源等方面。

由于始终将澳美同盟视为不可撼动的战略基石，决定了其“自主防御”政策是在美澳同盟阴影下的有限的“自主防御”。

**2. “冷战”结束以来的海洋安全战略**

“冷战”结束后，世界政治格局出现“一超多强”的基本态势，经济全球化和区域经济一体化的日益加深。亚太经济的持续蓬勃发展和错综复杂的地区冲突同时并存。澳大利亚的海洋安全战略意图伴随着国防白皮书的逐步出台而日渐清晰。

1994 年的国防白皮书是在“冷战”结束后的新形势下出台的。政府认识到，国家未来的安全和繁荣是与整个亚太地区的繁荣和稳定息息相关的，但作为一个在地理位置上孤悬于南太平洋的国家，自身未来可能受到的威胁是全方位的和不确定的。1997 年，外交和贸易政策白皮书明确地提出今后 15 年地区安全的总体要求，就是要保持强大的防御性的国防能力，为东南亚提供一个“安全的”南方和为南太平洋地区提供一个“安全的西方”。澳必须首先考虑的是大力加强自身的综合性海洋军事力量。同时继续肯定澳美同盟作为澳整体防务政策的重要性，包括与美国的联合军事演习、接受美国先进的武器系统、军事人员培训和情报交流等等。另外也开始加强与东亚国家建立安全对话机制，发展海上防务安全合作。这三个方面构成了澳整体实施海洋安全战略的基本政策。

在这样的过程中，澳对海洋安全的认识有了更为切合自身实际的变化，树立较为清晰的海洋观并调整其海防政策，从20世纪50—70年代的那种一味追随美国的国防政策和70—90年代对“自我防卫”而“摇摆不定”的国防政策中走出来，逐渐将自身的国防安全政策（主要是海防）同澳美同盟之间的关系摆清楚：就是这两者是不可偏废的，而是相互依存、相互依赖的。

有了这样的整体的政策导向，澳坚定地认为澳美同盟是其有效地维护独立国防政策的基础，加强与美国军方的合作对于保证其海上安全至关重要，同时也必须努力发展一支能够在东南亚地区具有攻防能力的海上作战力量，这对于实施海洋安全战略才具有主体的意义。在具体实施方向上，其基本判断是北部海域，来自东南亚方向的威胁是最主要的，同时要注意西南太平洋和印度洋两个方向。要加强和扩大同东盟国家和中国等国海军的交流与合作，这有助于维系和加强澳自身在东南亚地区的军事影响力，保证其在亚洲的海上贸易线路的通畅和经贸利益的实现，也可以保证其周围海上环境的安全。澳还宣布将采取“向西看”战略，寻求印度洋国家和地区的经贸合作，旨在通过经济合作来确保西部海洋的安全。随着海洋经济时代的到来，特别是东南亚恐怖主义问题，澳更加迫切地要保卫本国辽阔的各个海区、港口、重要海湾和贸易交通线的安全，维护和实现自身海权必须要有明确的海洋安全战略摆上议事日程。

具体而言，可以从如下几个方面说明：

第一，继续巩固和加强以海防安全同盟为鲜明特点的澳美关系。《新西兰安全条约》是澳外交和防务政策的基石，也是澳美关系的基础。早在海湾战争时，皇家澳大利亚海军舰队成为多国海上拦截力量的一部分。澳大利亚海军舰队包括2艘护卫舰、4艘战舰和1艘油艇等。这些舰艇有力地配合了美国的海军舰队。澳大利亚海军海上作业队还担负爆破和拆除任务。[11]

1996年台湾海峡危机发生时，澳是亚太地区唯一公开表示要为美国提供军事援助的国家。1996年澳美举行国防部长和外交部长的联席安全会议，认为“日本和澳大利亚是美国亚太地区战略中的北南两锚”[12]。1997年，两国在澳北部举行了20年规模最大的联合军事演习。澳还准备将美澳联合管理的松峡通信基地作为导弹防御的核心基地，积极配合美国的军事行动。

以霍华德为首的澳政府在对外政策中最大的调整就是从工党的“面向亚洲”转变为“倾向美国”。适应“冷战”后国际形势的发展和美国的战略需要，澳美关系大幅提升。在澳大利亚政府的日程表上，澳美联盟毕竟是排在第一位的。[13]

澳美同盟使得澳积极支持美国参与亚太事务。“冷战”后每次对华政策调整几乎都与美国对华政策紧密相连。而在数次因台海危机导致的中美关系紧张之时，澳还付诸行动。比如中美因南海撞机事件关系紧张之时，澳3艘舰艇驶过台湾海峡，被认为是澳海军为“配合美国在东亚加强军事前沿部署的安排”[14]而做出的举动。

从澳美联盟的历史和现状来看，在可预见的未来，澳美海防安全合作仍将占据双方安全关系的主流，这也正是澳海防安全实现的重要外交联盟途径之一。

第二，继续加强与东亚国家如中国和日本等国的海军交流与合作。地区安全和防务上，澳寻求同中国在内的亚洲大国的多边安全合作。“冷战”后澳认识到在新的安全环境中依靠美国军事保护这种单一的安全战略已难以应付复杂的安全形势，必须重新估价本国综合国力和所处的安全环境，面向亚洲制定新的国家安全战略和地区安全机制，以维护本国安全和亚太地区的稳定。[15]“冷战”后新的不确定因素使澳在亚太的地缘战略地位更加凸显。澳十分重视同中国、日本、美国三大国的关系。对于中国的大国崛起，澳大利亚是有疑虑的。澳希望通过各种制约关系来达到地区力量平衡。1994年国防白皮书首次提出发展对华军事合作和对话，“鼓励中国充分参与地区与其他多边安全讨论”[16]。基廷政府停止把中国说成是本地区和澳大利亚的威胁，废止了许多针对中国的防务条款。中澳两国军方交流与互访日益频繁，从1994年到2009年两国几乎每年都进行多种形式的接触、交流和合作。澳国防部部长尼尔逊2007年访华，称中澳是“地区稳定的好伙伴”，并邀请中国海军赴澳，参加澳大利亚、新西兰和中国三方举行的首度海上联合演习。

澳日关系是澳美同盟关系之外最重要的对外关系，重视将两国关系由原来以经济性质为主逐步向政治和安全合作方面发展。2007年3月，澳日签署了《防务与安全合作的声明》。这是战后日本与美国之外的国家所签订的第一个防务协定，也是澳美签订同盟条约之后的又一个着眼于国家安全的防务协定。这使国际社会普遍认为“美日澳构筑战略铁三角，欲打造亚洲版北约”[17]。

第三，调整海军部署，加强东南亚方向的维护海洋权益的力度。澳认为未来对自身威胁最大的地区是来自北部海域的东南亚区域，为了防范可能来自北部海域外来的入侵，必须将海军防卫力量由东部和南部重点挪移到北部和西部。海防力量在北部海岸设置了警戒雷达体系，还在重要海域和水道布设海底声呐以监控外国潜艇的行动，并加强了北部海域的海上巡逻力量。海军舰艇按照“三级保卫网”配置，以北部和西部为防御重点。第一级保卫网由导弹驱逐舰和护卫舰组成，在多数情况下可以单独对付来自空中、海上和水下的各种威胁；第二级主要由各种护卫舰组成，其任务是使用自身的反舰和防空武器支援第一级保卫网作战；第三级主要由大型巡逻艇和水雷战舰艇组成，平时主要用于对经济特区的巡逻。[18]通过调整防御战略，澳加强了西北沿海的基地建设，由海军和空军组成海空防御屏障，而以机动的地面部队配合作战，确保“挫败任何来自陆地和海空的威胁”。政府还决定将22艘太平洋巡逻艇更新设备，延长使用30年。此外，澳大利亚作为典型的海洋性国家，海域辽阔，海洋资源丰富，如何确保和维护自身的海洋权益变得愈加重要。澳组织海上巡逻艇在北部海域的专属经济区打击非法捕鱼等活动颇有成效。这也有效地适应了海上安全形势的需要。

为了积极主动地应对可能来自东南亚方向的海上威胁，保护海上通道，维护其在亚洲的经贸利益，保障海上周边安全，确保澳自身在东南亚一定军事力量的存在，澳加强了同东盟国家海军合作和交流，充分发挥海军的外交职能，积极派出海军舰艇访问有关国家和地区的海军基地。此外，澳还积极促成防务协定的签署和多种形式的地区联合军事演习，如多国海军联合军演、多国海空联合演习、多国多兵种协同演习、“五国联防”军事演习、澳新海军联合演习等。澳还十分重视海军军事人员的培训和交流，通过“太平洋巡逻艇”计划，向西南太平洋国家提供巡逻艇及相应的海上行动与技术顾问、训练、后勤和修理支援。同时，澳还积极向东盟国家“出借军事基地”，提供军事人员培训，等等。这些措施有利于增强澳与周边国家的军事互信，确保周边海域的安全，也有利于扩大地区影响力。

另外，澳致力于建设一支具有在东南亚“无与伦比”的攻防力量的海上作战力量。20世纪90年代以来，澳加大了海上力量的建设力度。目前，澳海军人数12700人。海军装备有3艘驱逐舰，6艘护卫舰，4艘潜艇。皇家海军还购置了8艘本国制造的“澳新军团”级护卫舰替换老式的护航驱逐舰。从90年代中期起，海军已逐步起用6艘新建造的“柯林斯”级潜艇，以替换过时的“奥伯隆”级潜艇，该计划耗资50.1亿澳元，极大地提高了澳大利亚的海防能力。[19]澳大利亚海军已成为一支在东南亚地区乃至整个亚太地区的重要的海防军事力量。

## 二、澳大利亚海洋安全战略的主要特点

### （一）强烈的依附性及集体安全机制作用较大

澳大利亚的安全问题具有强烈的依附性，曾一度将国家安全完全委托给英国来处理，甚至到“二战”前期，仍保有对母国情感依赖的惯性，暂缓考虑本国防御的需要，将全

部现役海军舰艇归英国海军部指挥。“二战”结束之后，随着国际“冷战”格局的到来，澳新美同盟的形成，澳将国家安全绑在美国战车上，向美国预付国家安全的保险金。这实质上是一种依附美国的安全战略。

无论是英国还是美国，都距离澳相对较远。因此，在应对地区安全问题上，澳很大程度上不得不依靠自己的努力去维护区域安全。当然，另一种有效途径则是通过与东南亚国家的一定程度上的结盟或者是地区联防的形式来达到自己的目的。在20世纪70年代前，澳作为西方阵营中的一员，参与地区联防具有浓烈的“冷战”色彩，如战后初期澳积极参与东南亚条约组织的筹划。英国政府宣布放弃在“苏伊士运河以东”的军事义务，在很大程度上影响了澳“前沿防御”总的战略部署。澳单方面做出了在没有美英两国合作的情况下继续给予马来西亚和新加坡军事援助的决定。1971年，澳还正式签署了《五国防务协定》，包括五国海军顾问工作小组在内的主要机构建立起来。进入新世纪以来，特别是巴厘岛爆炸事件，恐怖主义成为影响澳安全的现实威胁。为了保持先发制人的态势，澳曾一度拒绝东南亚国家提出的签署互不侵犯协定的要求，海上集体安全防务战略仍然面临诸多现实复杂国际关系的考验。

### （二）发展海上整体力量，凸显皇家海军的作用

霍克工党政府执政后，虽然受制于两极“冷战”格局，基本保持澳美同盟关系，但比以往历届政府都更强调两国关系的平等和澳大利亚的独立性。

在这种思想的主导下，工党上台之初便决定将当时仅有

的一艘航空母舰“墨尔本”号退役，并不再造新航母，这表明了澳将不再继续配合美国在西太平洋上实行“前沿防御”。[20]经过一系列政策准备，澳国防政策完成了从过去一味依赖美国军事保护向在保持澳美军事同盟关系下逐步实现“自主防卫”目标的过渡。

两极格局解体后，澳对西太平洋地区的朝鲜半岛问题、南中国海主权之争、台海局势等热点问题密切关注，这种情况在步入新世纪后仍然得以保持。由于澳长期以来对亚洲的不安全感，陆克文刚上任就暗示要扩充自身的军力。他宣布将快速加强海军力量，并耗资600亿澳元加强军备。[21]他还说：“我们必须加强海军实力，以保护我们的海上运输线，并在陆军进行部署时提供支援。”[22]军方已开展为期10年的现代化计划，以建立一支规模更大的军队，所将增添的军备包括大型两栖攻击舰、导弹驱逐舰。[23]澳大利亚还将继续改进其拥有的全球最先进的常规潜艇——“科林斯”级潜艇。[24]2009年白皮书指出，未来20年政府将加强海军军备力量的建设。大部分资金将用于购置新型潜艇、驱逐舰、护卫舰，用以加强对领海的控制能力。

澳大利亚重点发展海军的思想在2001年公布的《21世纪的澳大利亚海军》发展规划中体现得较为充分。该文件要求澳海军提升海上快速反应能力、支持登陆作战能力和区域防空能力。澳海军不但要在周边地区，还要能配合盟国遂行远征作战。规划是澳海军的“现存舰队”到2015年蜕变为“增强舰队”，到2025年发展成“未来舰队”。这是澳海军走向“蓝水海军”的标志，也代表着澳海军成为一个非谨守领海，而是逐渐扩张的战略角色。[25]台湾学界也看到了澳海军转型的这一特点，认为到了2020年后的战力必将有很大的提升，其将具有区域兵力投射，并掌握区域制海、制空权的能力。除此之外，澳海军还将会发展出新的军事思想，藉以达成澳成为区域性的军事和海上强权的目标。

### （三）西南太平洋和印度洋方向的双向性趋于明显

澳大利亚海洋安全战略除了集中体现在西南太平洋方向，也表现在印度洋海域方向，以政治互信、海上经贸交流和地区核不扩散为主要内容。由此，澳大利亚海洋安全总体表现出双向性特征。

澳大利亚也是印度洋上的海洋性国家，随着印度实施海洋战略，澳自然也把目光转向这一地区。1994年，澳宣布将采取“向西看”战略，寻求印度洋国家和地区的经贸合作。其“向西看”战略在澳海洋安全中成为重要的组成部分。

澳大利亚“向西看”战略，主要有以下三点理由：第一是防卫澳西部海上通道和海洋资源，要有两个大洋的海军。第二是保护澳贸易和交通路线的安全：澳有25%的贸易要穿过印度洋。第三是澳尤为担心核扩散尤其是南亚核扩散的问题，因为印巴均不是核不扩散条约的签字国。

从海上经贸的关系上看，澳向印度出口的商品主要有煤炭和羊毛。1997年印度洋沿岸国家成立了环印度洋合作联盟（环印联盟）。这是是继欧共体、北美自由贸易区和亚太经合组织之后的世界第四大经济集团。随着时代的发展，澳大利亚“向西看”的海洋安全战略必将继续涵盖更多的实质性内容。

## 三、澳大利亚海洋安全战略对中国的影响

### （一）美国因素及澳美印日靠拢在战略上围堵和遏制中国的意图更加明显

澳大利亚的海洋安全战略具有强烈的依附性，集体安全机制发挥着较大的作用。澳美同盟是澳外交和防务政策的基石。2007年，澳日实际上构成了准军事同盟的关系，被国际社会普遍认为“美日澳构筑战略铁三角，欲打造亚洲版北约”。此外，澳还实施“向西看”的海洋安全战略，加强与印度的关系。澳美印日四国战略合作和靠拢十分明显，一旦与中国存在某种问题，四国之间的松散同盟必然会遥相呼应，在战略遏制中国方面发挥彼此作用。

2009年，澳新的国防白皮书指出，未来20年政府尤其要加强海军军备力量的建设。大部分资金将用于购置新型潜艇、驱逐舰、护卫舰，用以加强对领海的控制能力。这份名为《2030年的军力——在一个亚太世纪里保卫澳大利亚》的国防白皮书花费长达140页的篇幅渲染“中国威胁”。虽然澳政府一再辩解扩充军力并非针对中国，但无论是澳舆论还是国际媒体均将二者紧密联系起来。《澳大利亚人报》一篇报道的题目则是“国防白皮书紧盯中国”[26]。澳在此次白皮书中散布“中国威胁论”，在其官方文件中首次公开把中国作为对手，其实是秉承美国国防白皮书散布“中国威胁论”的传统，是以美国为主的西方国家散布“中国威胁论”的延续。它一方面反映了中国军力发展确实引起了澳

的关注，另一方面也反映了澳在积极寻求加强与美国的关系。

### （二）搅浑本来就错综复杂的南中国海安全形势

我国海上形势近年来极为严峻，大量岛礁被侵占，海洋资源被掠夺，海上通道经常受到干扰，海上纠纷与争端不断，周边国家海上力量发展迅速，海洋大国又纷纷介入。这种情况最为突出地体现在南中国海，特别是南沙诸岛被瓜分殆尽。

澳大利亚的海洋安全战略虽然不会对我海上安全构成直接威胁，但澳大利亚的对美安全的依附性及其集体安全联防的总体思路，为东南亚国家拉拢更多的区域外大国、以形成大国平衡的战略态势提供了某种便利之处。东盟最近酝酿的10+8模式（包括中日韩、澳新、印度、美俄）就是证明。这在客观上与东盟、日本、印度的各自意图具有利益链条和战略博弈的关系，也符合美国亚太战略整体构想（如构建澳日“亚洲版北约”和所谓美日澳印“四国同盟”），澳自觉不自觉地都要置身于这个总的战略格局中。这都使中国的海洋安全面临更加严峻的挑战。

## 四、中国应对澳大利亚实施海洋安全战略的策略

澳大利亚的海洋安全战略符合其自身安全和经济利益，但其动辄以“中国威胁论”为借口，客观上对我国海洋安全利益构成一定的潜在威胁，我们需要在错综复杂的国际形势中准确判断，把握和应对澳大利亚实施的海洋安全战略。

### （一）以东盟为协商平台，促进地区安全防务合作

澳高度重视澳美同盟、澳日“准军事同盟”关系、“向西看”的海洋战略；同时重视同东南亚国家（东盟）的集体安全合作。无论从澳自身安全诉求还是服从美国亚太海上安全战略部署来看，这都会对我国海洋安全环境造成不利影响。

基于此，除了要妥善处理好中美、中日和中印这三大双边关系，更要以东盟为平台，促成和展开东亚区域安全防务机制的建立。因为这里国家多、海洋安全环境复杂，我国的海洋利益最为关切。最为重要的是，从澳大利亚的角度来看，澳也特别重视东南亚地区，也是未来可能与我国在南海的利益发生冲突的地带。随着澳大利亚和新西兰逐步纳入与东盟的自由贸易区合作，澳在东南亚的利益会更加凸显。当然，澳自身和东南亚国家尚有安全上的龃龉，特别是与印尼，与马来西亚和新加坡的防务协作较为紧密。澳曾设想提出一个类似于“欧洲安全与合作委员会”的地区性安全机制，加强双边安全防务合作，但时机并未成熟。“冷战”结束后，东盟国家逐步形成了新的安全观：树立全方位外交安全意识，建立保障综合安全的多边安全合作机制。澳开始在“东盟区域论坛”等平台上开展“协商安全”。澳还加强了同新加坡、泰国、文莱和菲律宾等国家的双边防务合作。

我们应当加强与东盟的安全磋商与对话，避免东盟的“大国平衡”战略将更多的国家扯入东南亚而造成的更为复杂的困境，近来酝酿的东盟10+8模式，包括中国、日本、韩国、澳大利亚、新西兰、印度、美国和俄罗斯8个国家，

这无疑应当值得我们深思，应尽快采取相应的举措来消除不利的影响。

## （二）加强中澳两军防务交流、增进彼此安全互信

中澳两国没有根本利益冲突，但是澳对中国的崛起怀有疑虑，最近维基解密的外交文件更加印证了我们的论断。[27]加强两国的军事交流，特别是海军交流，从而加深了解、增进互信，是我们应采取的重要手段。

澳在考虑亚太地区引发大国战争的最大威胁时，将目标指向崛起中的中国。此前对中国的军力和威胁评估基本上与美国同调，而2009年新版国防政策白皮书则以独立的国防标准评估中国，认为中国是未来亚太地区可能的危机爆发点，因此必须把中国视为重要的考虑因素。澳认为“中国军事现代化的速度、规模和结构可能会使其邻国感到不安”[28]，必须做好独立防御的准备。

近来的中澳两国海军交流充分说明了在复杂的国际形势下，到底应该采取什么样的举措能够更好地增进互信，维护海上安全。2010年9月中澳海军在黄海海域举行联合军演。中澳军事官员都认为此次海上联合演练时间长，科目多，很务实。在打击海上目标科目中，双方均使用实弹演练，这在中外海军演练中比较罕见。在澳舰访华的同时，中国海军舰艇正访问悉尼港，这在两国海军友好交往史上尚属首次，推动了两国海军的务实性合作关系。海军互访，特别是两军联合演练有效地增进了两国军队之间的相互了解和信任，也促进了两国关系的发展。

## （三）共同推进东南亚海上战略通道的安全

一是澳大利亚同东盟的关系发展迅速，特别是在经贸领域。新加坡、马来西亚、印度尼西亚、泰国、菲律宾在澳大利亚对外经贸关系中日益重要。东盟已成为澳大利亚继日本、欧共体后第三大出口市场。2010年元旦，澳新—东盟自由贸易区开始分阶段实施。目前澳大利亚与东盟贸易额年均800亿美元，而澳大利亚从东盟进口货物的价值是其出口的2倍。[29]澳同东盟的关系步入新的阶段。总之，日益加深的经贸关系，需要加强海上战略通道安全的关注。澳外长斯蒂芬·斯密斯多次以“后院”形容东南亚国家对澳大利亚的重要。[30]这种说法固然有待商榷，但从一个侧面说明了澳同东南亚日益加深的海上经贸利益。

二是东南亚海上战略通道安全问题日益突出，中澳存在着安全合作的巨大空间。澳与东南亚的关系、中国与东南亚的关系是中澳推进海上安全利益需要共同协作应对的。目前中国—东盟自由贸易区建设发展势头迅猛。中澳自由贸易谈判也在紧锣密鼓地进行。这也必然会与正在建设的东盟—澳新自由贸易区相连接。中国—东盟—澳新的海上经贸交流必然会更加密切。要确保东南亚地区的海上贸易交通要道的安全和畅通，不仅符合中国的利益，也符合西南太平洋地区整体的经济利益和安全利益。

### ［注释］

［1］Neville Meaney, *A History of Australian Defence and Foreign Policy 1901—1923*, vol. 1, Sydney University Press, 1976, p. 94.

［2］同上，p. 100.

[3] 张炜、冯梁主编：《国家海上安全》。北京：海潮出版社，2008 年，第 323 页。

[4] 参见汪诗明：《20 世纪澳大利亚外交史》前言部分，北京：北京大学出版社，2003 年。

[5] 刘樊德著：《澳大利亚东亚政策的演变》。北京：世界知识出版社，2004 年，第 28 页。

[6] 吴桢福主编：《澳大利亚历史 1788—1942》。北京出版社，1992 年，第 294 页。

[7] 张天：《澳洲史》。北京：社会科学文献出版社，1996 年，第 307 页。

[8] 张秋生：《澳大利亚与亚洲关系史 1940 ~ 1995》。北京：北京大学出版社，2002 年，第 82 页。

[9] 汪诗明：《20 世纪澳大利亚外交史》。北京：北京大学出版社，2003 年，第 103 页。

[10] 宫少朋：澳美安全合作的纠葛及其前景，《美国研究》1992 年第 2 期，第 63 - 64 页。

[11] 汪诗明：《20 世纪澳大利亚外交史》。北京：北京大学出版社，2003 年，第 239 页。

[12] *Sydney Morning Herald*, 8 August 1996.

[13] Stewart Firth, *Australia in International Politics*: *An Introduction to Australian Foreign Policy*, Allen & Unwin, 1999, pp. 37—38.

[14] 苏浩：《从哑铃到橄榄：亚太合作安全模式研究》，北京：世界知识出版社，2003 年版，第 112 页。

[15] 张秋生：《澳大利亚与亚洲关系史 1940 ~ 1995》。北京：北京大学出版社 2002 年，第 219 页。

[16] *Defense White Paper*, 1994.

[17] 2007 年 3 月 17 日新华网军事新闻：http：//news. xinhuanet. com/mil/2007 - 03/17/content_ 5859883. htm

[18] 张炜主编：《国家海上安全》。北京：海潮出版社，2008 年，第

333页。

[19] 参阅沈永兴、张秋生、高国荣：《列国志—澳大利亚》。北京：社科文献出版社，2003年，第245页。

[20] 宫少朋：澳美安全合作的纠葛及其前景，《美国研究》1992年第2期，第64页。

[21] *New Chinese Marketing Weekly*，澳大利亚《新市场报》（周报），2008年9月12日—18日。

[22] 同上。

[23] 同上。

[24] 中国新闻网：《美国侨报：陆克文也有一版"亚洲威胁论"?》，2008年9月16日，http://www.chinanews.com.cn/gj/xwbj/news/2008/09-16/1383149.shtml

[25] 参阅汪照棠：《后"冷战"时期的澳洲海军》，台湾淡江大学硕士学位论文，2010年1月11日。

[26] http://www.anti-cnn.com/forum/cn/viewthread.php?tid=162082

[27] 维基解密网公布了一份机密电报，文件透露澳大利亚前总理陆克文曾建议美国国务卿希拉里，在其他方式无效的前提下，对华使用武力，对两国关系产生了很大的影响。参考链接：http://news.ifeng.com/world/special/weijijiemi/content-2/detail_2010_12/07/3381660_0.shtml

[28] *Defending Australia in the Asia Pacific Century*: *Force* 2030, p. 34: http://www.apo.org.au/sites/default/files/defence_white_paper_2009.pdf

[29] 张学刚：东盟的大国外交更趋务实灵活，参见《东南亚纵横》2010年第1期编辑部所编专家访谈录。

[30] 沈旭晖：港评：澳大利亚的"东南亚后院论"，《联合早报网》2008年11月17日，http://www.zaobao.com/special/newspapers/2008/11/hongkong081117n.shtml

## 作者简介

**甘振军**，博士，现任安徽淮北师范大学历史与社会学院讲师，主要研究方向为澳亚关系。（Email：ganzhenjun2006@ yahoo. com. cn）

**李家山**，海军指挥学院训练部干部。

# 7

# 澳大利亚的南海政策解析*

王光厚

当前，南海问题正呈现出扩大化、复杂化和国际化的态势。这一局面的出现，一方面源于某些南海声索国的单方面行为，另一方面与区域外部势力的介入有着十分密切的关系。传统上，美国、日本、印度等国是影响南海局势发展的主要外部因素。近两年来，伴随澳大利亚逐步向东亚靠拢，它对南海局势的发展亦开始予以密切关注。尽管就国家实力而言澳大利亚无法同美、日、印等国相提并论，但是，澳毕竟是一个"中等强国"，其对南海问题的介入将给南海问题的发展带来新的不确定性。深入探究澳大利亚南海政策的意图及其影响，可为中国应对南海局势提供一定的参考借鉴。

## 一、澳大利亚在南海地区的战略利益

国家利益是一国对外政策的基本出发点和最终归宿。澳大利亚的南海政策是以其对南海在澳大利亚生存与发展中的

---

* 本文原载于《东南亚研究》2011 年第 6 期。

作用的研判为基础的。澳大利亚政府认为“（南海）问题对澳大利亚而言非常重要”[1]。

具体而言，澳大利亚在南海地区的战略利益主要表现在以下几个方面：

首先，南海地区对澳大利亚而言有着重要的经济价值，澳大利亚的经济发展离不开南海地区的和平、稳定与繁荣。其一，南海周边的中国与东盟诸国都是澳大利亚的重要经济伙伴。长期以来，东盟一直是澳大利亚的主要贸易伙伴。据统计，2010 年澳大利亚与东盟的双边贸易额达到 520 亿美元，东盟整体位列澳第三大贸易伙伴。[2]2010 年 1 月 1 日，东盟—澳大利亚—新西兰自由贸易区正式启动。该自由贸易区的创建将会大大降低区域内国家间商品与服务贸易的诸多障碍，这将为澳大利亚与东盟国家经济关系的发展提供新的动力。由于近年来对华铁矿石和煤炭出口激增，中国现已迅速成长为澳大利亚的最大贸易伙伴和第一大出口市场。据统计，2010 年中国与澳大利亚的贸易额达到 880.92 亿美元，其中中国对澳的出口为 272.26 亿美元，中国从澳的进口为 608.66 亿美元，[3]澳处于明显的出超地位。目前，中国与澳大利亚正就建立自由贸易区进行谈判。其二，南海航线是澳大利亚开展对外贸易的重要通道。澳大利亚是一个以出口农矿产品为主要经济支柱的国家。东北亚是澳大利亚的主要贸易区，经济高速发展的中国和资源较为匮乏的日本、韩国对澳大利亚的农矿产品需求量极大。目前，除了中国外，日本、韩国分别位列澳大利亚的第二和第四大贸易伙伴，而澳与东北亚国家的贸易额事实上已经超过了其国内的贸易额。[4]据统计，2010 年澳大利亚与中、日、韩三国的贸易额占澳对外贸易总额的比重分别为19.1%、12%和5.4%。[5]澳大利亚地处大洋洲，海洋运输是澳大利亚与东北亚诸国贸易往来的主要方式。出于运输成本和运输安全的考量，目前澳大利亚很大一部分国际贸易是经由南海到达东北亚市场的。[6]南海在澳大利亚对外贸易全局中的位置由此可见一斑。这条贸易通道如果被切断，澳大利亚的经济发展也将陷入困顿。其三，参与南海资源开发是澳大利亚在南海地区的又一项重要经济利益。南海地区蕴藏着各种丰富的战略资源，其中石油和天然气的储量更是引人注目，甚至有"第二个波斯湾"[7]之称。南海区域外部的某些国家之所以积极介入南海事务，其目的之一是试图在南海地区的油气勘探和开发上分得一杯羹。澳大利亚虽然是世界著名矿产大国，但是石油资源却较为匮乏。2011年，澳大利亚的石油产量为484千桶/日，消费量为1003千桶/日。[8]这意味着目前澳大利亚石油产量仅占其消费量的48.26%。如果能够参与南海地区的石油开发，澳大利亚就可以更为便利地获得石油。目前，澳大利亚的必和必拓集团（BHP Biliton）、全球勘探公司（AWE）、Neon能源公司等参与了在南海海域进行的石油勘探与开发。

其次，南海所处的东南亚地区是澳大利亚安全防范的主要区域之一。在国家利益构成的诸要素中，安全利益居于基础与核心地位，是"决定国家战略关系性质的首要因素"[9]。对于任何国家而言，保证自身的生存是其首要的最基本的对外战略目标。澳大利亚地处南太平洋和印度洋之间，尽管四面环海且不与大国为邻，但是澳大利亚政府认为，"作为一个在地理位置上孤悬于南太平洋的国家，自身未来所可能受到的威胁是全方位的和不确定的"[10]。在澳大利亚看来，除了其本土和邻近海域外，澳大利亚在"从北部亚洲到东印度洋之间的亚太更广阔区域"亦有着"持久的战略利益"[11]。这其中东南亚地区的稳定对澳大利亚的安全至关重要。这是因为"在战略上，我们（澳大利亚）在东南亚的邻居地跨北部的门户。为了持续部署力量来对抗澳大利亚，敌对势力将会操控这一门户。一个稳定而团结的东南亚将会减弱这种威胁。"[12]目前，"为了防范可能来自北部海岸的入侵"，澳大利亚海军在努力成为一支在本地区具有"无与伦比"的海上攻防作战力量的同时，还将"战略防御重点由东部和南部改到北部和西部"。为此，澳大利亚海军以北部和西部为防御重点配置了"三级保卫网"、在北部海岸配置了警戒雷达体系、在北部海区的重要水域和水道布设了海底声纳基阵、加强了北部海区的海上巡逻。与此同时，澳大利亚还通过海军出访、联合军事演习、军事人员交流与培训等方式密切了同东南亚国家以及中国的军事合作，以保持自己在东南亚地区的军事存在。[13]南海地处东南亚的核心区域。如果南海海域出现动荡局面，那么整个东南亚地区都将会受到波及。届时，与东南亚毗邻的澳大利亚亦难以独善其身。就此而论，保持南海海域的稳定系澳大利亚的重要安全利益之一。

最后，介入南海事务有助于澳大利亚扮演更重要的国际角色。除了经济发展需求、国家安全需求外，在国际社会争取一定的话语权、发挥一定的作用等政治诉求也是一国追求的主要国家利益。自"二战"结束以来，澳大利亚历届政府都坚持澳"中等强国"的国家定位，力求在国际舞台上发出自己的声音。[14]近年来，随着澳大利亚国家力量的提升，澳渴望发挥一定政治影响的愿望更趋强烈。陆克文时期，澳大利亚进一步提出了成为“富有创造力的中等强国”的外交目标，力求实现澳国际形象的“破”与“立”[15]。与超级大国不同，“中等强国”所赖以发挥关键性作用的舞台主要是区域性的。对澳大利亚而言，亚太是其开展独立外交的主要区域，而东南亚则是其扮演重要国际角色的理想平台。这是因为：其一，除了大洋洲诸国外，东南亚在地理上与澳大利亚最为临近，事实上澳大利亚与一些东南亚国家的距离要近于与某些大洋洲国家的距离；其二，不同于亚太其他主要地区，东南亚并不存在一个居于主导地位的大国，这为澳大利亚这样的“中等强国”发挥政治作用奠定了良好的地缘政治基础；其三，长期以来澳大利亚与东南亚国家一直保持着较为密切的政治经济关系，早在1974年澳大利亚就成为东盟的对话伙伴国，而目前澳大利亚业已加入东盟主导的一系列区域性国际机制；其四，东南亚是近年来全球经济社会发展最为迅速的地区之一，积极参与该地区的事务有利于推动澳大利亚的经济增长；其五，就东南亚方面的情况来看，后“冷战”时期的东盟积极推行“大国平衡”战略，欢迎包括澳大利亚在内的国家参与本地区的事务，东盟邀请澳参加首届东亚峰会就是一个典型的例证。基于上述因素，近年来澳大利亚通过多种方式不断扩大自己在东南亚地区的影响并积极介入本地区的有关事务之中。目前，澳大利亚无论在政治—安全领域还是在经济领域都与东盟建立起非常密切的关系。[16]其标志性事件是，2010年10月30日，澳大利亚与东盟在越南首都河内召开了首次峰会。南海问题不但直接牵涉到东盟几个国家，而且与整个东南亚地区的安全和稳定息息相关，因而，介入该问题无疑会提升澳大利亚在整个东南亚地区事务中的影响力。

从理论上看，一国国家利益的实现是以其国家力量为基础和后盾的。对于澳大利亚这样的中等国家来说，上述三项战略诉求之间是存在一定的内在矛盾性的。例如，防范敌对势力控制东南亚与寻求外交独立性两项利益诉求就很难得兼。这就需要澳大利亚根据具体的国际环境来平衡这三项战略利益诉求。当前，澳大利亚在南海问题上的政策选取就是此种平衡的结果。

## 二、澳大利亚在南海问题上的基本政策取向

澳大利亚是新近介入南海问题的外部力量。不容否认，如同印度等国一样，目前澳大利亚对南海问题的介入“很难说已经形成某种具有全局意义的战略内涵”[17]，并且澳大利亚政府自身也并没有出台明确针对南海问题的外交文件，因而我们无法对澳大利亚的南海政策进行精细的探讨和分析。但是，通过澳大利亚的有关对外活动，我们依然可以判断出其在南海问题上的基本政策取向。

首先，在南海问题上与美国保持相近立场，紧密跟随美国在南海区域的有关行动。自 1951 年《澳新美安全条约》签署以来，澳大利亚一直保持着同美国的军事同盟关系，并将美澳同盟视为国家生存与发展的基点。澳大利亚认为，美国在军事领域处于支配地位这一现实确保了过去几十年亚太地区经济令人瞩目的增长。[18]在澳大利亚看来，尽管当前全

球性的经济危机使得美国的实力有所下降，但是，“在2030年以前，美国在政治、经济和军事方面仍将是最富实力和影响力的战略角色”，“没有其他强国能够具备挑战美国主导地位的军事、经济和战略实力”。对澳大利亚来说，美澳同盟“是澳最重要的防务关系”，“当澳大利亚处于一个军事力量超过其抵抗能力的大国的威胁之下时，澳大利亚只能够依靠美国提供帮助”[19]。有鉴于此，尽管近年来澳大利亚在外交上表现出了很大的独立性，但是在事关国家安全的战略问题上澳依然保持着与美国亦步亦趋的关系。在南海问题上，澳大利亚亦唯美国马首是瞻。其一，继美国国务卿希拉里于2010年7月宣布美国在南海地区有着“自己的国家利益”[20]之后，澳大利亚外长陆克文也明确表示南海问题关乎澳的利益，澳成为公开就此问题表态的又一个南海域外国家。值得特别指出的是，2010年9月15日，澳大利亚与美国“2+2”年度部长级会议发表的声明中专门阐述了两国在南海问题上的基本立场。声明明确指出：“与国际社会一样，澳大利亚和美国在南海的航行自由、保持和平与稳定、尊重国际法以及畅通的合法商贸方面，拥有国家利益。”[21]这一声明的发表凸显了澳大利亚与美国在南海问题上利益与政策的一致性。其二，澳大利亚参与了美国在南海附近海域所进行的有关军事活动。例如，2011年7月，当中国与东南亚有关国家之间的南海争端不断升温之际，澳大利亚海军会同美国海军、日本海上自卫队在濒临南海的文莱附近海域举行了一次联合军事演习。此次军事演习规模虽小，但是鉴于演习时间和地点的特殊性，人们依然可以从中捕寻到若干政治信号。其三，澳大利亚积极配合美国加强对南海战略威慑力的军事部署。2011年11月16日，澳大利亚总理吉拉德和到访的美国总统奥巴马在堪培拉举行记者会，宣布了美国在澳大利亚的永久性驻军计划。根据美澳签署的军事合作新协议，从2012年年中开始，美军在澳大利亚的达尔文港部署一个连（200～250人），5年内增加到2500人，此外美国还将分步骤扩大在澳大利亚的军事活动。

其次，对中国存有一定的防范心理，担忧南海为中国所“控制”，但是却力求在此问题上不“触怒”中国。在南海争端各国中，中国是唯一的大国。南海问题之所以引起国际社会的普遍关注，除了南海本身所具有的战略价值外，还因为一些国家将中国在南海的行动看作是中国外交政策走向的“试金石”[22]。近年来，伴随中国综合国力的迅猛提升，中国外交政策的走向日益成为世人关注的焦点。尽管中国政府向世界庄严承诺中国坚定不移地走和平发展之路，但是在国际社会有关中国崛起后将会改变现状、建立霸权之类的“中国威胁论”却不绝于耳。澳大利亚虽然在经济上保持着同中国的密切联系以求分享中国经济快速增长的红利，但是，在安全问题上澳对中国却有着较强的防范心理。澳大利亚于2009年发布的题为《在亚太世纪保卫澳大利亚：2030年军力》的国防白皮书专门就中国的未来发展进行了研判，认为“到2030年，中国将成为地区和全球经济活动的主要驱动力，而其战略影响力将超越东亚”。该白皮书还重点探讨了中国军事力量的发展情况，认为中国将成为“亚洲最强大的军事强国。其军事现代化将以不断深入地发展力量投射能力为特征。中国将发展一支与其规模相适应的、全球性的军事力量。但是，如果中国不能对其军事计划进行详细解释，同时也不能为建立信任而与其他国家就其军事计划进行沟通，那么中国军事现代化的步伐、规模和结构将有可能使其邻国有理由产生疑虑”[23]。该白皮书虽未直接将中国列为澳大利亚现实的对手，但是其背后却隐含着视中国为潜在威胁的意味。就南海问题而言，澳大利亚认为中国的“海上武断行为”将引发“同邻国甚或美国的冲突”[24]。此外，澳大利亚还在战略上对中国加以防范。如前所述，防范“敌对势力”控制东南亚是澳大利亚的重要安全利益。澳大利亚虽然没有公开言明“敌对势力”有可能是哪个国家，但是考虑到意识形态、地缘政治、国家力量等因素，澳对中国的防范将会更多一点。对澳大利亚来说，如果中国“控制”南海，进而掌控整个东南亚，澳在安全上将陷入被动，因而澳应当努力防范这种局面的出现。然而，需要着重指出的是，由于澳大利亚将中国看作是“全球经济增长的关键推动者和地区及国际事务的自信参与者，是澳大利亚有重大利益需要接触的对象”[25]，所以尽管澳在南海问题上对中国有所防范，但是却力求避免在此问题上“触怒”中国。因而，从中国的视角来看，澳大利亚的南海政策取向呈现出一定的两面性。

最后，力倡南海局势的和平与稳定，避免出现选边站的困局。澳大利亚“作为地处东方的西方国家，外交政策一直有偏东还是偏西的选择”[26]。后“冷战”时期，随着东亚在世界政治、经济格局中地位的提升以及澳大利亚独立外交意识的增强，澳的外交重心逐步向东亚一方倾斜。当前，澳大利亚在安全上依赖美国、在经济上与东亚同行的战略态势基本形成。这使得澳大利亚不但在安全上无后顾之忧，而且在经济上搭上了东亚这趟快车。顺应此种战略态势的需要，澳大利亚希望南海局势能够保持和平与稳定。这是因为，一旦南海出现动荡局面或战争，澳大利亚的经济利益和战略利益都将严重受损。从经济层面看，这种局面的出现不但会直接影响到澳大利亚与有关国家的贸易，而且澳大利亚通往东北亚主要贸易伙伴的海洋通道也会因之受阻。从战略层面来看，南海局势的恶化很可能会引发美国的军事介入，届时，澳大利亚将不得不面临选边站的困局。[27]在这种情况下，不但澳大利亚在美国和东亚的中国之间同时获益的局面将被彻底打破，而且澳大利亚所忧虑的“敌对力量控制东南亚”的梦魇将成为自我实现的预言。为实现南海局势的和平与稳定，澳大利亚积极倡导南海有关各方通过和平方式解决争端。早在 1999 年，澳大利亚外长多纳在东盟地区论坛曾就南海行为准则提出了一些非正式建议。[28]其后，澳大利亚多次表示明确支持 2002 年的《南海各方行为宣言》，并希望各方能够达成具有约束力的准则。此外，澳大利亚还表达出成为南海问题调停人的意愿。[29]对澳大利亚而言，成为这一角色不但有利于推动南海地区的稳定，而且还可以使自己在地区安全事务中发挥一定的作用。

众所周知，走和平发展道路的中国并不是南海争端的“麻烦制造者”，且中国一直积极维护南海海域的航行自由，因而澳对中国的“防范”本身是没有任何依据的。当前，“南海局势总体是和平的、稳定的”[30]，因而澳大利亚的介入只能给南海局势的发展带来负面影响。

## 三、澳大利亚介入南海事务对南海局势的影响

南海问题之所以近年来变得更为复杂，其根源主要在于外部势力的介入。澳大利亚虽然不是南海的声索国，但是它却在南海问题上有着自身的利益关切并且已经在此问题上表现出了一定的政策意愿，这不可避免地给南海局势的发展带来新的影响。

一方面，澳大利亚的介入加剧了南海问题复杂化、长期化和国际化的态势，给南海问题的解决带来新的不确定性。中国人最早发现并开发了南海的岛屿礁滩，因而，无论从历史上看还是从法理上看，中国对南沙群岛及其附近海域都拥有无可争辩的主权。然而，东南亚一些国家却罔顾这一历史事实，强占我南海岛屿、瓜分我南海海域、掠夺我南海资源。为了增强抗衡中国的实力，这些国家积极施展所谓的"大国平衡"战略，妄图将区域外部大国拉到自己一边，这为外部势力介入南海问题提供了良机。区域外部势力的介入使得南海问题呈现出复杂化、长期化和国际化的态势，这不但阻碍了南海问题的解决，而且还恶化了南海地区的安全形势。澳大利亚虽然不是亚太地区居于主导地位的国家，但是，有鉴于美澳同盟框架的存在以及澳所处的地缘位置等因素，澳大利亚在南海问题上依然起着不可令人忽视的作用。正是看到这一点，东南亚一些南海声索国在倚重美国、日本、印度等区域外部大国的力量来抗衡中国的同时，还积极拉拢澳大利亚站在自己的一边。例如，2011年6月，在澳大利亚和菲律宾于堪培拉举行的部长级会谈上，双方专门就

南海问题进行了探讨并在联合声明中阐述了它们在南海问题上的共同立场。[31]又如，2012年8月，澳大利亚国防部长访问越南时亦专门谈到南海问题。此外，由于美澳特殊关系的存在，还存有澳大利亚通过东亚峰会等机制就南海问题在前台向中国“发难”、而美国背后操控的可能。澳大利亚介入南海问题无疑会加剧业已十分复杂的南海博弈态势，给南海争端的解决带来更多困难和不确定性。众所周知，为寻求南海局势的稳定，中国政府一贯主张通过双边友好协商来解决与有关国家之间的南海分歧，反对任何外部势力介入南海争端。因而，澳大利亚介入南海问题不言而喻将给中国应对南海局势带来一定的负面影响。

另一方面，澳大利亚在南海问题上紧随美国而动的政策取向，增强了美国在亚太地区的战略威慑力，为美国应对中国崛起提供了战略平台。始于2008年的全球金融危机加速了亚太地区“权力转移”的进程。目前，“如何应对中国日益崛起的影响”已经成为既有“主导国”美国“外交政策的一个核心问题”。[32]尽管美国明确表示欢迎“一个强大、繁荣和成功的并在世界事务中发挥更大作用的中国的崛起”，但是在美国看来，“缺乏透明性、中国军事发展的性质和决策过程，使人对其未来在亚洲和以外的地方的行为和意图提出合法性的问题”[33]。为防范中国，奥巴马政府上台伊始就采取了诸多措施来强化美国在东亚地区的战略存在。鉴于近两年来台海局势日趋稳定，美国转而介入南海事务，以塑造对己有利的区域安全格局，从而平衡中国在亚太地区日益上升的影响力。正是基于这一战略考量，2009年以来美国在南海问题上采取了一系列举措。澳大利亚是美国在亚太地区历史最悠久和最亲密的军事盟友之一，美澳同盟是美国的“亚太战略之锚”。在协助美国应对南海局势、掌控南海地区安全格局方面，澳大利亚亦可发挥不可替代的作用：其一，澳大利亚海军拥有较强的实力，可以在南海地区出现危局的时候协同美军进行有关军事活动；其二，部署在澳大利亚北部和西部的超视距雷达站、电子监听站、通信站等设施，可为美国监控南海局势以及美军的有关行动提供信息、情报；其三，澳大利亚在地缘上与南海相距较近，可为美国在南海的有关行动提供后勤给养、人员休整等帮助；其四，从战略层面看，澳大利亚、美国、日本三边安全合作的强化将增大美国在南海海域乃至整个东亚地区的战略威慑力。目前，美澳两国就扩大美国在澳大利亚的军事存在问题所达成的协议正处于落实之中，这将强化美国对“第二岛链”的控制并有助于美国落实其专门针对中国而设计的“空海一体战”战略，而整个亚太地区的安全环境亦将随之产生连锁变化。中国是美国在亚太战略防范的主要对象，美国在本地区战略威慑力的提升无疑会增加中国的安全压力。

对于澳大利亚介入南海问题给中国所带来的负面影响，中国方面不应仅仅局限于南海问题本身，而应立足对外战略全局，采取多种措施加以有效应对。其一，增加中国与澳大利亚在政治、安全领域的互信。从战略层面来看，近两年来澳大利亚对南海问题所表现出来的浓厚兴趣和有关介入行动，主要是澳为了应对中国的迅速崛起而做出的政策反应。澳大利亚对于中国崛起的认知具有两面性：既认识到了中国的经济发展给澳所带来的机遇，又在安全上对日益发展壮大的中国有所防范。设法减弱乃至消除澳大利亚的对华“顾虑”，有利于中国的和平发展。为此，中国应当依托中澳“业已形成的良好互动态势，紧紧抓住澳对中国高度关注的历史性契机，大力推进和平外交，以经济、文化为先导，积极拓展双边共同利益范围，建立互信，构建起一种良性的外交循环机制”[34]。中国与澳大利亚之间并不存在直接的、涉及国家核心利益的冲突，且不同于美、日、印等区域外部势力，澳大利亚对于南海并没有任何战略上的企图。因而，如果中国和澳大利亚在政治、安全领域的互信能够有所提升，澳大利亚介入南海问题的动力将会随之弱化。其二，从中、美、澳三边关系的角度出发来思考问题，推动中美关系持续稳定发展。由于美澳之间在多领域有着共同利益，所以在可预见的未来，澳大利亚仍将会以澳美同盟为其对外战略的轴心。[35]有鉴于美国在美澳同盟中居于主导地位，中国应当从中美澳三边关系的角度出发来应对澳大利亚介入南海问题所带来的挑战。尽管中美之间存在一些“分歧和敏感问题”，但是“新形势下，两国共同利益越来越多，合作领域越来越宽”[36]。因而，在推动中美关系持续稳定发展方面中美双方是大有可为的。中美关系如能实现健康发展，不但澳方在安全问题上对中国的顾虑将会随之减弱，而且整个南海局势也将会大大降温，而前述的澳美同盟在南海问题上给中国带来的安全压力也将会大大降低。其三，回归南海问题的基本面，处理好与有关南海声索国之间的关系。尽管南海问题引起包括澳大利亚在内的诸多域外国家的关注，但是就其本质来看，此问题是中国与东南亚一些南海声索国之间的问题。中国如果对域外国家在南海问题上的有关举措给予积极回应，反陷入其彀中，致使东南亚南海声索国与域外势力形成联合向中国施压的“软同盟”。反之，如对其进行冷处理，并坚持通过双边友好协商来解决与有关国家之间的分歧，南海局面将更易于管理和控制。需要重点指出的是，上述几对关系的处理实际上面临着一个共同的挑战，即如何增进中国与相关国家之间在政治和安全领域的互信的问题。能否有效应对这一问题，不但关乎南海局势的稳定，而且关系到中国的和平发展。

总的来看，尽管澳大利亚介入南海事务给南海问题的解决带来新的不确定性并对南海地区安全格局的走势产生一定的影响，但是，只要中国方面能够处理好中国与澳大利亚、中国与美国、中国与南海有关声索国这三对关系，这些影响是可以控制、减弱，甚至是消除的。

## [注释]

[1] Daniel Flitton, Spratly Spat Threatens to Overshadow Summit, *The Sydney Morning Herald*, 22 July, 2011.

[2] ASEAN Secretariat, Overview of ASEAN-Australia Dialogue Relations, http: //www. asean. org/23213. htm.

[3] 中华人民共和国商务部综合司、国际贸易经济合作研究院：《中国对外贸易形势报告（2011 年春季）》，http: //zhs. mofcom. gov. cn/aarticle/cbw/201104/20110407511679. html。

[4] 芮捷锐：澳大利亚外交政策与中国维度，《当代亚太》，2008 年第 3 期。

[5] Australian Government Department of Foreign Affairs and Trade, *Trade at a Glance* 2011, http: //www. dfat. gov. au/publications/trade/trade-at-a-glance - 2011. html#sect02.

[6] Carl Ungerer, Ian Storey and Sam Bateman, *Making Mischief: the Re-*

*turn of the South China Sea Dispute*, Special Report of Australian Strategic Policy Institute, Issue 36, December 2010, p. 2.

[7] United States Institute of Peace, *The South China Sea Dispute: Prospects for Preventive Diplomacy*, http://www.usip.org/files/resources/SR18.pdf.

[8]《BP 世界能源统计年鉴（2012 年 6 月）》, http://www.bp.com/liveassets/bp_ internet/china/bpchina _ chinese/STAGING/local _ assets/downloads_ pdfs/Chinese_ BP_ StatsReview2012.pdf, 第 6、8、9 页。

[9] 阎学通：国家安全比经济利益更重要，《环球时报》，2003 年 2 月 14 日，第 5 版。

[10] 甘振军、李家山：简析澳大利亚海洋安全战略，《世界经济与政治论坛》，2011 年第 4 期。

[11] Department of Defence (Australia), *Defending Australia in the Asia Pacific Century: Force* 2030, http://www.defence.gov.au/whitepaper/docs/defence_ white_ paper_ 2009.pdf, p. 12.

[12] Department of Defence (Australia), *Defending Australia in the Asia Pacific Century: Force* 2030, http://www.defence.gov.au/whitepaper/docs/defence_ white_ paper_ 2009.pdf, p. 12.

[13] 参见张炜主编：《国家海上安全》，海潮出版社 2008 年版，第 332－334 页。

[14] See Carl Ungerer, The "Middle Power" Concept in Australian Foreign Policy, *Australian Journal of Politics and History*, 2007, Vol. 53, No. 4.

[15] 唐小松、宾科：陆克文"中等强国外交"评析，《现代国际关系》，2008 年第 10 期。

[16] See ASEAN Secretariat, *Overview of ASEAN-Australia Dialogue Relations*, http://www.asean.org/23213.htm.

[17] 王传剑：印度的南中国海政策：意图及影响，《外交评论》，2010年第3期。

[18] *Australia's National Defense: a defense update* 2007, http://www.defence.gov.au/ans/2007/pdf/Defence_ update.pdf, p.19.

[19] Department of Defence (Australia), *Defending Australia in the Asia Pacific Century: Force* 2030, http://www.defence.gov.au/whitepaper/docs/defence _ white _ paper _ 2009.pdf, p.32, p.93 and p.50.

[20] Hillary Rodham Clinton, *Remarks at Press Availability*, http://www.state.gov/secretary/rm/2010/07/145095.htm.

[21] *Australia-United States Ministerial Consultations (AUSMIN)* 2011 *Joint Communiqué*, http://www.foreignminister.gov.au/releases/2011/kr_ mr_ 110916b.html.

[22] ASEAN Studies Center, *Energy and Geopolitics in the South China Sea: Implications for ASEAN and Its Dialogue Partners*, Institute of Southeast Asia Studies, Report No.8, 2009, p78.

[23] Department of Defence (Australia), *Defending Australia in the Asia Pacific Century: Force* 2030, http://www.defence.gov.au/whitepaper/docs/defence_ white_ paper_ 2009.pdf, p34.

[24] Dennis Richardson, *Australia: Foreign Policy in a Changing World*, http://www.dfat.gov.au/media/speeches/department/111013 _ zelman.html.

[25] 芮捷锐：澳大利亚外交政策与中国维度，《当代亚太》，2008年第3期。

[26] 沈世顺：澳大利亚外交新走向，《国际问题研究》，2006年第2期。

[27] Hugh White, The Limits to Optimism: Australia and the Rise of China, *Australian Journal of International Affairs*, 2005, Vol.59, No.4.

[28] Alexander Downer, *Australia Welcome Declarations on South China Sea*, http://foreignminister.gov.au/releases/2002/fa162_02.html.

[29] Rowan Callick, Australia Enlisted as Regional Mediator, *The Australian*, 21 August 2010.

[30]《杨洁篪外长在第18届东盟地区论坛外长会议上的发言》，http://www.fmprc.gov.cn/chn/pds/wjdt/wjbxw/t842181.htm。

[31] *Joint Ministerial Statement Philippines-Australia Ministerial Meeting* (*Canberra*, 16 *June* 2011), http://www.foreignminister.gov.au/releases/2011/kr_mr_110616a.html.

[32]《佐利克：应对中国崛起影响是美国外交政策的核心》，http://world.people.com.cn/GB/1029/42355/4363546.html。

[33] U.S. Department of Defense, *Quadrennial Defense Review Report* (*February* 2010), http://www.defense.gov/qdr/images/QDR_as_of_12Feb10_1000.pdf, p.60.

[34] 张露、黄楫：中国周边战略中的澳大利亚："大周边"战略理念与外交谋划的新探索，《现代国际关系》，2007年第2期。

[35] Paul Dibb, U.S.-Australia Alliance Relations: An Australian View, *Strategic Forum* (*Institute for National Strategic Studies*), 2005, No.216.

[36] 胡锦涛主席接受《华尔街日报》和《华盛顿邮报》联合书面采访，《人民日报》，2011年1月18日，第1版。

## 作者简介

**王光厚**，博士，现任东北师范大学政法学院副教授。主要从事中国外交、东南亚政治等问题的研究。(Email：wanggh818@nenu.edu.cn)

# 8

# “融入亚太”背景下澳大利亚媒体视域中的中国国家形象分析*

刘　琛

1989 年，《澳大利亚与北亚崛起》（Australia and the North Asian Ascendancy）的发表标志着澳大利亚正式从政治、经济与文化层面全面开启其融入亚太地区的时代。1993 年，澳大利亚广播公司（Australian Broadcasting Corporation）开播了澳大利亚电视台（Australia Television）并使用印尼的帕拉帕（Palapa）卫星传送节目。以此为起点，澳洲的大众传媒步入了“融入亚洲”（enmeshment with Asia）的新阶段。从这个意义上说，澳大利亚对国内媒体的国际传播功能与任务做出了重大调整。

出现这种调整与当时国际传播发生的变化有着直接关系。伴随着全球化的进程，世界的样貌发生了深刻的改变，这直接影响到了国际传播的外延与内涵。根据图苏（D. K.

* 本论文为教育部重大项目资助成果（项目合同号为07jzd0036）。论文原载于《暨南学报》2012 年第 3 期，收入本文集前作者对材料进行了更新并对论文做了适度修改。

Thussu）的研究，“传统上，国际传播首先是政府与政府间（government-to-government）的信息交流，由几个大国控制传播议程。但是，在当代社会，国际传播变得更加广泛和多层次，辐射政治、经济、社会、文化和军事等诸多领域”[1]。

在这样的时代背景下，人们开始重新评价大众传媒对一国形象以及舆论的影响。20 世纪 90 年代以来的公共领域学说指出：“公共领域是公共空间（public space）的民主视角。在此，由普遍的社会规范和集体的政治决定形成舆论。（媒体）对于这些意见的构成和接受发挥着重要作用。”[2] 以 CNN 对“海湾战争”的报道为例，世界各国都从中体会到国际媒体实际上是在左右（shape）事件并成为事件的组成部分。这种改变不仅为大众传媒吸引到了新的受众，也迫使传媒再次界定新闻和传播的属性。正因如此，BBC 和 NHK 等国际传媒巨头才开始重新反思自己的功能，而其他国家也认识到了国际传播已经赋予传播技术以新的用途[3]。

显然，全球化带给大众传媒最为深刻的影响是传媒对一个国家的介绍与展示已经不再只是简单地提供信息和知识。相反地，当今的大众传媒正在借助国际传播，力图塑造一个虚拟的现实。在国际局势因各国、各地区的密切联系而逐渐复杂化的背景下，国家形象成为赢得各国人民的尊敬与认可的关键影响因素。一国的形象是积极的还是负面的，是真实的还是虚假的都“直接左右我们对其他地方，那里的人和那里的产品的态度”[4]。

那么，自 90 年代，伴随着澳大利亚对亚洲和对华政策的不断调整，其国内媒体展示的中国形象在不同阶段具有怎样的特征？变化的规律以及今后的走向又是如何呢？

针对这一问题，本研究依据我国学者对国家形象构成的定义[5]，从政治形象、经济形象和文化形象等三个方面对90年代以来中国在澳大利亚的形象展示进行历史分析与评价。

## 澳大利亚“融入亚太”政策下的中国政治形象

国家政治形象的主体是政府，它的构成主要包括两个部分，“一部分是政府代表国家所从事的政治、经济、军事、外交活动……另一部分是政府代表国家通过媒体直接发布的信息，包括有关国家法律法规、方针政策制定、颁布方面的信息，对重大国际事件或两国关系处理表态性的信息”等[6]。

根据这一界定，本研究集中梳理了澳大利亚主流媒体对中国政治话题的报道。通过研究发现，澳大利亚媒体展示的中国国家形象是一个较为动态的变化过程，主要可以分为三个阶段。下面依据各阶段中澳政治交流的具体背景和不同特点，抽离和剖析不同阶段澳媒体展示的中国政治形象特点与背后原因。

从1989年到1996年，澳大利亚自由党（Liberal Party of Australia）和国家党（National Party of Australia）组成联盟政府，约翰·霍华德（John Winston Howard）出任总理。这一时期的澳主流媒体对中国的关注主要集中于人权问题。对华报道的话题比较集中和单一，而且在新闻内容上呈现出较强的议程设置色彩。可以说，虽然当时澳大利亚提出的是

“亚洲优先”政策，但是中国作为一个重要的亚洲国家却被澳主流媒体边缘化了。

此外，由于澳传媒业自身构成的特点，这一阶段默多克（Rupert Murdoch）打开中国传媒市场受挫，然而却在印度获得巨大成功，这也成为澳媒体解读中国政治形象的突出热点。1993 年，默多克看重了亚洲传媒市场并聚焦于中国和印度。为此，他的新闻集团投资了星空电视（Star TV）。该电视台总部设在香港，通过亚洲一号卫星（AsiaSat 1）向亚洲 38 个国家传送卫星电视节目。然而，中国和马来西亚却禁止其卫星信号落地。对此，澳媒体的结论是“中国不希望让国内民众收到来自西方的信息”[7]。同样地，默多克也声明，“从根本上说，自由市场不会导致垄断，（垄断）只有在得到政府支持时才可能存在”[8]。

1996 年到 2001 年，作为第二个阶段，澳主流媒体对中国的立场继续呈现出鲜明的对抗性特征，但是对中国政治话题的关注视角与前一个阶段相比，日趋丰富和多元化。此外，聚焦的热点开始包括台湾和西藏等问题。1996 年，霍华德执政伊始就连续与中国发生摩擦，主要包括：当中美因李登辉访美而交恶时，澳大利亚公开支持美国、派遣部长级官员访问台湾、允许时任台北市市长的陈水扁参加在布里斯班（Brisbane）举行的亚太城市峰会（Asia Pacific Cities Summit），以及会见达赖喇嘛等。此外，1996 年澳外交与贸易部（Australian Department of Foreign Affairs and Trade）宣布，人权问题是澳中关系中最为敏感的问题。

很快地，霍华德政府鉴于中澳的经济合作需要，对对华政策做出了调整，以防止两国关系进一步倒退。1997 年，霍华德访华，与中国建立人权对话机制。

然而，1999年发生的美军飞机轰炸我国驻南斯拉夫使馆让中澳关系再次处于紧张状态。在上述事件中，中美关系一度陷入危机。对此，澳大利亚的态度却是积极支持美国，以“亚太地区治安副官”的心态参与其中。这种外交政策加剧了中澳两国的分歧。2001年4月，中美因海南岛撞机事件爆发外交冲突。值此敏感时刻，澳大利亚派遣三艘军舰经过台湾海峡，招致中国政府的严正抗议。

在对这些“中国事件”进行报道时，澳媒体的新闻立场与政府是基本一致的。从政府的角度看，在澳大利亚的总体外交战略中，国家安全是一个核心支柱，澳美军事同盟一直是澳外交和安全政策的基石，是其最重要的对外关系[9]。因此，澳大利亚在这一时期释放的信息是美国是澳的战略盟友而中国则是敌对力量。从媒体的态度看，它们一方面是顺应了政府的政策，同时也是在服从美国等主流媒体的议程设置，继续强化对中国的刻板印象。例如：在谈及中国与西方世界的关系时，澳媒体认为最本质的问题是“中国会愿意逐步融入国际社会吗？还是更可能的是它会致力于提升自己的实力并最终成为亚洲邻国和美国的安全威胁?”[10]。在谈及“中国威胁”的时候，澳媒体与政府一样强调地区安全问题，指出伴随着中国经济的崛起，澳大利亚需要关注的是“中国的军事实力（military strength）也在提升”[11]。在报道其他事件的时候，澳媒体也经常会扯上“人权问题”。例如：“中国艺术家举办展览需要政府批准。在中国仍然对艺术家有一种控制机制……政治话题是禁区”等[12]。

2001年美国“911”事件是中澳两国关系的重要转折

点。霍华德政府在对待中国的问题上不再采用过激的手段，开始注重平衡美中两个大国在澳外交战略中的作用。其中，最具有代表性的案例是2003年10月，当时新当选的国家领导人胡锦涛主席与美国总统布什同时访澳，霍华德政府安排两位国家元首都在国会发表演讲。此举被认为是澳大利亚愿意重视发展对华的友好关系。胡锦涛主席发表了《携手共创中澳全面合作关系的美好未来》的演说。对此，澳各界的评价是为新世纪中澳关系发展描绘了长远框架。从2001年开始，中澳关系的基本走向是强调经济合作、共同发展和地区稳定，这标志着两国的双边关系建设日渐成熟。

在中澳关系迅速发展的背景下，澳主流媒体对中国政治形象的展示也发生了变化。2003年，在评价澳新闻界如何看待胡锦涛主席与布什总统的同台亮相时，《纽约时报》写到，“澳大利亚立场保守（conservative）的商报《金融观察报》（*The Financial Review*）在头版头条发表了题为《布什来了，胡锦涛征服了》（Bush came, Hu conquered）的文章，认为（两个领导人）最大的区别是风格（style）。他们的表现令人们大感意外。中国领导人平易近人（gregarious），而美国总统却拒人于千里之外（aloof）”[13]。2008年，中国奥运会期间，与个别西方媒体对中国的戒备态度不同，澳主流媒体高度肯定了中国的政治民生，指出“中国人的满意度从2002年的48%跃升至2008年的86%。分析家认为这并不是人民迫于政府的压力才这么表态的……即使因为对中国有偏见（bias）而减去15%，那么该统计结果仍然非常有力”[14]。

总体上，自90年代以来，澳大利亚媒体对中国政治形象的塑造是与国家对“融入亚太”的解释相互呼应的。当政府强调与美国的同盟关系时，媒体上的中国政治形象会充斥着规避的色彩。进入21世纪以来，澳大利亚逐渐明确了对华的基本战略，其国内媒体也有了更多的渠道和愿望去发现一个更加真实的中国。然而，有必要指出的是，虽然中澳的政治对话在不断深化，澳媒体对中国的关注仍然较为有限。以澳大利亚两大电视媒体ABC和澳大利亚特殊服务广播公司（Special Service Broadcasting，SBS）的对中国报道统计为例：

**表1　ABC/SBS对2010中国重大事件相关报道数量统计**

| 事件名称 | ABC报道数量 | SBS报道数量 |
|---|---|---|
| 中国取代日本成为世界第二大经济体 | 1 | 0 |
| IEA宣布中为能源消费第一大国 | 1 | 1 |
| 上海世博会 | 4 | 27 |
| 玉树地震/舟曲泥石流 | 14 | 0 |
| 十七届五中全会 | 3 | 0 |

可见，与其他话题相比，澳大利亚媒体对中国重要的政治活动的参与和报道，从报道数量来看，是无法满足需求的。也就是说，澳大利亚人如果仅凭国内媒体是无法真正了解中国的建国思想，政治体制与文化的。

## 澳大利亚“融入亚太”政策下的中国经济形象

国家经济形象主要是由该国的经济行动决定，其中企业也是经济形象的重要塑造者[15]。

与上文“政治形象研究”一致，对于澳媒体视角下的中国经济形象的评价也需要剖析出不同阶段的特点，以及其主要的影响因素。

在中澳的经贸关系上，两国一直保持着密切联系。截至2009年12月31日，澳大利亚与中国已经签署了贸易协定和经济合作协定、双边投资保护协定和税收协定。据商务部2010年年鉴统计，全世界共有79个国家与中国签有全部上述三种协定。

1981年10月，中澳两国签署了《中澳技术合作促进发展计划》，两国政府都非常重视与对方的经贸合作。在霍华德执政期间，澳大利亚始终积极肯定中国经济增长带来的商机。通过共同努力，两国在经贸、投资和经济技术合作等领域的交流与合作不断扩大。据中国海关统计，“2009年中澳双边贸易总额达600.8亿美元。其中，中国对澳出口206.5亿美元，下降7.2%，从澳进口394.4亿美元，增长5.4%。澳大利亚为中国第八大贸易伙伴，中国为澳第一贸易伙伴”[16]。

对于澳大利亚媒体来说，经济因素同样不容小觑。90年代以来，其国际传播范式（paradigm）的转变与看重包括中国在内的亚洲国家在传媒产业方面的经济潜力有很大关系。以澳大利亚电视传媒为例，业界认为，“东亚将是未来世界最兴旺的新兴市场，潜藏巨大商机，毕竟这个地区拥有全世界近三分之二的人口和300万亿美元的税收”[17]。

在这一时期，中国的传媒业也进一步加快了全球化进程，加大了与国际传媒公司的合作力度。仍然以电视业为例，据澳大利亚电影委员会（Australian Film Commission，AFC）的统计，“上海电视台经营的两个电视频道中40%到50%的节目是国外进口的，主要来自美国、日本和香港。其中，用于购买电视剧的费用是30万美元。1991年，该电视台在中国—昆士兰友好协会的帮助下，在澳制作播出了为期一周的电视节目。通过此次合作，上海电视台认为澳大利亚是一个理想的合作伙伴”[18]。

这种传媒贸易的切实需要形成了澳大利亚媒体上的中国经济形象一个值得重视的特点，即：其基本调子（general tone）是温和的，可以称为是“平衡性的批评”（balanced criticism）。这与美国媒体形成了较为鲜明的反差。

在报道中，澳大利亚媒体基本是能够客观地报道中国的经济政策、取得的成绩和对世界做出的贡献。这些信息有助于国内民众从不同侧面了解到了相关信息，并做出判断。通过分析ABC和SBS对1999年江泽民主席访澳、2003年胡锦涛主席在国会的演讲以及随后签订的一系列双边经贸合作协议的报道中，可以得出结论，虽然澳对华政策不可避免地要受制于美国因素，但是澳大利亚绝对不会因此而忽视与中国进行经济合作的巨大的现实利益。与澳各大政党的立场一样，澳大利亚的媒体也相当认同需要进一步推动与中国的经贸关系。正如美国媒体所发现的在澳大利亚“工程师们，包括行政主管、商人和制造商都恨不能工作得再快些以满足他们的最新的最大客户：中国的需求。许多人已经认为，未来是属于中国的。不论是天然气还是铁矿石，与中国签订的合同利润之大战胜了澳大利亚对外国人拥有自己的自然资源的敏感。同样地，中国和澳大利亚无论在外交领域还是企业界都迫切希望建立一种着眼于未来发展的互惠关系”[19]。

综上所述，澳大利亚主流媒体对中国经济形象的展示突出体现了该国在中美之间奉行的“平衡策略”，承认中澳间的经济互补利益，希望借助两国的经贸关系提升澳大利亚的经济能量。从这个角度上说，自 90 年代以来的关于中国经济话题的议程设置会因两国经济依存度的不断提高而在今后相当长的时间内保持不变。

## 澳大利亚“融入亚太”政策下的中国文化形象

文化是国家形象中最为重要的组成部分。我国学者认为，国家形象的内容首先是“一种主体意识，是国家或民族精神中的闪光点。它是在历史文化传统的基础上，融入现代化的要素，经萃取、提炼而成的”[20]。同样地，西方相关研究也指出，“（全世界）没有几个国家可以说是幸运到足够富裕，但是所有的国家都具有丰富的隐形财富（intangible assets），即文化、历史、地缘、人文和知识资本……当全球经济日渐以服务、知识资本和虚拟产品为推动力时，一国的人文资本就成为其经济发展的核心要素了”[21]。

一般说来，我国从国际政治领域入手的澳中关系研究对两国的文化交流基本持乐观态度，认为目前中国已经成为澳大利亚最大的留学生来源国和新移民来源国，是其最大的旅游客源国之一，而且汉语已经成为该国的第二大语言，因此澳大利亚会自然而然地深化对中国文化形象的理解。与这种观点相似，澳政府也赞同要在最大程度上增进对亚洲的了解，中国显然是其中的主要国家。很多为国家亚洲政策服务的研究报告都详尽阐释了关于了解中国文化的重要性。有些研究者还呼吁澳大利亚应该比世界上任何国家都付出更多的努力，以增强对中国的了解。

然而，通过分析主流媒体对中国文化的报道质量和数量，得出的结论却与上述推断相去甚远。以 ABC 和 SBS 的中国文化话题节目为例，总体上，从国内的电视荧屏上，澳大利亚人是难以了解中国的文化认同和理念的。笔者于 2008 年曾在墨尔本主持完成了一项相关调查。受访者表示中国文化是“陌生的”(estrange)、“神秘的”(mysterious)和“异质的”(eccentric)。此外，对于中国文化崇尚的“勤劳”、“艰苦创业”等美德也非常不了解。例如，在问及“你心目中的澳华商形象”时，受访白人大多会认为：“华人店跟本地（local citizen）店不同，全年 365 天营业，（这些中国商人）也许希望一年有 367 天，一天有 26 小时，这样他们就可以赚更多的钱了……但是，不能一天到晚地工作就为了钱吧?”或者认为：“华人旅行社收费低，还不要小费。这是因为他们的人工低，愿意加班挣一点点加班费。我想我不会为他们工作。他们的理念（idea）有问题。”

正是由于主流传媒的淡漠，导致了中国文化在澳大利亚的影响力始终较为有限。根据笔者主持的《20 世纪中国古代经典文化在澳大利亚的传播》研究结果显示，澳大利亚本土的中国学研究几乎处于空白，绝大多数的研究成果是从中国直接引进的中文著述，少部分是美国、英国和日本等国家学者的作品。

就澳华文媒体而言，虽然对中国文化有传播热忱，但是缺乏厚重感。华文报纸对“中国文化”的定义大多局限于中医、饮食、宫廷、习俗等话题。这也在一定程度上说明了为什么在澳大利亚被视为“中国经典文化”的总是“致公堂”、“四邑会馆”、“宫庙”和“华人古坟场”等“刻板印象”式的中国文化符号。

可以说，从中国文化在澳传播的发展状况看，澳主流媒体并不熟悉中国文化，中澳两国交流的日益深化并没有带来中国文化影响力的自然提升。值得一提的是，这种对中国文化的异质化解释也是澳国内媒体对待亚洲文化的普遍态度。从报纸、广播和电视中，公众所能看到的只是“亚洲文化与政治体系与西方不同。在这些国家，政府的导向和控制要显著得多”[22]。因此，澳本土受众仅凭借国内的主流媒体是难以理解和体会中国人及蕴育了中国民族精神的中国文化的。这个问题甚至已经影响到在澳出生的第二代和第三代华人。

## 结　论

早在上世纪 60 年代，伯纳德·科恩（Bernard Cohen）就指出，“传媒在告诉读者怎么想时并不成功，但是在告诉读者该想什么却是相当有效（The press may not be successful much of the time in telling people what to think, but it is stunningly successful in telling its readers what to think about）”[23]。

从中可以看到，大众传播对国家形象国际传播的重要影响。

通过分析90年代澳大利亚实施“融入亚太”战略以来，澳媒体视域下的中国国家形象可以得出结论：澳大利亚主流媒体在对中国的政治话题进行说明时会强调选择（对于两岸关系等敏感问题甚至会显示出遏制的意味），在介绍中国经济政策时会比较客观，在阐释中国文化时还是基于传统的刻板印象。在华文媒体方面，由于实力有限加上自身的不足，例如，很多经营者没有能够成为会通中西的意见领袖等，在对澳展示中国方面发挥的作用较为有限。因此，以目前的传播状况来看，澳大利亚民众还难以通过自己国家的大众传媒全面地了解中国、中国社会生活和中国人的理想与追求。

值得注意的是，中国与澳大利亚在地缘上同属亚太，在经济上有着互补优势，在政治上有着较为一致的外交基本理念，即：在解决国际争端和冲突时，倚重对话、不干涉别国内政等原则，在文化上，随着两国民间交流的日益广泛，相互学习和融合会成为赢得普遍共识的符合历史规律的文化态度。从这个意义上说，澳主流媒体应该为客观地了解中国、分析中国和介绍中国做出更多的努力，并在国际传播中发出更加响亮的“澳大利亚声音”。同样地，中国也应该更加重视在澳大利亚的对外传播，为澳媒体和民众了解中国创造条件、提供信息和帮助。

全球化时代的世界样貌有一个基本特征，那就是国家间、地区间的联系日益紧密。在面临问题时，可以说没有哪个国家能够完全做到“独善其身”。因此，中澳之间在对外传播中如果能够继续做出更多、更符合国际传播精神和新闻精神的努力，促进国家间、民族间和不同文化间的相互理解、相互学习和共同发展，这将不仅是中国与澳大利亚媒体为中澳两国做出的贡献，也是为亚太地区做出的贡献，最终是亚太为世界做出的贡献。值得肯定的是，中澳两国政府愿意为此携手合作。2010 年 6 月 9 日，以“想象澳大利亚”为主题的澳大利亚中国文化年正式开幕。澳驻华大使芮捷锐在致辞中指出，“这次交流是澳中文化关系史上的里程碑”。根据协议，2011 至 2012 年，中国在澳大利亚举办“中国文化年”。这些交流活动无疑有助于双方加深理解、全面合作。

### [注释]

[1] Daya K. Thussu, *International Communication: Continuity and Change*, London: Oxford University Press, 2000, p2.

[2] S. Benhabib, *Situating the Self: Gender, Community and Postmodernism in Contemporary Ethics*, Cambridge: Polity, 1992, p87.

[3] Lewis A. Friedland, *Covering the World: International Television News Service*, New York: Twentieth Century Fund Press, 1992.

[4] Simon Anholt, *Competitive Identity: The New Brand Management for Nations, Cities and Regions*, New York: Macmillan, 2007, p113.

[5] 周明伟主编：《国家形象传播研究论丛》。北京：外文出版社，2008 年。

[6] 程曼丽：国家形象塑造及其问题与对策，载周明伟主编，《国家形象传播研究论丛》。北京：外文出版社，2008 年，p18 - 19.

[7] Ranggasamy Karthigesu, Television in the Asian Cultural Map, *Media Information Australia* 1994, (73): pp90 - 96.

[8] 安东尼·吉登斯著，赵旭东，刘琛等译：《社会学》（第 4 版）。

北京：北京大学出版社，2006年，p460.
[9] 杨明星：透视澳大利亚霍华德政府对华政策及其走向。北京：国际论坛，2005年，(2)：pp34－38.
[10] Jennifer Hewett, What image now, butcher or benefactor: China, *The Age*, February 22, 1997.
[11] Peter Hartcher, Analysts challenge China's threatening image, *The Australian Financial Review*, December 24, 1996.
[12] Elizabeth Fortescue, Brushing up on images of China, *The Daily Telegraph*, April 12, 1996.
[13] Jane Perlez, "Bush came, Hu conquered," paper says Chinese president impresses Australians, *The New York Times*, October 2, 2003.
[14] John Garnaut, East does not meet West on China's self-image, *Sydney Morning Herald*, July 24, 2008.
[15] Keynote speech by Simon Anholt at the Opening Session of EuroPCom, 2011.
[16] 中国商务年鉴编辑委员会：《2010年中国商务年鉴》。北京：中国商务出版社，2010年，p400。
[17] Ranggasamy Karthigesu, Television in the Asian Cultural Map, *Media Information Australia* 1994 (73): 90－96.
[18] Australia Film Commission, *South East Asian Television Study*, Sydney: AFC, 1994, p29.
[19] Jane Perlez, Across Asia, Beijing's Star Is in Ascendance, *The New York Times*, August 28, 2004.
[20] 程曼丽：国家形象塑造及其问题与对策，载周明伟主编，《国家形象传播研究论丛》。北京：外文出版社，2008年，p16。
[21] Simon Anholt, *Competitive Identity: The New Brand Management for Nations, Cities and Regions*, New York: Macmillan, 2007, p2.
[22] Annette Hamilton, The Mediascape of Modern Southeast Asia,

*Screen*, 1992, (vol. 15, 2): pp81 – 92.

[23] Bernard C. Cohen, *The Press and Foreign Policy*, Princeton NJ: Princeton University Press, 1963.

## 作者简介

**刘琛**，博士，现任北京外国语大学英语学院副教授、北京外国语大学英语学院跨文化研究中心主任、中国跨文化交际学会常务理事，中国高校影视传播学会青年研究会理事。主要从事跨文化传播研究和中国国家形象研究。（Email：fenine@163.com）

# 9

# 澳大利亚公共外交探析*

黄　忠　唐小松

作为中等强国并且致力于在周边地区有所作为的国家，澳大利亚公共外交值得关注，它为我们提供了研究中等强国公共外交的一个典型标本，具有极其重要的理论意义和实践参考价值。本文拟在探讨澳大利亚公共外交的主要成就、发展动因的基础上，总结其局限，以抛砖引玉。

## 澳大利亚公共外交的主要成就

澳大利亚公共外交历史悠久，其萌芽最早可以追溯到"二战"时期的对外信息和文化关系项目。[1] 其后，它在曲折中前进，终于在21世纪初形成了较为完整的运作体系。当前，澳大利亚公共外交立足亚太、辐射全球，其所涉及的范围是"多样而广泛的"，成就也令人印象深刻。[2]

---

* 本文为2010年教育部人文社会科学研究规划基金项目"网络外交对中国社会发展的影响及对策研究"（项目批准号：10YJAGJW014）研究成果的一部分，原文发表于《国际观察》2012年第4期，收入本文集时略有修改。

第一，初步形成了议会与政府结合、中央与地方结合、官方与非官方相结合以及国内与国外相结合的公共外交组织体系。

国会积极为公共外交出谋划策。2007 年 8 月，它在详细搜集大量资料并举行多次听证会的基础上，发表了《澳大利亚的公共外交：塑造我们的形象》（Australia's public diplomacy：building our image）这一长达 244 页的外交政策报告。该文件立足国内外形势，对澳大利亚公共外交发展的成就和问题做出了细致分析，并提出了 20 条政策建议。它标志着澳大利亚公共外交已经超越了传统意义上由政府单独谋划、主导实施的范畴，进入到一个新的发展阶段。政府方面，外交贸易部（Department of Foreign Affairs and Trade）特别是其下属的澳大利亚形象局（Images of Australia Branch）主要负责公共外交事务。[3] 外交贸易部的另外两个机构澳大利亚国际开发署（AusAID）和澳大利亚贸易委员会（Austrade）也在公共外交中扮演重要角色。在外交贸易部之外，以教育、国防和旅游为代表的诸多政府部门和机构同样积极参与公共外交。[4] 2002 年，国际形象局开始组织召集政府 21 个相关部门参与的公共外交跨部门协调委员会（inter-departmental committee），以便共享资源、协调行动。[5] 地方政府议会在澳公共外交中的作用也很明显，墨尔本议会就是其中的典型。它通过树立墨尔本在城市设计（city design）和城市管理上的国际声誉、参与对外经济文化交流和环境保护活动等方式，长期致力于同世界各地的不同组织深化和拓展合作关系，它还积极支持草根阶层接触政府、参与国际事务。[6] 进入 21 世纪，非政府组织（NGO）

和个体行为体在澳大利亚公共外交中的战略地位日益突出。在2007年的公共外交报告中，澳国会高度评价了非政府行为体在公共外交方面的重要作用，阐述了它们在对话、交流和沟通等方面相对于政府的独特优势，还特别表扬了相关NGO为推动澳大利亚公共外交的发展做出的出色贡献，指出了澳海外移民侨民、科学家、作家、商务和体育人士等对公共外交的积极作用。[7]为了做好对外联系，澳还先后成立了澳大利亚—中国理事会（Australia-China Council）、澳大利亚—印度理事会（Australia-India Council）和澳大利亚国际文化理事会（Australia International Cultural Council）等十大致力于双边或多边交流的理事会、基金会和研究机构。[8]澳大设置的海外工作岗位（overseas posts）也采取了一系列富于创新的有效公共外交活动服务于国家的外交目标，相关活动仅在2008—2009年度就执行了5054个。[9]

第二，初步建立了从电台广播、有线电视到互联网等新旧媒体服务全面覆盖的公共外交传播体系。

澳政府积极干预、影响和管理媒体以推动公共外交的发展，海外工作岗位就常常与负面媒体信息作斗争，并且强力执行前瞻性的媒体管理战略，以提升澳大利亚的国际形象。[10]在对媒体的使用方面，除了传统的书籍出版之外，它在国际广播和互联网领域的工作最为瞩目。在国际广播领域，澳大利亚主要通过澳大利亚国家广播电视公司（Australian Broadcasting Corporation）进行。该公司“建于1932年”，是澳大利亚“最著名也最有影响”的广电公司，其“广播已存在70多年，电视有50多年，网站有20年，杂志有15年”。它“在世界50个国家和地区设立办事处，包括华盛顿、伦敦、东京、北京等。"[11] 2007 年，该公司在重组中设立了澳大利亚国际广播电视公司（ABC International），它毫不掩饰自己在国家公共外交中的战略作用，声称自己是澳大利亚以电视、电台和计算机联网的方式在海外展示自己的一个主要行为体，其功能之一就是促进海外对澳大利亚的了解、使国际社会理解澳大利亚对于世界事务的态度。该公司由两个部分构成，即澳大利亚广播电台（Radio Australia）和澳大利亚电视网（Australia Network）。[12] 其中，澳大利亚广播电台的历史较为悠久。它开始短波广播于 1939 年，最初被应用于同"二战"时期日本对澳大利亚周边地区的广播宣传做斗争，其后它也一直就在澳亚太公共外交舞台上占有举足轻重的地位。到 1945 年，其广播的语言种类就有德语、西班牙语、荷兰语、法语和意大利语等，达十五种之多。20 世纪 90 年代末，它在帮助澳大利亚应对亚太地区的动荡局势方面发挥了重要作用。例如，在东帝汶决定是否独立于印度尼西亚的公民投票时期，它在东帝汶的公共外交活动对于支持澳大利亚的相关政策和国际维和部队在当地的行动就至关重要。1999 年下半年，其关于选举的使用东帝汶和印尼语的双语网站受到特别欢迎，在 9 月和 10 月的点击率超过 200 万次。2007 年，它开通了对柬埔寨的广播服务。2008 年，它开通了对老挝的调频广播服务，成为老挝唯一允许一周七天 24 小时全天候广播的英语外国电台。[13] 澳大利亚电视网诞生于 1994 年，起初目的是对澳广播电台在亚太地区的活动起补充作用。[14] 由于澳政府也将其作为公共外交的重要平台来扶持，因此它发展也很快。外交贸易部 2009—2010 年度的报告显示，它已覆盖了 44 个国家的

2,200万个家庭。[15]此外，互联网在澳大利亚政府本身的公共外交中也具有重要地位。以外交贸易部为例，它非常重视传统网络媒体在信息服务和沟通服务中的作用，并且根据国家战略的需要，不断更新内容、改进表达风格。比如外交贸易部网站的周点击率就呈现出不错水平，其中2008—2009年度，外交贸易部网站的周点击率约为755,000次，2009—2010年度为980,703次。在社交新媒体方面，2011年8月，外交贸易部设立了推特（Twitter）账户，就旅游、新闻、贸易、领事签证等事务发布信息、提供咨询或建议，它也设立了优酷（YouTube）频道，发布与部门工作有关的视频，以拓展对外交流。[16]

第三，初步打造了国际教育、文化外交与其他各种对外沟通联系项目等一系列公共外交品牌活动。

澳大利亚现在已经是世界上第五大国际学生教育的提供者，其教育水准和国际学生的满意度都很高，曾经有调查显示，83%的接受过高等教育和88%的接受过职业与技术培训（VET）的留学生都愿意推荐家人和朋友去澳大利亚学习。据经济合作与发展组织（OECD）的统计，澳大利亚高等教育体系中外国留学生的比例远远高出其成员国7.2%的平均率，达到了最高的19.3%。[17] 2010年，有62万留学生通过澳大利亚的教育机构注册学习，其中的40万直接移民澳本土学习。[18]另需补充的是，澳大利亚政府于2009年11月设立了澳大利亚国家奖学金（the Australia Awards），该项奖学金将以往由不同部门分管的国际奖学金项目合而为一，以加强澳大利亚奖学金项目发展的稳固性和品牌性，从而使其收益最大化并且尽可能支持澳与周边地区发展持久的联系，更好发挥出国际教育的公共外交作用。[19]在文化外交方面，澳大利亚致力于通过各种文化项目和广泛的海外联系传播本土文化、艺术和音乐。例如：2009—2010 年度，澳大利亚的主要文化外交机构国际文化理事会就在拉美、亚太、印度、加拿大和英国等地支持了 17 个文化项目，其中 11 个在中国。2010—2011 年度，它又支持了 21 个文化外交项目，其中 5 个在韩国，10 个在中国。[20]这些活动当中，以澳大利亚参与上海世博会的优异表现为代表。世博会期间，"澳大利亚国家馆总体运营时间为 2,622 个小时，迎接了 8,182,259 名公众访客。"所有访客都尽情观赏了"主映剧场播放的 10,800 场演出，享用了 42,000 个澳式肉派和 114,000 多个冰激凌。"其"服务态度获得 100% 游客的好评"，这种杰出表现也"收到了 7,500 多篇中国媒体的正面报道"。[21]除了这两大品牌之外，澳大利亚其他多种形式的对外沟通联系项目也是其公共外交的特色所在。如特别访问者项目（Special Visits Program）、国际媒体访问项目（International media visits）、国际关系资助项目（The International Relations Grant Program）和对外直接援助项目（Direct Aid Program）等。其中，国际关系资助项目是澳外交贸易部主管的最大资助项目，这个项目旨在通过"加强人与人之间的联系"，推动澳大利亚与中、法、韩、日等重点国家，在农业、社会和贸易等诸多领域展开富有成效的公共外交活动。比如，2010—2011 年度，仅澳大利亚—日本基金会（Australia-Japan Foundation）就利用其资助扶持了 60 多个双边活动。[22]

## 澳大利亚公共外交的动因

就本质而言，澳大利亚与其他国家开展公共外交的原因都是一样的，即在熟悉和接触外国公众，告知他们有关自己的价值观、文化与目标的基础上，吸引、影响他们，进而诱导其政府支持自己的外交政策目标，帮助它实现战略利益。[23]具体而言，澳大利亚公共外交的动因主要表现为如下方面。

其一，澳大利亚发展公共外交是其中等强国地位尤其是顺应地区战略格局演变的内在要求。

澳大利亚的中等强国地位有着两层含义。首先，与荷兰、瑞典和加拿大等其他中等强国一样，澳大利亚虽然不是一个可以被忽略的处于全球舞台边缘的国家，但它也不可能像美国、俄罗斯和欧洲某些大国那样，有着足够的硬实力支撑自己的国际地位。它要想在国际社会中赢得注意，就必须在外交中更加注意培养软实力。其次，澳大利亚还有着其他中等强国所没有的独特地缘政治特点。与加拿大不同，澳大利亚没有与一个经济军事超级大国为邻，相对而言不那么方便分享美国繁荣稳定的红利；与荷兰和瑞典不同，它不能享受欧盟成员国的利益；不仅如此，它还没有加入像北约这样的安全联盟和类似于北美自由贸易区的地区经济集团。尽管它是一个近代历史和传统盟友都与亚太地区无关的国家，但随着国际权势向亚太地区的转移，它目前必须经营亚太，并且要以亚太为依托走向世界。[24]不仅如此，随着全球化的发展，恐怖主义、武器扩散、气候变化与食品和资源匮乏导非传统安全问题也日渐超越国家界限，并影响澳大利亚的切身利益。解决这些问题不仅需要政治决心和勇气，也需要澳大利亚广泛接触国外尤其是周边地区的大众，特别是其中的精英阶层。这种情况下，它要想在国际社会中发出自己的声音，解决发展困境，赢得发展机遇，就必须在外交中更加注意发挥软实力的影响。由此，作为发展软实力的重要工具——公共外交自然而然就受到了澳外交决策者的关注，当然这反过来也成为澳公共外交不断发展创新的内在源泉。[25]其实早在1990年，时任澳外交贸易部长就说过，“不能将公共外交视为外交与贸易政策中的一个可有可无的配角”，“作为一个依赖于国际贸易的国家”，“一个决心从事亲密靠近和建设性参与多元文化的亚太地区的国家”，“一个有着独特国家身份的自信社会（community）”，“公共外交对于增进澳大利亚的许多国际利益很重要”。[26]

其二，澳大利亚的国际形象有着诸多被世界误解的地方，其民众对外了解也存在很多不足，它需要公共外交发力以树立积极正面的和负责任的国家形象，同时增进国内社会对世界的了解。

中等强国在树立国际形象方面都面临这样的基本挑战：世界对其了解不是很多，或者更坏的是，只了解其刻板陈旧的负面形象，这一点对于澳大利亚也不例外。[27]当前，澳大利亚的国际形象和它实际想要树立的形象之间存在很大差异。澳政府认为如下国际形象与其国家利益直接相关，即国际社会的负责任成员、国际法的遵守者、人道主义援助的积极参与者以及周边地区经济发展的建设性贡献者。它想要被认为是一个充满想象力和创造力的、真诚致力于地区稳定与繁荣并且有着丰富实践经验的国家。然而，迄今为止，澳大利亚的国际形象仍旧是老套过时的。经济形象上，尽管澳大利亚成就明显，但在外界看来，澳大利亚首先仍旧是充满阳光、海滩、袋鼠和沙漠的旅游胜地，它经济的成功仅仅只能归因于人口少、国土面积大与资源丰富的运气。政治形象上，由于历史上白澳政策的影响，澳大利亚至今一直被误解为种族歧视严重的国家。尽管澳政府当前致力实现种族平等、消除种族歧视，以树立种族包容的国际形象并且在这方面取得很大进步，但目前澳国内种族歧视的温床并没有完全消失，偶而仍会有相关的恶性事件发生。澳大利亚需要消除这种偶发事件的不良影响，尤其是要防止国际社会做出将这些偶发事件视为澳境内普遍现象的负面解读。[28]在周边地区，以上情况显得更为严重。这种严重性不仅表现为周边地区的民众对澳大利亚不够了解，也表现为澳大利亚民众对周边地区不够了解，双方彼此之间均缺乏足够的理解和信任。以中国为例，罗伊研究所2011年的澳大利亚民调显示，50%的人认为澳大利亚应该与其他国家一起限制中国的影响力，58%的人认为政府在施压中国改进人权方面做得不够，57%的人认为澳政府已经允许中国在其本土投资过多，44%的人认为在未来20年中国有可能会对澳大利亚构成军事威胁，仅有34%的人同意澳大利亚的利益不会因中国获得更多的权力和影响而受到损害。[29]同样，它2009年的中国民调显示，48%的中国人认为澳大利亚是一个对中国持怀疑态度的国家。[30]尽管当前中澳经贸关系已经很紧密，中国是澳大利亚第一大贸易伙伴、第一大出口市场、第一大进口来源地和第二大外资来源国，两国官方也积极发展关系，但两国民众之间的相互认知显然未能达到双方关系应有的程度。[31]在解决方法上，就澳大利亚方面而言，它必须更加熟悉和了解周边地区，并树立正面的形象，这也需要公共外交发挥作用。正如澳前外交贸易部长所言，"公共外交不仅仅是我们在海外做什么"，"它同样是与国内社会接触，与其就政府的政策和目标进行对话，它还包括帮助人们更好地了解周围的世界"，"邻近地区人民之间的相互理解和熟悉并不必然带来和平与繁荣"，但是"相互无知一定会是一个更大的危险"。[32]

其三，澳大利亚公共外交的发展还是对全球公共外交发展的回应，一定程度上也可以说是全球公共外交刺激的结果。

随着国家利益的拓展尤其是全球公共外交的发展与激烈竞争，澳国内的有识之士特别是政界和学术界相关人士不断奔走呼吁，强调自己的声音不能被别人盖过，否则那将是"非常危险的"。它同样推动了澳大利亚公共外交的与时俱进。[33]澳国会 2007 年的公共外交报告指出：公共外交是一项竞争日益激烈的活动，无论大国还是小国都面临着争夺有限国际空间的斗争，即让自己是能够被"看得到的和听得见的"，这对于澳大利亚也不例外。尽管资源有限，但为了确保它不会在这场争夺国际空间的比赛中失去光彩，澳大利亚必须从战略上慎重设计公共外交项目，并证它能够得到有效执行。[34]再以它在国际教育和网络公共外交方面的发展为例。2008 年 8 月 8 日，吉拉德在一次论坛中提到，尽管国际教育的需求日益增多，且澳大利亚在其中拥有诸多优势，但是竞争也日渐激烈。澳大利亚的地位不仅受到美国、英国、加拿大等传统教育强国积极创新国际教育战略、拓展国际教育市场的竞争，也面临着中国、新加坡和马来西亚提升本土教育质量和服务水平的挑战，甚至传统上并非以英语为母语的国家，如日本、德国和韩国等，也在向海外输送英语课程，与澳大利亚争夺市场。因此，为了维护澳国际教育的“全球联系（globally connected）”局面和“世界领袖”地位，“我们必须不断寻求改善和创新”。[35] 在网络公共外交方面，澳学者梳理了网络公共外交这一新公共外交工具的特点和发展趋势，包括它的基本功能、它在突尼斯和埃及等国政变中的作用以及美国、英国和加拿大的外交部门对其使用的情况，指出网络公共外交并非外交部门可有可无与华而不实的奢饰品，它在21世纪的国家外交运作中将日渐占据中心位置。因此，澳外交贸易部需要与技术的发展同步，以提升国内外交流的效率，加速信息的流通和聚集。否则，外交贸易部将会被切断与重要受众的联系，越来越难传递信息和在政府层面协调国家的外交政策。[36] 在此也不难看出，正是这种在深刻洞察国际公共外交发展趋势的基础上，充分立足自身优势抢占制高点的发展思路，才推动了澳大利亚公共外交的不断进步。

## 澳大利亚公共外交的局限

尽管成就明显，而且发展的动力十足，但澳大利亚公共外交所面临的问题也不少，有些甚至很突出。

首先，澳公共外交的全员参与意识不足，其组织体系、运作机制、战略规划力和执行力有待提高。

在学术研究上，尽管以罗伊研究所为代表的学术机构和某些优秀学者从多个视角对澳公共外交展开了认真审视，并提出了不少有价值的建议，但是，澳国会在2007年公共外交报告中认为的澳学术界对公共外交的研究缺乏应有的重视这一局面没有得到根本改变。除此以外，澳公共外交的社会参与意识和氛围也有待提高，比如“公共外交”这个术语就尚未在普通大众中得到广泛理解和使用。[37]在组织体系和运作机制上，三大问题最为突出。首先是在中央政府层面，由外交贸易部单独主导的公共外交跨部门协调委员会对于公共外交的组织领导已经力不从心，因为它只是一个协调机构，决策能力和执行能力有限。其次是澳地方政府和议会参与公共外交的组织协调也待优化，比如尽管它们广泛参与公共外交，但绝大多数并未对此展开系统总结。澳国会2007年就曾指出在公共外交调研中，它只收到了墨尔本议会的相关报告。虽然国会已经敏锐意识到这些问题，并提出了相关改革建议，但政府并未做出有力回应。比如，国会曾经建议政府重组公共外交跨部门协调委员会，以提升其地位和相应的决策力，改善公共外交的战略规划能力。国会甚至还建议政府如果觉得这一措施不可行，就成立一个永久独立的机构来代替它履行职能。澳国会也曾经建议，中央政府应创造利用机会与地方加强协调与合作以促进公共外交发展。但是，从外交贸易部近几年的年度工作报告来看，政府并没有将这些事提上日程。[38]不仅如此，国会在2007年提出了针对公共外交的20条建议仅4条被政府采纳。[39]这也就是澳大利亚在公共外交组织与协调方面的第三个大问题，即国会与政府未形成合力。

在这种情况下，澳大利亚公共外交整体的战略规划能力必然是不足的，其活动的执行缺乏长远规划、整合力差，有时甚至会发出自相矛盾的信息，效率也收到严重影响。比如，尽管澳大利亚国内已经普遍认识到公共外交主要有在海外树立正面形象和引导他国执行有利于自己的政策这两大战略目标，但是在实际操作中它却往往给人以专注于前者，后者则常常被忽略的印象。这些都造成了“公共外交全局的整体影响效应不如其各分支机构单独打拼所产生的效果之和”这一尴尬局面一直持续，甚至有评论称，它目前已再次沦落到被排斥于主流外交活动之外的边缘化境地。[40]

其次，澳公共外交的传播体系和品牌活动还有许多缺陷和亟待解决的挑战。

这些问题表现在三个方面：第一个方面是语言文化交流和移民政策问题的困扰。以国际教育为例，在语言文化交流上，向海外派出本国留学生对发挥澳大利亚国际教育的影响有重要作用，但澳大利亚年轻人明显缺乏有效接触周边地区多元文化的语言技巧和心理准备。2009 年的研究显示，在澳大利亚 12 岁的学生中，学习第二语言的比例只有 12%，而这其中又仅有 5.4% 在学习亚洲语言。澳大利亚高校提供的语言学习课程近几年也在大幅下降，只有 3% 的大学生可能愿意学习亚洲语言。[41]“澳大利亚移民政策缺乏稳定性和可预见性”。曾经一度，澳大利亚抓住美国的留学生招收工作因为官僚主义和后 9·11 时代的种种偏执而陷入签证困境的机遇，在世界尤其是亚洲招收了大量学生。但自 2010 年以来，澳大利亚也收紧了移民政策，“新南威尔士州国际部主任阿列克桑德尔·伏宁斯基表示，不少留学生和外国政府认为，澳大利亚的政策表明，澳政府想要把留学生挡在国门外。”这个问题加上澳元升值、以及学校关闭风波等因素影响，赴澳大利亚求学的外国学生人数大幅萎缩，使澳国际教育产业出现近年来少有的困难局面。“从2008—2009学年至2009—2010学年，申请来澳留学的国际学生签证数量萎缩18.9%。”2010年下半年，移民当局受理的国际学生签证申请，“同比下滑超过2.27万份。”[42]

第二个方面是对公共外交各活动项目的资助缺乏科学合理的分配。如2010年，澳大利亚将近80%的公共外交预算（2亿澳元）投资于国际奖学金领域——澳大利亚奖学金。在剩下的预算中，澳大利亚电视网获得了1900万澳元，文化外交获得了750万澳元。当国际奖学金项目被排除的时候，澳大利亚对公共外交投资很小的局面就变得明显了。此外，尽管对公共外交的贡献显著，澳大利亚广播电台和澳大利亚电视网还是周期性地受到关闭或预算削减的威胁。澳大利亚的人均国际广播投入也远远落后于英法德等国家，甚至不如同为中等强国荷兰的一半，[43]澳大利亚国际广播电台和各种国际电视服务企业也还没有属于自己的独立传播基础设施（transmission infrastructure）。[44]

第三个方面是澳大利亚尚缺乏有效的评估机制来评价公共外交活动的成效。比如外交贸易部在其年度报告对公共外交的陈述中，就将篇幅主要聚焦于表达他们在公共外交上都做了哪些活动，而非这些活动都产生了什么结果，带来了什么影响。[45]

最后，澳大利亚外交战略的内在缺陷成为了限制公共外交起作用的根本因素。

中等强国发展公共外交的可能性受政治意志和经济实力的双重约束，[46]这对澳大利亚也不例外，上述所总结的澳大利亚公共外交一系列问题的根源也在于此。就外交传统而言，澳大利亚现实主义的外交传统使得它依赖在力量和文化上志趣相投的强大盟友，并且重视实用主义的贸易和安全框架。软实力尽管被认识到，甚至被不少有识之士不断提及，但是它在当前的外交部门并没有被引起普遍重视，在外交决策中也没有被置于战略优先地位。[47]近几年，澳政府着力扩充军备，2009年，“澳大利亚提出了在未来20年花费700多亿美元的全面提升军力的计划。在这份计划中，我们不仅看到了增强边境和能源保卫的力量，还有一系列大规模采购名单，包括把潜艇舰队翻倍至12艘，购入100架F-35战机，并希望购入8艘新型护卫舰和3艘驱逐舰等。此外，澳还将改进卫星及网络技术，以提高信息作战能力。”与之相对应的是，“澳大利亚总理陆克文强调，为保证国防建设的资金准确到位，澳政府计划逐年增加国防经费，2018年前每年增加国防经费3%，2018—2030年间将增加幅度调至2.2%”。[48]2008—2009年度，澳国防部的预算超过了220亿澳元，而外交贸易部的预算则不足12亿澳元。并且由于连年下降的预算长期捉襟见肘，其应对外交事务的能力也相应下降，甚至难以满足澳国家利益的正常需要。在这种情况下，它在公共外交方面的精力和资金投入必然会受到限制，公共外交的发展自然而然也就变得“暗淡无光”。[49]更令人忧虑的是，吉拉德政府上台后，为了应对持久的国家财政赤字，势必实行缩紧财政预算，对国内政治优先性的考量必然会导致其更加不可能有改变公共外交资金投入不足这个局面的意愿。[50]由此，我们也不难得出这样的结论：当前澳大利亚公共外交的发展正处于新一轮困境中，其复兴尚需时日。

## [注释]

[1] Rosaleen Smyth, Managing Australia's Image in Asia, *Australia Journal of International Affairs*, 1995, Vol. 49, No. 2, p224.

[2] The Senate, *Australia's public diplomacy*: *building our image*, Printed by the Senate Printing Unit, Parliament House, Canberra, August 2007, p46.

[3] 同上，p31.

[4] 同上，pp96 - 98.

[5] 同上，p101.

[6] 同上，pp110 - 113.

[7] 同上，pp129 - 141.

[8] 相关内容参见澳外交贸易部网站：http://www.dfat.gov.au/councils/index.html（访问时间：2011 年 11 月 14 日）

[9] *DFAT Annual Report* 2008 - 2009, p190, http://www.dfat.gov.au/dept/annual_reports/08_09/downloads/DFAT - 08 - 09 - Complete.pdf（访问时间：2011 年 11 月 15 日）；*DFAT Annual Report* 2009 - 2010, p128, http://www.dfat.gov.au/dept/annual_reports/09_10/downloads/DFAT - AR0910.pdf（访问时间：2011 年 10 月 28 日）

[10] Mohd Azizuddin Mohd Sani & Irene Limberis Twombly, Australian Government Media Strategies, *Journal of Asia Pacific Studies*, 2010, Vol. 1, No 3, p631.

[11] 丁曦林：澳大利亚传媒竞争态势，《中国新闻出版报》，2010 年 2 月 3 日，第 4 版。

[12] The Senate, *Australia's public diplomacy*: *building our image*, Printed

by the Senate Printing Unit, Parliament House, Canberra, August 2007, p40.

[13] Annmaree O'Keeffe & Alex Oliver, International Broadcasting and its contribution to public diplomacy, *Lowy Institute for International Policy*, September 2010, pp49 – 66.

[14] Alex Oliver and Annmaree O'Keeffe, Struggling to be Heard: Australia's International Broadcasters Fight for a Voice in the Region, 22 June, 2011, http://publicdiplomacymagazine.com/struggling-to-be-heard-australia%e2%80%99s-international-broadcasters-fight-for-a-voice-in-the-region/（访问时间：2011年11月15日）

[15] *DFAT Annual Report* 2009 – 2010, p137, http://www.dfat.gov.au/dept/annual_reports/09_10/downloads/DFAT-AR0910.pdf（访问时间：2011年10月28日）

[16] *DFAT Annual Report* 2009 – 2010, p126, http://www.dfat.gov.au/dept/annual_reports/09_10/downloads/DFAT-AR0910.pdf（访问时间：2011年10月28日）；*DFAT Annual Report* 2010 – 2011, p. 121, http://www.dfat.gov.au/dept/annual_reports/10_11/downloads/DFAT-AR1011.pdf（访问时间：2011年11月17日）

[17] Julia Gillard, Globally Connected, AEI Industry Forum 2008, Melbourne Convention Centre, http://mediacentre.dewr.gov.au/mediacentre/Gillard/Releases/GloballyConnected.html（访问时间：2011年11月21日）

[18] Caitlin Byrne & Rebecca Hall, Australia's International Education as Public Diplomacy: Soft Power Potential, July 2011, p1, http://www.clingendael.nl/publications/2011/20110700_cdsp_discussion_paper_cbryne_rhall.pdf（访问时间：2011年11月21日）

[19] *DFAT Annual Report* 2009 – 2010, p136, http://www.dfat.gov.au/dept/annual_reports/09_10/downloads/DFAT-AR0910.pdf（访

问时间：2011 年 10 月 28 日）

[20] *DFAT Annual Report* 2009－2010，pp130－132，http：//www. dfat. gov. au/dept/annual_ reports/09_ 10/downloads/DFAT-AR0910. pdf（访问时间：2011 年 10 月 28 日）；*DFAT Annual Report* 2010－2011，pp124－126，http：//www. dfat. gov. au/dept/annual_ reports/10_ 11/downloads/DFAT-AR1011. pdf（访问时间：2011 年 11 月 17 日）

[21]《澳大利亚国家馆闭幕》，澳大利亚国家馆网站，http：//www. australianpavilion. com/CN/news_ media/Pavilion_ Closed_ last_ day. aspx（访问时间：2011 年 11 月 22 日）；刘康，《上海世博会 各国对华公共外交的大舞台》，凤凰网，http：//news. ifeng. com/mainland/special/PublicDiplomacy/anli/detail_ 2011_ 02/22/4794546_ 1. shtml（访问时间：2011 年 11 月 22 日）

[22] *DFAT Annual Report* 2010－2011，pp123－130，http：//www. dfat. gov. au/dept/annual_ reports/10_ 11/downloads/DFAT-AR1011. pdf（访问时间：2011 年 11 月 17 日）

[23] Annmaree O'Keeffe & Alex Oliver，International Broadcasting and its contribution to public diplomacy，*Lowy Institute for International Policy*，September 2010，p44.

[24] 同上，pp42－44.

[25] Caitlin Byrne & Rebecca Hall，Australia's International Education as Public Diplomacy：Soft Power Potential，July 2011，pp7－8，http：//www. clingendael. nl/publications/2011/20110700_ cdsp_ discussion_ paper_ cbryne_ rhall. pdf（访问时间：2011 年 11 月 21 日）

[26] Gareth Evans，Australia and Asia：the role of public diplomacy，15 March 1990，p4，http：//www. gevans. org/speeches/old/1990/150390_ fm_ australiaandasia. pdf（访问时间：2011 年 11 月 25

日）

[27] Eytan Gilboa, The public diplomacy of middle powers, http://publicdiplomacymagazine.com/the-public-diplomacy-of-middle-powers/（访问时间：2011年11月27日）

[28] The Senate, *Australia's public diplomacy: building our image*, Printed by the Senate Printing Unit, Parliament House, Canberra, August 2007, pp53-57.

[29] Fergus Hanson, Australia and the World: public opinion and foreign policy, *The Lowy Institute Poll* 2011, pp6-12, http://www.lowyinstitute.org/Publication.asp?pid=1617（访问时间：2011年11月27日）

[30] Fergus Hanson & Andrew Shearer, China and the World: public opinion and foreign policy, *The Lowy Institute China Poll* 2009, pp6-7, http://www.lowyinstitute.org/Publication.asp?pid=1193（访问时间：2011年11月27日）

[31] 习近平：携手推动中澳经贸合作再上新台阶——在中澳经贸合作论坛午餐会上的主旨演讲，人民网，http://politics.people.com.cn/GB/1024/11930000.html（访问时间：2010年06月22日）

[32] Gareth Evans, Australia and Asia: the role of public diplomacy, 15 March 1990, pp1-10, http://www.gevans.org/speeches/old/1990/150390_fm_australiaandasia.pdf（访问时间：2011年11月25日）

[33] 同上，http://www.gevans.org/speeches/old/1990/150390_fm_australiaandasia.pdf（访问时间：2011年11月25日）；谭利娅：澳智库称应关注公共外交警惕“声音被中国盖过”，环球网，http://world.huanqiu.com/roll/2011-03/1537566.html（访问时间：2011年3月3日）

[34] The Senate, *Australia's public diplomacy: building our image*, Printed by the Senate Printing Unit, Parliament House, Canberra, August 2007, p xi & pp20 - 25.

[35] Julia Gillard, Globally Connected, AEI Industry Forum 2008, Melbourne Convention Centre, http://ministers.deewr.gov.au/gillard/globally-connected（访问时间：2012 年 06 月 07 日）

[36] Fergus Hanson, The new public diplomacy, *Lowy Institute for International Policy*, April 2011, pp1 - 5; Fergus Hanson, A Digital DFAT: Joining the 21st Century, *Lowy Institute for International Policy*, November 2010, pp1 - 14.

[37] Caitlin Byrne, Not Quite the Sum of its Parts: Public Diplomacy from an Australian Perspective, *Exchange: The journal of public diplomacy*, Fall 2010, p45; The Senate, *Australia's public diplomacy: building our image*, Printed by the Senate Printing Unit, Parliament House, Canberra, August 2007, pp27 - 31 & 129 - 143.

[38] The Senate, *Australia's public diplomacy: building our image*, Printed by the Senate Printing Unit, Parliament House, Canberra, August 2007, pp103 - 114.

[39] Annmaree O'Keeffe & Alex Oliver, International Broadcasting and its contribution to public diplomacy, *Lowy Institute for International Policy*, September 2010, p45.

[40] The Blue Ribbon Panel, Australia's Diplomatic Deficit: Reinvesting in our instruments of international policy, *Blue Ribbon Panel Report*, pp30 - 32, http://www.voltairenet.org/IMG/pdf/Australia_Diplomatic_Deficit.pdf（访问时间：2011 年 12 月 5 日）; The Senate, *Australia's public diplomacy: building our image*, Printed by the Senate Printing Unit, Parliament House, Canberra, August 2007, p46; Caitlin Byrne, Not Quite the Sum of its Parts: Public Diplomacy

from an Australian Perspective, *Exchange*: *The journal of public diplomacy*, *Fall* 2010, p45.

[41] Caitlin Byrne & Rebecca Hall, Australia's International Education as Public Diplomacy: Soft Power Potential, p14, http://www.clingendael.nl/publications/2011/20110700_cdsp_discussion_paper_cbryne_rhall.pdf（访问时间：2011年12月23日）

[42] 傅云威：澳收紧移民政策重挫国际教育产业，《经济参考报》，2011年3月25日，第4版；Nicholas J. Cull, Australia's Public Diplomacy Crisis, 6 September, 2009, http://uscpublicdiplomacy.org/index.php/newswire/cpdblog_detail/australias_public_diplomacy_crisis/（访问时间：2011年11月21日）

[43] Annmaree O'Keeffe & Alex Oliver, International Broadcasting and its contribution to public diplomacy, *Lowy Institute for International Policy*, September 2010, pi & pp47 – 48.

[44] 同上，p55.

[45] The Blue Ribbon Panel, Australia's Diplomatic Deficit: Reinvesting in our instruments of international policy, *Blue Ribbon Panel Report*, pp32 – 33, http://www.voltairenet.org/IMG/pdf/Australia_Diplomatic_Deficit.pdf（访问时间：2011年12月5日）

[46] M. A. Rudderham, Middle Power Pull: Can Middle Powers use Public Diplomacy to Ameliorate the Image of the West?, p1, http://www.yorku.ca/yciss/publications/documents/WP46 – Rudderham.pdf（访问时间：2011年12月23日）

[47] Caitlin Byrne & Rebecca Hall, Australia's International Education as Public Diplomacy: Soft Power Potential, p5, http://www.clingendael.nl/publications/2011/20110700_cdsp_discussion_paper_cbryne_rhall.pdf（访问时间：2011年12月23日）

[48] 千亿扩军：澳大利亚军事大国梦，时代周报网，http://news.

time-weekly. com/story/2009 - 07 - 16/101205. html（访问时间：2011 年 12 月 24 日）

[49] The Blue Ribbon Panel, Australia's Diplomatic Deficit: Reinvesting in our instruments of international policy, *Blue Ribbon Panel Report*, p. v-viii, http://www. voltairenet. org/IMG/pdf/Australia_ Diplomatic_ Deficit. pdf（访问时间：2011 年 12 月 5 日）

[50] Caitlin Byrne & Rebecca Hall, Australia's International Education as Public Diplomacy: Soft Power Potential, pp18 - 19, http://www. clingendael. nl/publications/2011/20110700_ cdsp_ discussion_ paper_ cbryne_ rhall. pdf（访问时间：2011 年 12 月 23 日）

## 作者简介

**黄忠**，青岛理工大学外国语学院讲师，从事公共外交、网络外交和亚太安全研究。(Email：huangzhong8309@163. com)

**唐小松**，博士，现任广东外语外贸大学外交学系教授，广东国际战略研究院首席研究员。主要从事公共外交、网络外交和美国研究。(Email：xstang2006@163. com)

# 10

# 澳大利亚：移民、多元文化与身份困惑*

钱超英

已故美国政治学家亨廷顿在其名著《文明的冲突与世界政治的重构》写道："（20 世纪）90 年代爆发了全球的认同危机，人们看到，几乎在每一个地方，人们都在问'我们是谁?''我们属于哪儿?'以及'谁跟我们不是一伙?'。"[1]亨廷顿认为，这不仅适用于"冷战"结束后出现的新民族国家（如从前南斯拉夫分裂出来的人民）而且也属于"更一般的国家"。例如，对澳大利亚，该书就发表了这样触目的评说：

> 澳大利亚是试图背弃西方、追随正在崛起的非西方文明的许多可能的西方国家中的第一个。到 22 世纪初期，当历史学家回首往事时，可能会把

* 本文原载于《深圳大学学报》（人文社会科学版）2009 年第 2 期，收入本文集前作者对论文做了适度修改。

基廷—埃文斯[2]的选择看作是西方衰落的一个主要标志。[3]

澳大利亚这个仅仅两千余万人口的南半球国家，之所以会让这位深谋远虑的美国政治文化策士如此大费周章，首先是因为澳大利亚对于今日世界具有特殊意义。而这种意义又是由其独特的国家身份问题所构筑的。

## 一、“太平洋国家”还是“亚洲国家”？

在全球版图上，澳大利亚作为孤立而完整的巨大陆岛偏处于南半球，东西两边分别被印度洋和太平洋包围，南方则和另一个孤岛国家新西兰一道，与无人的南极洲相望，仅北部与亚洲南端的少数岛国接近，印度尼西亚是其最大的北方近邻。尽管它（与新西兰一并）是与西方世界核心地区距离最远的地理单元，但却是扼守南半球海洋世界的最大、最稳定统一而又最具有战略纵深的政治地理实体。1770 年英国殖民探险家詹姆斯·库克船长“发现”了澳大利亚大陆，1786～1788 年间，英国政府正式开始对其统治和移民，在其东南沿海设立罪犯流放地，这成为澳大利亚大陆“文明”历史的开端。而原已在澳大利亚生息了数万年之久的土著民族则遭到白人的大量屠戮和驱逐，正是在土著的血泪和殖骨之上，英国人逐步把这个流放场兴建成了新国家。早先有多个殖民区分布于澳境的东南部、西部和北部沿岸地区，如同北美殖民地开始时的情形，各据一方自治经营。1900 年英国议会通过《澳大利亚联邦宪法》；次年，1901 年 1 月 1

日，各殖民区改为州，各州正式组成联邦，作为英国的自治领延续至今。

从全球视野看，这个新国家的孕育过程不过是西方早在15世纪就开启的全球地理探险、殖民扩张历史中的新一页：与澳大利亚几乎同时期兴起的西方外缘—新兴地区，包括北美和南非，都经历了极为相似的“开化”过程。例如，随着地理地质勘探活动的开拓、对大量矿产的需求和采掘手段的发展，这些地区相继发现了贵金属矿藏，特别是金矿，吸引了更多欧洲人和非欧洲人前往采集，于是在世界范围内引起了以这些地区为目标的越洋淘金潮。而这些地区基础设施建设的高潮——公路、铁路、城市和大片土地的开发也急需大量劳动力，也是第三世界海外契约劳工得以进入的原因。这些都促成了涌向北美、澳大利亚的短期或长期移民的浪潮，成为资本主义新兴国家早期发展的人口移动、汇聚景观。

进入20世纪，澳大利亚不仅幸免于成为两次世界大战的主战场，而且从战时、战后经济贸易中获益良多，故其社会经济发展很快。澳大利亚的发展不仅与作为西方“飞地”的一系列新兴国家具有明显的同步性和同构性，而且也使它成了全球政治经济体系中的重要一极。然而，澳大利亚却又始终有着其他西方社会所不多见的国家身份焦虑，因而被亨廷顿归入“无所适从”的国家之列。

这种国家身份上的严重的不确定，首先明显地表现在：它对于自身的世界地缘特点所可能赋予的意义和作用难以定义，具体地说，澳大利亚作为一个西方文化根源的现代国家，在处理与亚洲国家及其文化关系时始终面对深刻的矛盾。其在区内的国际交往和政治角色的反复演变呈现为一条相当曲折的历史线索。大致上说，这一线索可划分出六个阶段。

第一阶段是其立国至第二次世界大战前。这一阶段的基本特征是以“英国属土”为自足意义，对亚洲采取排斥、防范和自闭的态度。自 18 世纪后期英国人正式殖民澳大利亚直至成立联邦国家的 120 多年间，尤其是 19 世纪中叶发现金矿的时期，各个自治殖民区都通过了限制华人和其他亚洲人入境的法例。这些法例成为 1901 年澳大利亚联邦成立的宪政基础的重要部分。正是出于协调各区关防、限制华人和亚洲人利用各殖民区之间的管理漏洞迂回进入澳境的需要，这个新生的政治联合体才迅即实行了一项“白澳政策”（White Australia Policy）旨在把澳大利亚打造成纯种白人为主的社会。这一歧视性政策一旦奠定，竟执行了接近 70 年。这为这个新国家打上了一个与生俱来的暗淡烙印。

第二阶段是第二次世界大战之前和战时，其特征是初步发展了与亚洲各国的共同战略利益。此前的澳大利亚，与国内实行“白澳政策”相伴随，与亚洲国家的正式接触很少，外交政策基本以英国为轴心并多依赖英国代行。1909 年，即联邦成立近十年时，澳国才接受了当时清政府派出的总领事并与之签订了护照协议。“一战”结束之后，迟至 1931 年，英国议会才通过《威斯敏斯特法案》赋予澳大利亚自主处理内政外交的全权（自此澳大利亚作为英国臣属仅具形式，英女王只在名义上为澳国元首）。1934 年，澳国派外长访问了当时的中华民国和几个亚洲国家。不久，第二次世界大战酿成，英国在德国法西斯攻击下自顾不暇，迫使澳大利亚开展较为积极的区内交往，1940 年 9 月它相继向美、日、中派驻了外交代表，1941年在华建立了公使馆。“二战”炽热的1942年元旦，澳大利亚总理柯廷发表了一份具有历史转折意义的新年贺词，宣称澳大利亚将与亚太国家积极发展团结互助的关系。作为反法西斯联盟的一员，澳大利亚的北部领土曾受到南侵的日本战机的轰炸。战争危机促使澳大利亚认识到：它除了与亚洲邻国协同战斗，共担安危命运和国际责任以外别无选择，这为澳大利亚社会打开了一个全新的历史视界，也孕育了新的区内认同。

第三阶段是20世纪五六十年代。其特征是追随美国“抵抗共产主义”，成为西方对东方“冷战”中的亚洲“斗士”角色。澳大利亚在“二战”中出现的国际关系的良性转折，因“冷战”格局的形成而转向变调：从战前的“英国臣属”、战时的亚洲盟友，突变成战后的美国仆从，快速滑入美国全球战略的轨道，而与亚洲多个国家的发展再度脱节和严重抵牾。1949年新中国成立时，澳国采取了拒不承认的立场；次年（1950）朝鲜战争爆发，澳大利亚视之为“共产主义在亚洲地区入侵、扩张”的证明，把新中国作为头号敌人。它是美国之后第一个应“联合国”要求派兵朝鲜的西方国家。1951年9月，它和新西兰、美国联合签订“澳新美安全条约”，三年后（1954）的9月，再与美、英、法、新西兰等联合签署《东南亚集体防务条约》。这两大条约帮助美国构建了针对所谓共产主义威胁的弧形军事同盟体系。紧接而来的1955年，澳大利亚就派兵镇压了发生在马来西亚的暴动，初显其国际准宪兵的角色；1965年，又以“遏制北越共产主义渗透”为名参与了美国主导的侵越战争。这样，整个50～60年代，澳大利亚的区内活动便基本上为美国的全球战略所左右。

第四阶段是20世纪70年代至90年代中期，这一阶段的特征是亚洲政策大转向，多元文化主义崛起，其巨大变化用翻天覆地来形容并不为过。尽管此前已有迹象显示，为了平衡“冷战热角”的形象和发展国内社会经济，澳大利亚也采取了两手政策：一方面紧跟美国战略，另一方面也局部地修补其区内关系。例如50年代推行的“科隆坡计划”就旨在为南亚和东南亚发展中国家提供国际援助，包括资助亚洲学生赴澳留学。1958年它取消了“白澳政策”一项核心内容“语言听力测试”，即不再用严格的英语标准来阻挠、限制亚洲移民，到1968年甚至正式宣布废除“白澳政策”。然而最显著的变化还是要等到1972年工党政府上台之时。这一年，惠特拉姆领导的新政府对国家政策大转向做了这样的宣布：“澳大利亚将成为对亚洲事务不作军事干涉和反对任何种族歧视之国。”这一讲话清晰显示了澳大利亚国内和国际政策之间的关联。在这一年里，澳大利亚与中华人民共和国建交，随后也与北朝鲜、越南等国建交，并从越南、新加坡、马来西亚撤回了军队。1973年，它颁布名为《非歧视性移民政策》的新移民法，表明其移民事务“全球一致，无人种、肤色和国籍歧视”，一举洗脱了这个国家和南非并列作为制度化种族歧视国家的恶名。尽管惠特拉姆政府在执政三年后（1975年）即被弗雷泽领导的自由党政府所取代，但已经开始的革命性转变仍然获得了延续。这种转变的部分契机，固然是70年代初中美关系“破冰”在西方激起的连锁反应，但澳大利亚的“过度抢进”也显示了其意欲重新开始寻找自己的道路的迹象。1977年，澳大利亚政策的调整甚至促使《东南亚集体防务条约》在签署23年之后被迫终止（这或许应被视为亨廷顿所谓“背弃西方”的较早一步）；1988年，在澳大利亚国庆200周年的同一年，中国政府总理李鹏作为非西方联盟的亚洲大国领导人首访澳大利亚。1989年初，澳国总理霍克在汉城首倡亚太经济合作论坛（APEC），同年11月即在澳国首都堪培拉主持召开了APEC首次部长级会议，澳大利亚由此成了APEC机制的策源国；1989年12月，澳大利亚外长伊文思第一次使用了“全面融入东南亚”的提法，1990年7月，这位伊文思再次提出一个仿效“欧安会”模式创设“亚洲安全合作会议”的倡议；1991年12月，新任总理的保罗·基廷更进一步提出了“澳大利亚的未来在亚洲”的战略思想，发展了一套“融入亚洲”的国内国际政策陈述，包括在国内民众中发动脱离英国的共和运动。1992年，保罗·基廷提议召开亚太首脑会议；1994年再次提出把澳大利亚—新西兰自由贸易区与东盟自由贸易区合并为一的设想。这一时期，随着澳国申办2000悉尼奥运会的成功，澳大利亚多元文化宽容共存的文化特色和社会愿景进一步为亚洲和世界所认识。这也是澳大利亚随亚洲经济起飞而获得巨大发展的时期，它的对外贸易份额从侧重于欧洲转变为以亚洲为重。

顺便一提，正是这一阶段的发展引发了本文开头引述的亨廷顿对澳大利亚忧心忡忡的评说。并且，针对这个国家对外关系的摆动所体现的国家身份问题，亨廷顿还提议澳大利亚应转而与美国建立更深的同盟关系，把自己“确定为一个太平洋国家而不是一个亚洲国家”，因为他认为，澳大利亚像美国一样具有英国本源，也是欧洲人占绝大多数的移民国家，价值观相近，因此不应竭力挤入一个"文化上相异的（亚洲）集团"。亨廷顿提议"把北美自由贸易协议扩大成北美-南太平洋联盟，包括美国、加拿大、澳大利亚和新西兰"，以便"协调文化和经济，并为澳大利亚提供一个坚定而持久的认同"[4]。事实上，在下一阶段，人们看到，亨廷顿的这一提议对澳大利亚并非没有产生实际影响。

第五阶段，从1996年至2007年，随着"后冷战"形势的发展，澳大利亚的角色再次出现明显转变。在约翰·霍华德政府的操作下，它的国内国际政策逐渐向"右"突击。约翰·霍华德本人在上台前就提出过"一个国家"理论（意即反对澳大利亚被不同来源的文化分裂为"多个国家"），上台后即与保守民间兴起的反移民、反多元文化的"汉森主义"默契互动。1997年，澳国发表了一份《澳大利亚战略政策》，通过扩展定义其安全战略利益区，从传统的东南亚、南太平洋扩至东亚、美国和南亚地区，显示了与美国"安全"概念交叉重合的态势；1999年，霍华德借出兵东帝汶维和之机，提出了所谓"霍华德主义"的"交叉理论"（即干涉主义）。2000年，澳军再次出兵平息斐济和所罗门政变；同年12月，发表新的国防白皮书，这一文件在2003年又进行了重要修订，重点在于改变70年代惠特拉姆以来的非（军事）干涉政策，宣称对"邻近国家以远"的危机也有权采取军事行动——事实上，它既是对已在东帝汶、斐济、所罗门等地实施的军事行动合法性的"追认"，也是为其后来在2001年和2003年以反恐名义参与美国在阿富汗、伊拉克的战争提供的政策依据。2003年12月，澳大利亚还宣布加入美国的导弹防御计划。澳大利亚的这一系列动作，大有重返当年作为美国仆从阶段的态势。

然而，时代毕竟不同了，“霍华德主义”操控下的“倒退国家”在一个政治经济面貌急速改变的亚洲和世界面前举步为艰。目前，澳大利亚正处在国家定位的第六个阶段，态势再次扭转。2007年，由凯文·拉德（陆克文）领导的工党在大选中全面胜利。新政府甫一上台就通过加入《京都议定书》、撤军伊拉克和促使构建中的美、日、澳、印同盟机制缓行等举措，来拉开与美国国际政策的距离。当然，人们必须看到，如同上一阶段霍华德时期一方面跟进美国战略，另一方面也竭力维持和亚洲日益增多的联系（霍华德向其西方伙伴解释说，这种发展着的联系是“实用主义”的）一样，新生的陆克文政府虽然显示了回归区内信任的决心，也未必意味着最终要与“美国优先”的对外关系主轴脱钩。当此全球化时代，澳大利亚一个逐渐成形的主流选择是：经济发展倚重于亚洲，安全战略维系于美国，总体上运用其文化身份的多元、模糊不定所形成的弹性，左右逢源地充当区内和世界多种力量的协调人，以此来维护和发展自己的利益，尽管这并非没有代价和风险——尤其是对于其自立于世界强大国家的政治文化雄心而言。目前的澳大利亚似乎尽量在“亚洲国家”和“太平洋国家”之间谋取一个平衡、兼容的“亚太”国家身份。历史的回顾显示，这种国家身份的探索和实验仍未有穷期。

## 二、“白澳”国家还是移民国家?

从上所述，对澳大利亚的考察有几个要点：第一，澳大利亚在国际格局中的定位变化始终是比较激烈、明显的，政策摆动幅度之大，确为其他西方国家所少见；第二，这种变化和其国内因素有着深度的牵连（通过选民影响的政府更替和政策调整来体现）；第三，虽然这个国家的基本政治经济制度自立国以来一直稳定至今（除“二战”时期外，社会生活基本没有发生剧烈振荡），但与其自身存在意义相关的文化身份问题始终没有很好解决，这是一种有别于领土的、物质的“意义”问题，但绝不因此而缺少其严重性。以亚洲崛起为诱因，这一问题导致90年代兴起的一场“文化战争”（恰好和本文开头所引亨廷顿描绘的全球“认同混乱”同一时期，而且也成为其标志之一）。这种“文化战争”提供了一个切入点，帮助人们理解与澳大利亚在世界格局中的立场变动和反复选择有关的内部情势。当然这种情势是一种动态的结构。其中包含了三大问题：土著问题、移民问题和多元文化主义问题。因本文篇幅关系，下面重点以头两个问题作考察。

第一是土著问题。

澳大利亚的“文化战争”涉及到对世居土著族民的处置，乃因它与世界上其他新兴西方国家（日本除外）一样，有一个共同的历史噩梦：土著居民早在欧洲白人“发现”诸新大陆之前即已先行存在，并在白人移民国家建立后遭受巨大苦难。相较于北美，由于澳大利亚没有大规模贩卖黑奴的过程，因此也没有北美那样尖锐的“黑白”矛盾，但肤色灰黑、浅棕的土著人口仍成为历史和现实中严峻的社会难题。白人立国之前，土著已在澳大利亚大陆生活数万年，白人抵达时的土著人口约有五六十万，伴随着白人逐渐占领大陆所有最宜居地区，数以十万计的土著被屠杀，剩余的数万土著居民大部分被驱逐到条件艰苦的中部沙漠保留地。实际上，进入 20 世纪，澳大利亚土著群体在社会主流结构之外的生存状况已极为恶劣，甚至濒临灭绝。在“白澳政策”之下，白人政府的一个“善行”是从这些土著家庭中强行收去大批婴儿，转交给白人家庭管养，以利“同化”。这不仅令土著再增家庭离散之苦，而且造成今日土著中有大量找不到原生父母的后裔，被称为“被盗去的一代”。土著及其文化的急速衰亡不仅在澳大利亚所宣称的文明价值体系中裂开了一个刺眼的伤口，成为国家的耻辱，而且也有碍于来自西方的白人在完成殖民后转而扮演“属于当地传统的守护者”[5]这一角色。在国际国内压力下，尤其是在 60 年代末、70 年代初“白澳政策”被废除之后，土著在人口养育、就业、教育、政治参与和文化保存等方面都获得了很大改善。然而与此同时，权利意识的觉醒也使土著的索偿诉求冲击着现代澳大利亚社会，其标志性的事件是“马宝法案”：土著岛民艾迪·马宝及其同胞在上世纪 80 年代提出了一项诉讼，要求索回他们在澳国北部马尔岛的土地拥有权，其理由是世代早居于此，先于白人殖民者的“发现”和占领。该案的审理延绵 10 余年，中经多级法院“驳回—上诉”的循环周折，直到马宝本人 1992 年逝世后近半年才在联邦高等法院胜诉。终审判决认为，假如土著能够证明其与某一块土地有着“不可分割的联系”，即应享有地权，但这一规定仅适用于占全澳境 12% 的土地，而且必须是公地，而非已确立了私人业权的土地。这一历史性的判决成就了土著争取恢复原住民权利的一大胜利，尽管它也给其他援引这一案例争取同样权利的土著人民设下了限制。这些限制不仅体现了这个白人移民国家作为既成事实的制度基础（完全推翻这一基础则使现实社会崩溃），而且还体现了西方法理与土著文化的冲突：要举证自己和一块土地有“不可分割的联系”，必须有现代法律认可的证据，而大多数土著有的只是传统的神话、传说、歌谣中饱含伤感的祖先家史，何况这些材料也因土著生活流徙和环境激变而面目全非，难于复原，只有沦为“文化记忆”的价值。这种“文化记忆”既断裂于西方白人的殖民史诗，也很难在西式法律的意义上生效。土著坚持把现代澳大利亚的国庆节称为“入侵纪念日”。土著权利的完整恢复事实上是一条困难重重的无尽之路，这成为对于国家统治结构合法性的历史文化根源的一个长久质疑。2008 年，凯文·拉德领导的新政府在胜选后的数月，首次发布了其前任霍华德政府一直不愿表达的对土著的郑重道歉，这是澳国土著关系历史上的一个标志性事件，尽管它并不足以冰释这一历史疑难，但也充分显示土著问题对澳大利亚国家文化身份的重要性。

第二是移民问题。

作为本来就是由移民建立的国家，现代澳大利亚的移民问题是今日国家生态的一部分，这不仅是指澳大利亚需要通过不断补充外来移民以维持、推动社会经济和技术的提升，移民政策通常成为各政党和社会团体的日常议题，而且也是指移民问题维系着澳大利亚对自己国家身份的动态建构。它其实仍和上述土著问题有隐秘的意义关联（很少研究者指出这一点）。对澳大利亚（以及其他移民立国的新兴西方国家）来说，持续地接受外来移民，适足淡化、缓解对早期白人占领历史的批判压力，而强化作为移民“共享”国家的意涵，把统治的既成事实变成一个长期的国家特性展现过程，以修补西方文明华美约言的伦理漏洞（这样，统治阶层不仅在面对土著时看起来是保护“本土”传统文化的守护神，而且也是面向外来文化“开放”并以之不断“丰富”既有文化结构的进步天使），这可以使当年西方白人殖民的黑暗往迹被编织进一个由不同的移民参与其中的、不断“丰富”、“进步”的时间序列之中，国家身份也就在移民动态中获得某种合法化、合理化的意义资源，有关“移民国家”的持续叙事于是成为其“澳大利亚性”的正当性基础。笔者认为，这应是深度观察西方有关国家移民论述的一个重要视点。

然而，澳大利亚移民事业的发展和上述的意义探索过程是相当曲折的，充满了文化的困扰和利益的冲突。其中，华人移民在澳大利亚的经历又是一个最有代表性的指标。

尽管有历史学家相信，华人是本地土著以外最早进入澳大利亚大陆的人种，但有文献确切记载的华人入境始于1848年，即中英鸦片战争后的第8年，该年中国的第一批“契约劳工”被用轮船运抵澳大利亚。据记载，早期到达“这类苦力是从中国农民的低下阶层中招来的；他们体力不佳，品质低劣”[6]，大部分来自广东农村。随着1850～1851年间年澳大利亚发现金矿，更多的中国劳工被各种开发公司和劳务公司招往“新金山”（区别于稍早于澳大利亚发现金矿的北美“旧金山”），抵澳华人数量最多时达到42000人，占非白人人口之首位。受部分来自欧洲的白人淘金者嫉恨华人的影响，最早发现金矿的维多利亚殖民区也最先通过了限制华人法案（每十吨船载量限载 1 名华人，并征收 10 镑人头税）。此时各地排华暴行不断发生（如 1857 年发生了巴克兰河大屠杀）。1877 年，从另一个殖民区昆士兰引发了全澳性的第二次排华浪潮。1880 年，全澳各殖民区召开第一次区际会议，设立了一个有关“中国（人）问题”的议题，结果导致除西澳殖民区外的各区都通过了限制华人的移民法。这一情况和发生在世界其他“金山”（如北美）的情况如出一辙。例如，1882 年和 1885 年，美国、加拿大分别通过了排华法案。针对美国的案例，历史学家史景迁（Jonathan Spence）评论说：“这是美国历史上第一次以立法的形式做不利于其他人民的事。”[7] 同样的评价几乎可以一字不易地移用到澳大利亚的早期政治史上——1888 年召开的全澳第二次殖民区区际会议秘密议决要完全禁止中国人（含属于“英国臣民”的华人）移民澳土。1896 年，第三次殖民区区际会议上，再通过“有色人种限制规定”，除华人外，限制的对象扩展到其他所有有色人种，包括“亚洲、非洲、太平洋岛屿原居民”。可见移民特别是华人移民的命运，和澳大利亚土著的经验实有历史的关联。1899 年，邻国新西兰追随澳大利亚也通过类似的排华法案。至此，大洋洲的主要国家都向以华人为代表的非西方移民关上了大门。可以说，随之成立于 1901 年的澳大利亚联邦及其制订的“白澳政策”，就是以排华、排亚为要旨的。在这一政策下，延至新中国成立之前，在澳的原中国移民已锐减至约 9000 人，其中属于早前入澳的第一代移民仅残存 5000 人。他们大都艰难生活在一个“黄祸”意识盛行的社会的底层。

“二战”后，因澳大利亚推行“科隆坡计划”，亚洲国家开始有小量以留学生形式的赴澳移民。随着“白澳政策”在20世纪50年代后期的松动到60年代末的废除，特别是1973年非歧视性移民政策的颁行，亚洲和华人移民的规模化才逐渐成为国家的常态。这里有好几个高潮。一是七八十年代在联合国协调下，从越南、柬埔寨等印度支那战乱地区怒海逃生的难民被澳国大批接收，二是八九十年代担忧香港前途的香港移民，三是1993年底的一项特别决定，使大批海外留学生转变为定居者，约有5万名中国留学生及其亲属因此成为合法移民（这也是“淘金时代”之后最大一波华人移民潮）。这几次较大移民潮中，华人都是主体，而且尽管其各有不同的来源地、不同的历史事件为背景，但都发生在20世纪70～90年代澳大利亚积极面向亚洲的时期，因此绝非偶然。这些移民大大扩充了在澳的非西方族裔特别是华人社区，全面充实了华人的经济、技术和文化艺术资源，也为这个国家进入21世纪之后选择把发展天平进一步向非西方的亚洲偏重，奠定了一个重要的社会基础。中国现在已成为澳国的第一大贸易伙伴（澳大利亚则是中国的第六大贸易伙伴），正是这一点的部分证明。

然而，澳大利亚历史上始终没有停止过对移民问题的争议。甚至也就是在上述时期，亚洲移民的增减和待遇也成为“文化战争”的一大战场。最引人注目的几个事件是：1984年，杰弗里·布兰尼教授发表反移民观点，激起全国性的辩论，亚洲移民首当其冲；1988年，史提芬·费兹杰拉尔德博士发表研究报告，认为澳大利亚接受、增加移民是必要的，但只能以遵守“澳大利亚惯例”为条件，并且移民不应都拥有澳大利亚公民权（实际上是主张非西方移民回复到历史上二等居民的地位）；同一年，政治家约翰·霍华德提出了“一个国家”（One Nation）理论，发展了1984年的布兰尼教授的观点，即认为亚洲移民将改变澳大利亚国家认同（身份）并破坏国内人民团结，因为他们背景的文化传统与“澳大利亚文化传统”多有乖违，并且相对“坏”和低下；1996年，由霍华德领导的政治右翼联盟党团上台，在大幅扭转其前任总理保罗·基廷“脱英入亚”进程的同时，与民间兴起的汉森主义默契互动；1998年，“一个国家党”成立，服务于该党纲领的学者甘桑·黑格（Ghanssan Hage）论证说，基于自19世纪以来澳大利亚就是白人统治的历史事实，土著和别的“少数民族”参与和决定澳大利亚国家事务并无足够的法理依据。这些包含种族主义或准种族主义的思潮、运动沉渣泛起，也受到了批判和反击。如著名学者卡勒林·别特（Katharrin Bett）和钟·斯特拉登（Jon Stratton）等人于1998—1999年间数次著文强力批驳上述论述，认为它们无非是以纯种优等白人自居，无视不同背景移民对澳大利亚国家的历史贡献，无视这个国家本来就是移居者社会的特性，用虚拟的“西方白人认同”来坚持单一主流文化立场，以抵抗文化多样性。

## 三、“单一国家”还是多元（文化）国家？

与澳大利亚国家身份相关的文化战争的第三个问题——对多元文化主义的褒贬取舍，因涉及到西方社会思想的普遍困境，牵连甚广，此处不便详述，仅为收结本文顺作交代。

事实上，在澳大利亚语境中，多元文化主义与上述两个问题是互相涵括的关系。上世纪70年代，澳大利亚借鉴了加拿大政府首倡的多元文化主义政策，而其实施力度则有过之而无不及。在一个长期实行白澳政策的社会，这一选择为整个国家的行政设置、人口背景、文化风貌和资源分配结构都带来了巨大变迁。多元文化主义的政策要求从宪政到社会服务都满足人人有权“表达和分享他们独特的文化遗产，包括语言和宗教”，不论其来源地的文化背景如何都“有权获得平等的对待和机会”，以“维持、发展和有效地运用所有澳大利亚人的技能和才智”的指标[8]。这样，澳大利亚的多元文化主义就不仅一举包揽前述的土著历史和移民现状，而且面向更多的外来影响和内部变迁，从意识形态到社会风气都为国家身份的新建构规划出一个远大的、开放性的前景，并为各种文化的共处、兼容和分享设置了社会平台。然而，在多元文化主义实施多年之后，也有越来越多的知识精英和民间保守势力开始质疑多元文化主义的价值和社会成就，其高潮就是20世纪90年代中期“汉森主义”的崛起：一个名为波琳·汉森的国会议员，在一次国会演说中公开表达了对“真正的澳大利亚人”被“剥夺”的抗议，以此煽动一种“怨恨和仇视的政治学”[9]。它与其后在法国兴起的勒旁主义并列而为20世纪后期西方政坛两大种族主义—准种族主义现象，为世所瞩目，更在澳国引发政治地震。90年代后期执政的霍华德右翼政府，则承接了这种对多元文化主义的“突破”并与之朝野互动，标举名为“一个国家”的政治纲领（波琳·汉森本人也创建了“一个国家党”）。这种“一国论”，以防制不同的文化集团把国家带向分化、分裂和冲突，坚持和发展统一的国家文化身份为号召。从某种意义上说，这种主张几乎可以看作是亨廷顿有关国际政治"文明冲突论"的国内版，预设了不同文化具有不可变易和难以交汇的根性、纯粹性，其间关系或应区隔（国际），或应同化（国内），土著和外来移民如若不符"国家标准"，则不应纵容。汉森主义、霍华德主义并非没有抓住多元文化主义某些理论上和实践上的软肋，但他们的"一国论"却无法解决也无意解决这样的根本疑难：在一个本来就主要由移民组成国家里，怎样化解"盎格鲁体制"不证自明的主导地位这个文化上的"硬核"？正是这样的硬核始终梗阻、困扰着澳大利亚国家身份的解决进程。正如乌龙冈大学教授温卡·奥门森指出，问题的关键是谁才是"澳裔"？谁才是"我们"（"澳大利亚人"）？国家是谁的？在"一国"之内是否有些公民比其他公民更有资格来占有对这个国家的文化身份的定义权？[10]

另一方面，已有国际学界的澳大利亚研究认为，即使经历了"数十年来密集的多元文化影响"之后，其"社会的核心制度基本上没有改变，属于单一文化"。在多元文化百鸟朝凤的绚丽风光中，这个社会的真实图景，其实是"种族和文化多样性环绕之下社会建制的单一文化核心"，即"盎格鲁体制"对社会资源的牢牢掌控[11]。从这样的意义上看，澳大利亚作为"一个国家"本来就不成问题，问题只是在于随着多元文化的发展对社会基础越来越大的改变，保守的主导势力是否愿意出让按照多元文化主义的理想本应分享的国家资源——包括物质的、制度的和意义上的资源。

从澳大利亚的案例可知，一国身份涉及文化、政治、经济等多方面的权力、利益及其动态调整的方案选择，它既与一国所处的世界格局有关（这种格局限定了可供其选择的空间），也受国内历史传统、社会势力和人口的族群文化背景结构的变化牵制，而有关意义的思想观念也在其间具有巨大作用。在此，本尼迪克特·安德森的民族（国家）“想象”理论可以获得必要的补充：现实格局并不排除想象的参与、介入，甚至它就是经由这种想象设计、创造出来的，但已经被创造的东西即有其现实性。新的“想象”固然可以对既有现实挑战、超越（比如多元文化主义的理想、保罗·基廷式的亚洲身份“想象”等都一度得势），但既有现实格局又使想象运作受制于其中的语境。不难理解，上述涉及澳大利亚国家身份规划的意义疑难与其国内、国际现实是高度混合交集的：澳大利亚在20世纪后期亚洲移民的涌入无疑改写了其内部的文化地图，加强了它和亚洲在贸易上和精神上的联系，并为一度冒升的“走向亚洲”、“融入亚洲”的自我想象提供了基础和动力，而其盎格鲁文化核心的征服历史及其在现实社会结构中的支配性，又使它不能不和国际性的西方主导势力保持关联与有机互动；澳大利亚历经多番“共和运动”和“脱英入亚”的热议，却至今没有摘去头上一顶“大不列颠属国”的帽子，这是新兴西方国家中的唯一例外。这已经无关任何实际利害，而主要与其部分国民历史想象的象征需要和平衡政治地理疏离感的“意义”沿习有关。所有这些都使澳大利亚在不同方向的巨大力量的撕扯之下，经历国家身份上的深重疑难。但在可见的未来，无论发生怎样的演变（甚至出现奥巴马式的非主流族裔领导人），澳大利亚仍将是这样的“一个国家”：它被迫因自己特有的多样性去不断追问自己的身份。

澳大利亚案例提供了这样的启示，不仅第三世界的人民和文化有其“后殖民处境”，而且某些西方国家，特别是那些通过西方势力移民建立的新国家——原属老帝国的殖民地后来转变为独立政治实体的西方国家，也有其“后殖民处境”。这两种后殖民问题当然具有很不相同的性质和特点，但这至少说明了，“西方”并不是铁板一块和同质的。对澳大利亚式的年轻西方成员国来说，它们总体上有一种双重身份：一方面作为昔日的“臣属”和今日的“新贵”，面临着如何摆脱历史负累（这种负累与其国内、国际新的发展机遇不相称），而为自己重定位、重定义的难题，另一方面作为西方的一部分，又扮演着西方全球主导权（霸权）的协同角色，而需要依从西方的整体利益和意义设置来调节其面对国内国际形势变化的立足点。在今日世界上，它们处于一种“中心的边缘”或“边缘的中心”的地位：在西方世界中，它们的角色有某种边缘性，而在面对第三世界的时候，它们又具有协同于西方霸主的中心性、主导性优势，从而与第三世界的后殖民问题相区别。

同时，澳大利亚案例也说明，对世界文化政治的版图，不宜总用“极化”的理解来简单处置，无论世界已经进入、即将进入或正在进入“单极”、“数极”或“多极”的时代，总存在广大和多样的中间地带。如果“极”的概念包含着能量和实力指标的话，那么，正是在这些中间地带的复杂生态之间，孕育着权力关系变动的无限可能。既然世界结构此消彼长的变化不会终结，对各种中介、桥接、复合、转换的因素的关注也就不会是多余的。这种关注还提示人们，一个国家（无论其是否为现实之“极”）的内部和外部、自我和他者的种种界线并不是绝对的（比如对澳大利亚式的国家而言，有关移民的思想和制度就是一种非常重要的“越界”因素，既是国内问题也是国际问题，这大有别于中国问题的研究），这样的界线当然也就需要动态的考察去穿越。

新时代出现了移民激增、文化杂交、族群涌动的形势，使越来越多的人类面临文化适应和身份重构，也把国家水平上的社会组合带到身份认同的挑战的前线。面对这样一幅“多种后殖民处境，多重身份问题”的错杂图景，澳大利亚国家身份问题提供了一个重要的视点。

## ［注释］

［1］塞缪尔·亨廷顿：《文明的冲突和世界秩序的重建》（第三版）（周琪 等译）。北京：新华出版社，2002年，第129－130页。

［2］澳大利亚政治家。两人曾于20世纪90年代分别担任澳大利亚工党政府的总理和外交部长。

［3］塞缪尔·亨廷顿：《文明的冲突与世界秩序的重建》（第三版）（周琪 等译）。北京：新华出版社，2002年，第165页。

［4］同上，第165－166页（着重号为引者所加）。

［5］本尼迪克特·安德森：《想象的共同体：民族主义的起源和散布》（吴叡人译）。上海：上海世纪出版集团/上海人民出版社，2005年，第169页。

［6］C. W. 蔡：《中国人在澳大利亚的移植和定居》。悉尼：悉尼大学出版社，1975年，中译参见《华工出国史料汇编》（第八辑“大洋洲华工”），北京：商务印书馆，1984年，第5页。

［7］史景迁（Jonathan D. Spence）：《文化类同与文化利用——世界

文化总体中对话中的中国形象（北大讲演录)》。北京：北京大学出版社，1990 年。

[8] James Jupp, *Understanding Australian Multiculturalism.* Canberra: Australian Government Publishing Service, 1996, p9.

[9] Wenche Ommundsen, In backlash country: Revisiting the multicultural literature debate in the wake of Pauline Hanson, in Adi Wimmer (ed), *Australian Nationalism Reconsidered: Maintaining a Monocultural Tradition in a Multicultural Society*, Tubingen: Stauffenberg, 1999, 223 - 33。(中译参见温卡·奥门森《多元文化写作、后现代批评与澳洲文学界的汉森主义》，钱超英译，见钱超英编《澳大利亚新华人文学及文化研究资料选》，北京：中国美术学院出版社，2002 年，第 374 - 388 页。)

[10] 同上。

[11] Adam Jamrozik (with Cathy Boland & Robert Urquhart), *Social Change and Cultural Transformation in Australian*, Cambridge: Cambridge University Press, 1995, p11.

## 作者简介

**钱超英**，博士、深圳大学文学院教授、国际比较文学学会会员、中国世界华文文学学会理事、深圳华文文学学会副会长、澳大利亚新南威尔士州华人作家协会理事。主要研究领域为文艺学、比较文学、海外华文文学、西方文化与文学。(Email: qianchaoying@163. com)

# 11

## 澳大利亚对中国崛起的认知与反应*

喻常森

2009 年中澳关系波澜跌宕。先是年初澳大利亚政府公布新版《国防白皮书》，直指“中国威胁”。接着是“力拓案”引燃中澳媒体大战。加之是年秋季中国“疆独”分子热比娅“窜访”澳大利亚受到新闻界热捧，中方对此表示“强烈不满”。凡此种种，促使人们对中澳关系走向表示出极大的关注。实际上，中澳关系的上述发展变化，在一定程度上反映了一个处于崛起与复兴之中的大国与一个希望继续维持现状的中等强国之间的相互再认识与关系调适过程。本文重点分析澳大利亚方面是如何看待中国和平崛起的。

澳大利亚为南半球最大的国家，国土面积 770 万平方公里，全球排名第六位，相当于中国的 4/5。但是，澳大利亚的常住人口只有 2020 万，相当于中国的 1.6%，其中白人占 90%，华人 50 万，占 4% 左右。从政治制度上看，澳大

---

* 本文原载于《当代亚太》2010 年第 4 期。

利亚属英联邦国家，实行资本主义议会民主制。1972 年 12 月 21 日中澳建立正式外交关系。此后，双边关系发展相对比较平稳，互设大使馆和众多领事馆，缔结了一批友好省份和姐妹城市。近年来，中澳双方的教育文化交流十分活跃。据统计资料显示，2008 年有 12.7 万中国学生在澳大利亚注册留学，占外国留学生 23%。2008 年到澳大利亚旅游的中国大陆游客人数达到 35.6 万人次，占澳大利亚外国游客总数的 6.4%，中国成为澳大利亚第五大外国游客来源地国家。中澳两国经济贸易发展势头迅猛。2007 年，中国一度成为澳大利亚最大的贸易伙伴。双边货物贸易额为 444.8 亿美元。2008 年，中国是澳大利亚第二大贸易伙伴，双边贸易额（含服务贸易）为 573.0 亿美元，排在日本之后。澳大利亚向中国出口的主要商品为矿产品、纺织原料和农产品；澳大利亚自中国进口的主要商品为机电产品、纺织品、家具和玩具制品。两国从 2005 年开始商谈自由贸易协定，目前已经进行了 14 轮谈判。但是，就在中澳两国经济贸易关系不断加深的同时，必须看到，由于各自的文化传统和社会政治制度不同，以及安全战略分歧，澳大利亚从民间到官方，均存在一定程度的对华认知误区。随着近年来中国国家实力的不断提高，澳大利亚部分学术界和官方人士担忧亚太地区权力结构出现对自己不利的改变。这些认知误区或担忧，如果得不到及时澄清和舒缓，可能会损害中澳两国关系的进一步发展。

## 一、澳大利亚学术界对中国崛起的认识

近年来，在澳大利亚学术界中，有关“中国问题”的

研究成为一门显学。主要研究力量分布在各高等院校、智库、新闻媒体和政府相关部门。他们通过学术出版、新闻评论和咨询报告等形式影响政府对华决策，形成了一个中国事务的“认知共同体”（Epistemic community）和“政策网络”（Foreign policy networks）。[1]澳大利亚学术界对于中国崛起问题的评价，总的来说是持“谨慎的乐观”态度。根据学术观点差异，可以细分为三大流派：自由主义、现实主义和保守主义。

### （一）自由主义学派——乐见其成

在澳大利亚中国问题研究的学术圈子中，自由主义学派主要包括退休外交官、经济学家和汉学家等“知华派”人士。他们大都非常熟悉中国情况，对华持友好态度。他们主张澳大利亚应该以积极与平静的心态对待中国崛起。这一部分学者所持的基本观点是：①中国是一个文明古国，人口众多，富有创造性。自改革开放以后，中国取得了巨大的成绩，为人类社会做出了重大贡献。②中国政府采取和平友好的外交政策，积极参与多边合作，中国融入国际制度将产生积极的社会化（socialization）影响。③中澳两国经济结构存在较大的互补性，中国的经济发展为澳大利亚创造了繁荣的机会。早在20世纪80年代，澳大利亚驻华大使郜若素（Ross Garnaut）就向澳大利亚总理霍克提出要利用中国改革开放的机会，搭上东北亚经济发展的顺风车，为此，他大力倡导组建亚太经济合作组织，将中国大陆、台湾和香港纳入其中。[2]曾经担任澳大利亚外交贸易部高级官员的何睿斯（Stuart Harris）形容中澳两国存在双赢的贸易关系：“中国的经济发展，为澳大利亚产品提供了一个有利可图的出口市场；中国强劲及有效率的工业，为澳大利亚提供了大量的廉价商品，双方都从各自的优势中获益。”[3] 中国作为一个新兴的全球经济体，在亚太地区未来的经济格局中发挥领导作用。由于澳大利亚与中国在经济上有巨大的互补性，澳大利亚的繁荣有赖于中国经济的持续增长。“澳大利亚的繁荣与安全将取决于创造一种能够（同时）容纳中国经济容量和较小的亚太经济体利益的国际经济与政治体制。”[4] 因而，他们鼓励并建议澳大利亚政府继续推行与中国建设性接触政策，同时加强与中国坦诚的对话。针对近期两国经贸合作中出现的一些风波，澳大利亚国立大学中国研究院教授、著名经济学家彼得·德赖斯代尔（Peter Drysdale）指出，澳大利亚对于中国投资的忧虑毫无根据，澳大利亚应该鼓励更多中国企业投资其资源行业。他说，澳大利亚使用外资的历史久远，从长远发展的战略角度考虑，澳大利亚以及其他发达国家应该欢迎中国企业的投资，而不是对它们秉持狐疑的立场。只有实行强强联合才是硬道理。中国目前是世界上最重要的外国直接投资来源国之一，有望成为未来外国直接投资的重要力量。2008 年，全球外国直接投资同比大幅下降（21%左右），而中国的外国直接投资数量却翻了一番。中国的发展速度令包括澳大利亚政策制定者在内的很多人感到惊讶。但中国目前在澳大利亚的投资总额还很低，发展潜力巨大。[5] 针对有关中国威胁问题，大部分学者持否定态度。正如澳大利亚国立大学中国研究院任格瑞（Richard Rigby）院长所指出的那样，“对外部世界来说，一个更加富裕和强大的中国并不必然是一种挑战。而一个失败的中国比一个成功的中国对世界更加危险。”[6]由此可见，自由主义学派主要从中澳经济的相互依赖关系，特别是中国经济发展为澳大利亚提供的巨大机会方面着眼，希望分享中国经济发展的红利，对中国崛起做出积极、正面的评价。根据2009年最新统计数字显示，中国已经超过日本成为澳大利亚最大的贸易伙伴（含货物贸易及服务贸易），双边贸易总额达到851亿多澳元，占澳大利亚对外贸易总额的16.8%，[7]中国同时成为澳大利亚第二大的投资来源地，当年合同投资总额达到265亿澳元。[8]澳大利亚的发展与中国密不可分。

### （二）现实主义学派——两面下注

持现实主义立场的人士大部分是高校和研究机构从事国际政治教学和研究的学者。这一流派的学者认为，中国崛起是不争的事实，但中国未来发展走向至今无法预测。因而，澳大利亚一方面应该继续积极同中国打交道，但同时必须要谨慎防止中国单独主导亚洲事务。澳大利亚现实主义学派的中国观包括：①中国的经济发展必然会推进国防现代化，从而导致地区战略力量对比的失衡；②如何协调与美国的安全同盟关系和越来越重要的中国贸易伙伴关系已经成为澳大利亚主要的外交政策挑战；③澳大利亚必须致力于建立一种有效的地区多边制度，将中国纳入其中。学者们认为，澳大利亚尽管算得上是一个中等强国，但是，在大国竞争中，从来不具备独立的抗衡能力。无论在亚洲还是在其他地方均是如此。也就是说，仅仅依靠自己的力量，澳大利亚认为无法与中国竞争，更不用说与其抗衡。澳大利亚主要奉行的国家战略是“双管齐下”：一方面依靠自己的力量追求自己的利益，努力营造一个对自己有利的国际和地区环境；另一方面，借助联盟的力量，对外部威胁加以消化，维护和增强自己实力和利益。中国作为一个负责任的利益攸关方参与亚洲秩序，符合澳大利亚的地区政策。如果中国未来作为一个修正主义的侵略性大国崛起的话，澳大利亚就要和盟国一道对中国加以围堵和制衡，就像“冷战”时期那样。[9]鉴于未来中美冲突可能难以避免，澳大利亚与美国和中国的关系确实遭遇非常大的困境——甚至毫不夸张地说它是澳大利亚面临最大的问题——它需要堪培拉政府更加周密的考虑。[10]澳大利亚对澳美同盟的忠诚可能与她想避免引起北京的不快相矛盾。美国布什政府的副国务卿里查德·阿米蒂奇在 1999 年曾经明确指出：“在华盛顿发现自己与中国（大陆）就台湾发生冲突的时候，它将希望得到澳大利亚的支持。如果没有得到澳大利亚的支持，这就意味着美澳同盟关系的终结。”[11]所以，澳大利亚一方面要承担与美国的同盟义务，另一方面又必须避免刺激中国，澳大利亚必须致力于建立一种稳定和建设性的中—美—澳三角关系。有学者直言不讳地指出：“如何应对正在崛起的中国成为澳新美同盟（ANZUS）建立半个世纪以来最根本的挑战。”[12]澳大利亚必须很好地调和它在地理上和经济上在亚洲的利益与战后在战略和历史文化上与美国的一致性关系之间的矛盾。在这一进程中，澳大利亚必须制订出一种成功的政策，不至于疏远北京或者华盛顿。这影响未来十年内澳大利亚的国家安全。澳大利亚应该采取一种深思熟虑的对华对美关系的决策模式，以最大程度上保障国家利益。在重大战略问题上与两个大国保持持久和制度性的对话与协商，避免夹在中美冲突的中间。

除了借助与美国的同盟关系维护澳大利亚国家安全外，作为像澳大利亚这样一个没有自然区域的富有小国来说，多边制度是一个有益的再保险措施。多边制度不但能够降低国际体系中丛林规则所产生的副作用，而且能够为小国取得更大的话语权。[13]学者们建议，在安全战略上，应该致力于在亚太地区实现从“排他性的”双边主义到“包容性的”集合安全（Convergence Security）战略的转移。[14]“集合安全”设想在多边地区安全秩序建立过程中给予中国、美国等地区大国一个集体的利害关系，同时，鼓励像澳大利亚这样的中小国家在建立和捍卫这一合作框架方面承担合适的责任。因而，大部分现实主义学派的学者们主张对中国采取“两面下注”（Hedge Strategy）的战略。即一方面，对中国进行积极接触，另一方面，通过同盟关系和多边制度对中国进行适当约束，最大程度地确保澳大利亚的国家利益以及地区秩序的和平转换。现实主义学派主要是从传统国际政治中的权力转移视角来看待中国崛起。根据历史的经验，这些学者认为，中国是不满现状的国家，中国的崛起必然挑战美国的霸权体系，从而引发霸权国家针对不满现状国家的预防性战争。澳大利亚因为与美国结成了安全同盟，无论从同盟义务或者澳大利亚自身安全考虑，一旦中美爆发战争，澳大利亚将难以独善其身。所以，澳大利亚一方面应该加强自身的防御能力（自助），另一方面还应该通过国际机制，试图发挥中美之间的桥梁作用，消化中国崛起带来的不稳定因素，极力避免卷入两败俱伤的同盟战争。

### （三）保守主义学派——遏制与围堵

澳大利亚的保守主义学派人物主要为国防决策人员、部分智库高级研究人员和情报分析部门人员。他们主张澳大利亚应该未雨绸缪，遏制中国可能的地区霸权主义政策。澳大利亚保守主义学派对华的基本判断是：①伴随中国军事能力的大幅度提高，特别是信息战和反卫星武器的开发，中国可以随心所欲地对台湾使用武力，从而威胁美国海军的存在；②中国崛起所导致的地缘战略影响使美国的亚洲盟国面临严峻选择，中国经济可能会在未来几十年内赶上美国，而且其战略与政治力量都将随之提高，将会冲击美国在亚太地区已维持40多年的领导地位；③中国是在非西方集团中实行局部优化（sub-optimization）战略，这严重动摇和损害了西方主导的新自由资本主义制度，或者说是“华盛顿共识”以及西方民主价值观。这派学者们过分强调中国的军事能力和对外政策的扩张性，认为，将来最有可能的情况是，随着中国经济的持续增长，它的政治和军事权力也将随之进一步增强（中国出现衰退的可能性很低）。根据购买力平价衡量，中国的经济规模将在2020年或2030年与美国持平。同样按照购买力平价计算，中国的国防预算已经超过了日本和俄罗斯。伦敦国际战略研究中心（IISS）评估2007年中国的国防开支为1220亿美元，而美国国防部对中国军事开支的估计是850亿美元到1250亿美元之间。如果中国的国防开支继续按照11.8%的比例增长，到了2020年，它就到了4000亿美元——与美国不相上下。无论如何，到了2020年，中国的军费开支都是全世界排名第二的。中国将具有更加持续作战能力的核战略力量（陆基和海基洲际弹道导弹），除非日本也大规模增加国防支出，中国将毫无疑问地成为亚洲最强大的海空军力量。而且，中国正在按部就班地进行航空母舰和反导弹系统建设，从而具备一定程度反导弹能力。学者们推测，随着中国的实力上升，中国在东南亚和朝鲜半岛的影响力将超过美国。在国内民族主义的驱动下，中国很可能采取对外扩张政策。由于中国政治和军事力量的增强，它就可以毫不犹豫地对台湾使用武力，从而威胁美国海军的存在。对澳大利亚来说最大的挑战是，确保东亚地缘政治平衡关系转换不至于损害地区的基本安全环境。最严峻的威胁是一个专政而野心勃勃的中国的崛起成为东亚的主导力量，从而限制澳大利亚的行动自由。另外一个严峻挑战是，虚弱的美国没有作好遏制中国崛起的准备，导致包括日本和澳大利亚在内的盟国对美国维护地区战略秩序承诺信心的丧失。所以，澳大利亚必须为东亚地缘政治发展作好足够的准备。[15]对澳大利亚来说，这种选择尤为重要，因为美国优势的衰落意味自越南战争以后形成的亚洲秩序的终结。而这一秩序确保了最近数十年亚洲与澳大利亚的和平。这同时也预示着盎格鲁—撒克逊文明对亚洲海洋控制时代的终结，而这正是澳大利亚建国以来国家安全的必要条件。[16]中国崛起不仅挑战亚太安全结构和西方主导的秩序，而且将从根本上动摇西方民主价值观，而这是过去30年中受到经济学家、政府和产业界奉若神明的法宝。尽管中国和其他非西方国家也属于这一系统，但是，这一行为的后果是，它们是通过使更大集团遭到损失为代价来追求的相对获益，特别是在能源领域。中国式的政治资本主义的崛起（北京共识）将导致西方新自由主义主导模式（华盛顿共识）的结构性危机加剧。[17]为了保持原有的优势地位，避免地区权力结构漂移，这派学者建议澳大利亚应该放弃其传统的“均势”战略，增加国防投入，打造强大海军潜艇部队和空军，以应对中国崛起可能引发的战争危险。[18]学者们建议，鉴于中国军事现代化的步伐和规模可能给地区造成误判和不稳定，澳大利亚必须加强与美国、日本等民主国家之间团结与合作，建立和加固美、日、澳三边对话机制，强化三方政策协调能力，共同应对中国崛起的挑战。[19]由此可见，澳大利亚这部分保守主义学派学者主要从意识形态和“冷战”思维出发，对社会主义中国怀着非常强烈的不信任感和偏见，从消极的立场审视中国崛起。他们将中国崛起看成是一种挑战和威胁，甚至危言耸听地认为，中国的崛起不仅影响澳大利亚的国家安全，而且将严重地冲击和动摇整个世界自由资本主义体系，因此主张对中国进行遏制和围堵。

必须指出的是，本文上述对澳大利亚学术界有关中国事务研究的流派划分并不是非常严格和绝对的，主要是为了研究的方便起见。而且，如同国际政治研究领域的学术流派一样，各种流派之间具有某种相互渗透和彼此借重的关系。

## 二、澳大利亚公众及媒体对中国崛起的反应

中澳经济关系的不断加强，特别是中国超过日本成为澳大利亚最大的贸易伙伴，这是澳大利亚历史上第一次出现最大的贸易伙伴不是联盟体系成员（过去先后是英国——美国——日本），使得澳大利亚与中国关系变得非常复杂和微

妙。中国崛起的现实，给澳大利亚公众造成了一定程度的心理震撼，必须经过一个漫长的调适过程。

中国大张旗鼓的奥运火炬传递，西藏、新疆平暴和中澳之间贸易纠纷的发生，都在不同程度上对澳大利亚民众的中国印象注入了负面因素。就在2008年奥运火炬在澳大利亚首都堪培拉传递当即，一些当地媒体却纷纷炒作“中国大使馆给火炬接力活动‘租借人群’”。澳洲新闻网站报道称，澳大利亚首都特区总长斯丹霍普证实，中国驻堪培拉大使馆紧急行动，向堪培拉运送了近万名中国留学生，以确保爱国示威者在人数上大大压倒“藏独”示威者。这些文章称，中国“一手安排”了成千上万名留学生参与了在澳火炬传递活动，将当天的堪培拉变为“红色海洋”。[20]经过舆论的夸大宣传，近年以来，澳大利亚民众对中国的认识发生了一些消极变化。

有迹象表明，澳大利亚人对中国崛起的不适应感日益明显。根据澳大利亚著名智库罗伊国际政策研究所（Lowy Institute of International Policy）调查结果显示，2008年与2006年相比，有更多的澳大利亚人主张与其他国家一道来限制中国的影响力，并主张澳大利亚在人权方面应该给中国施加足够的压力。只有三分之一的受访者认同中国崛起不会损害澳大利亚的利益。不少人认为，在未来的十年时间里，中国崛起为世界性大国将对澳大利亚构成重大威胁，这个数字比2006年上升了9个百分点。[21]而根据2009年该研究所民调显示，澳大利亚民众的中国负面印象进一步加深。主要表现在以下几个方面：①对中国的态度趋于消极和冷淡，亲近度三年下降了近14个百分点（由2006年的67下降到2009年的 53)。②63% 的澳大利亚受访者认为目前中国是澳大利亚最重要的经济体，95% 的人认为中国已经或者将要成为亚洲的主导力量。③对于中国崛起的态度，52% 的人感到不快，48% 的人认为可以接受。④59% 的人相信中国是世界上一个负责任的国家，41% 的人不同意。91% 的人认为澳政府应该对中国实行友好合作与接触政策。46% 的人主张澳政府应采取有力的行动限制中国发展，52% 的人不赞成这样做。⑤大部分（57%）的澳大利亚人认为，在未来 20 年内中国不太可能成为澳大利亚的军事威胁，而 41% 的人认为有这个可能性。40% 的人认为中国成为一个世界性大国将对澳大利亚的核心利益构成威胁（比 2006 年增长了 15 个百分点)。[22]⑥关于外来投资问题，中国是最不受欢迎的外来投资者之一，排在阿联酋之后。其中，50% 的受访者认为澳大利亚政府允许太多的中国投资，42% 的人主张允许中国投资但是要加以适当限制。[23]

澳大利亚民众对中国的消极反应，在很大程度上受到本国媒体的不良宣传影响。2009 年度，中澳两国媒体围绕澳大利亚新版《国防白皮书》和力拓事件展开了激烈的交锋，其中，力拓事件成为引燃澳大利亚媒体仇华报道的导火线。该事件的起因是，2009 年 2 月，中国国有控股企业—— 中铝公司（Chinalco）与全球三大矿业公司之一总部设在英国(89% 总资产集中在西澳大利亚，澳大利亚总部在墨尔本)的力拓（Rio Tinto）集团签署了合作与执行协议，中方以总计 195 亿美元战略入股力拓集团，届时中国将持有该公司 18% 的股份。但是，澳大利亚媒体和部分反对党议员却反复强调中铝集团为“中国国有企业”，呼吁政府应设法保护国家资源行业利益和国家安全。澳大利亚商人伊恩·梅尔罗斯甚至私人出资20万澳元制作了一部宣传片，在澳大利亚电视台反复播放，矛头直指中铝与力拓的交易。澳大利亚反对党领袖马尔科姆·特恩布尔更是利用此事极力批评陆克文政府，指称陆克文政府为北京的“传声筒”。在各方面的合力作用下，澳大利亚外商投资审查委员会将中铝并购力拓的申请由一般的30天审查期延长了90天。到了6月5日，力拓集团董事会撤销与中铝达成交易协议，并依据事先约定向中铝支付了1.95亿美元的分手费，转而与总部设在澳大利亚的必和必拓（BHP Billiton）公司达成合作协议，交易额为58亿美元。一个月以后，即7月5日，力拓集团上海首席代表、力拓中国区哈默斯利铁矿业务总经理胡士泰等4名员工因“涉嫌为境外窃取、刺探中国国家机密”罪（后降格为商业贿赂罪）被中国政法部门刑事拘留。力拓事件本来纯属商业与司法问题，但澳大利亚媒体却加以大肆炒作。就在中铝注资并购力拓失败的消息发出第二天，澳大利亚媒体均大篇幅报道此事，总体上是“一片欢呼”。其中一份报纸在相关报道中精心配制了一幅漫画非常抢眼。画面中一条口吐火焰的红鳞黄鬃巨龙，正忿忿地被矿用铲车运走，而开车的正是力拓和必和必拓的两位老总。但是，在公布胡士泰等4人被捕消息后，澳大利亚媒体反应十分激烈。第二天，该国各大报纸都在头版刊登了这一消息，而且几乎众口一词地认为，逮捕力拓员工的事件是中国政府对中铝并购力拓矿业公司失败的报复行为。澳大利亚主流媒体《澳大利亚人报》发表的《不要向中国的欺凌磕头》评论文章最具有代表性。该文猛烈攻击陆克文政府的对华政策是一种胆怯行为，并认为学者的温和言论是一种无知误国。文章称，中国逮捕澳大利亚公民胡士泰的目的是胁迫澳大利亚，“胁迫我们的政府，胁迫我们的公司和整个公民社会”。“显然，北京是蓄意要惩戒和教训澳大利亚。”[24] 根据发表在《澳大利亚人报》网络版的该文读者 100 个跟帖，澳大利亚网民对此反应激烈。有读者认为，与中国的贸易会加强中国的军事力量和对西方盟国的优势，这对澳大利亚无疑是自杀，号召西方国家团结起来对中国进行制裁；有读者攻击中国是“帝国主义”，指出澳大利亚对中国经济的过度依赖已经暴露出自己的脆弱性；有读者主张对中国实施报复，包括停止与中国进行的矿山合作，并邀请达赖喇嘛和台湾政府官员访问澳大利亚等等。[25] 正是在这种不利的舆论环境下，8 月，澳大利亚新闻协会才一意孤行地邀请中国“疆独”分子热比娅窜访澳大利亚，并公开接受媒体采访，攻击中国的内政外交政策。在开放的公民社会里，媒体所反映出的民意，对国家的内政外交政策是一个不可忽视的重要干预变量。澳大利亚新闻媒体的上述仇华言行，极大地恶化了两国的外交环境，致使双方一度停止了高层往来。

## 三、澳大利亚政府对中国崛起的应对策略

中澳建交至今，澳大利亚对华政策重点在各个时期有所不同。从建交初期到“冷战”结束（1972—1990），澳大利亚对华政策的特点是，经济上充分利用中国改革开放的机遇，发展与中国的经济贸易关系，政治安全上利用中国作为制衡苏联南下太平洋的力量。“冷战”结束初期（1991—

1995），霍克和基廷执政期间，澳大利亚将主要精力放在与中国发展经济合作上，并致力于将中国（中国大陆、台湾和香港）纳入到澳大利亚倡导的APEC等地区合作制度框架中。到了自由党——国家党联盟霍华德政府执政时期（1996—2007），澳大利亚的对华政策又做了一些调整，在经济上将国家利益与友谊区分开来，而且更重视前者。在政治上，重点放在寻求建立澳大利亚、美国、中国三方平衡关系。2007年11月，澳大利亚工党领袖陆克文（Kevin Rudd）在联邦大选中击败了执政长达11年之久的自由党—国家党联盟领袖霍华德，成为澳大利亚第26任联邦总理。在施政纲领中，陆克文即提出“新领导”、“新思想”口号。在对外政策上，除了继续发展澳美同盟关系外，同时强调发展“富有创造力的中等强国外交”，[26]并表示将重点加强与亚洲各国的关系。上任伊始，陆克文即提出“亚太共同体”构想，期望以此取代APEC成为新的地区多边框架。2010年6月，吉拉德代替陆克文担任澳大利亚新总理，将致力于继续推行工党政府积极稳健的外交战略。

在对华政策上，澳大利亚政府较好地吸收了学术界有关中国问题的各种流派观点的合理之处。首先，澳大利亚工党政府在对华总体战略上主要基于现实主义的政策立场，将应对中国崛起作为首要任务和挑战。认为，中国的崛起，以及整个亚洲的崛起，改变了澳大利亚的国际环境，要求澳大利亚对此做出反应，并及时调整政策。其次，为了保持政策的连续性，如同霍华德领导下的自由党—国家党联合政府一样，陆克文—吉拉德工党政府执政时期，继续将经济关系与政治安全关系区分开来。在经济政策上充分吸收了自由主义学派的主张，继续全面加强与中国的经济贸易关系和技术合作。因为，这种合作符合澳大利亚的国家利益。在力拓事件的处理上，陆克文政府迁就于舆论，不断向中方施压。澳大利亚外商投资审查委员会有意拖延对中铝并购力拓的协议审批期限，对促成力拓摆脱资金困境以及毁约并转向新的合作伙伴——必和必拓的谈判赢得了时间。力拓事件并没有从根本上影响中澳两国正常的经济合作关系。2009 年 8 月，澳大利亚资源和能源部长马丁·费格逊访问中国，并与中国签订了价值 500 亿澳元的液化天然气合作协议。根据协议，中石油（CNPC）每年将从埃克森美孚在西澳大利亚海岸外的高庚项目（Gorgon）购买 225 亿万吨液化天然气，期限 20 年，这是澳大利亚有史以来最大的贸易协议。这笔交易将为澳大利亚创造 6000 个就业岗位。2009 年 9 月，澳大利亚政府又有条件地批准了中国山东兖州煤业股份有限公司以 29 亿美元收购澳费利克斯资源有限公司的交易案。2009 年 10 月底，中国国务院副总理李克强成功访问澳大利亚，标志着两国紧张关系时期的结束。2009 年，中国已经稳居澳大利亚最大的贸易伙伴地位，当年两国双边贸易额比上年增长了近 30%，达到 860 亿澳元（超过 800 亿美元）。如果这一趋势得以持续，预计 2010 年双边贸易额预计将达到 1000 亿澳元。为了推动双边贸易发展，中断一年多的中澳两国自由贸易区谈判也于 2010 年 2 月重新启动。两国自由贸易协定一旦签订，将在未来 20 年内为澳大利亚经济创造价值 1460 亿澳元的收入。第三，在政治安全上，澳大利亚当前工党政府的对华政策除了主要立足于现实主义的考量外，同时还部分采纳了保守主义的某些主张。例如，在人权、民主和宗教自由等方面继续对中国进行批评，并声称要做中国的“诤友”。[27]在国防政策上，重点加强了对中国的防范。2009年春天，澳大利亚公布了题为《2030年的军力——在一个亚太世纪里保卫澳大利亚》的新版《国防白皮书》，明确将中国崛起当成是亚太地区不稳定因素，把中国当成为未来澳大利亚国防建设的假想敌。白皮书大肆渲染“中国威胁”，称中国的军事现代化引发了周边国家的不安。随着中国等国军力的崛起，亚太地区在未来20年有可能发生战争。白皮书强调美国仍将是澳大利亚“不可或缺的”盟友。为了应对中国崛起所造成的不确定性，白皮书表示，澳大利亚将在未来20年里投入700多亿美元改善军备，将潜艇数量扩充一倍至12艘，购入100架F-35战机，并希望购入8艘新型护卫舰和3艘驱逐舰。[28]澳大利亚《国防白皮书》所包含的“中国威胁论”，在“很大程度上是澳大利亚政治生态和安全观念的一种综合体现，同时也折射出澳大利亚对国际体系转型带来的不确定因素所感到的不安。”[29]

中澳关系的上述发展，充分说明，尽管双方在政治理念和安全战略上存在一定分歧，但只要彼此更多地从共同利益出发，就一定能够找出化解矛盾和纠纷的办法。正如澳大利亚外长史密斯针对2009年本国媒体对华不实报道批评指出的那样：“中澳关系是一种复杂的关系，不能简单地对待。目前，非常遗憾地看到人们用一种简单的方法看待对华关系。出现了误判、幼稚和简单化倾向。”前总理陆克文也明确表示：“中澳关系总是充满挑战……它一直都是这样，在未来相当长的时间内也还会如此。”“这是因为，我们同在中国的朋友拥有巨大的共同利益和持续的分歧，他们的价值观与我们不同，而且往往利益也不相同。”[30] 事实确实如此，中澳关系的这种政经分离的双重性特征，为国际政治经济学的复合相互依赖关系理论提供了一个鲜活的案例。

## 四、结论与启示

总之，目前中澳关系的性质是崛起（或复兴）中的东方社会主义大国与倾向维持现状的西方资本主义中等强国之间的合作与竞争关系。反映了国际政治权力转移过程中的必然规律。同时，中澳关系发展也在很大程度上受到地缘政治、价值观、联盟关系、经济利益分配等多重因素制约，是一种复杂的相互依赖关系。鉴于近年来中国与澳大利亚之间的经济相互依赖程度不断提高，两国自由贸易协定（FTA）的签署具有重大意义。因为，它可以在某种程度上为缓解双方经济合作领域的纠纷提供稳定的指导性框架，并尽可能避免因经济纠纷演变为外交争端。中澳两国必须进一步加强政治互信建设，充分理解对方的关切和核心利益。健康和良性发展的中澳关系，不仅有利于实现中国的和平崛起，而且必将成为21世纪亚太地区稳定与繁荣的重要条件之一。

### ［注释］

[1] Allan Gyngell, Michael Wesley, *Making Australian Foreign Policy* (Second Edition). Cambridge: Cambridge University Press, 2007, p165.

[2] Ross Garnaut, *Australian and the Northeast Asian ascendancy: Report to the Prime Minister and the Minister of Foreign Affairs and Trade*,

Canberra: Australian Government publishing service, 1989, p2.

[3] Stuart Harris，蒲美译：中国在全球经济中举足轻重，《社会观察》2005年2期，第56页。

[4] Ross Garnaut, The sustainability and some consequences of Chinese economic growth, *Australian Journal of International Affairs*, 2005, Vol. 59, No. 4, pp509/518.

[5] 彼得·德赖斯代尔：西方担心中国投资无根据，《经济参考报》2009年07月20日。

[6] Richard Rigby, *Rising China on the eve of the Olympics*, Wednesday Lunch presentation at Lowy - 6 Aug 2008, http://www.lowyinstitute.org/Publication.asp?pid=867

[7] Australian Government Department of Foreign Affairs and Trade, *Composition of Trade* 2009, p33, http://www.dfat.gov.au/publications/stats-pubs/composition_ trade.html

[8] Australian Government Foreign Investment Review Board, *Annual Report*, 2008 - 2009, http://www.firb.gov.au/content/publications.asp? NavID=5

[9] Rod Lyon, Changing Asia, rising China, and Australia's strategic choices, *Policy Analysis*, ASPI, Australian Strategic Policy Institute, Friday, 17 April 2009.

[10] Michael Wesley, *The Howard Paradox: Australian Diplomacy in Asia*, 1996 - 2006, (ABC Books). 2007, p130.

[11] 同上，pp125 - 126.

[12] William T. Tow and Leisa Hay, Australia, the United States and a "China growing strong": managing conflict avoidance, *Australian Journal of International Affairs*, 2001, Vol. 55, No. 1, pp 37 - 54.

[13] Michael Wesley, Critical thinking needed to bolster ties with Asia, *The Australian*, April 30, 2007.

[14] William T. Tow, *Asia-Pacific Strategic Relations: Seeking Convergent Security.* Cambridge: Cambridge University Press, 2001, p213.

[15] Paul Dibb, *The Future Balance of Power in East Asia: What are the Geopolitical Risks?* Strategic and Defence Studies Centre, Australian National University, Canberra, ACT 0200, Australia, January 2008, Defence Studies Centre Working Paper No. 406.

[16] Hugh White, The geo-strategic implications of China's growth, in Ross Garnaut, Ligang Song and Wing Thye Woo (eds), *China's New Place in a World in Crisis: Economic, Geopolitical and Environmental Dimensions.* Beijing: Social Science Academic Press (China), The Australian National University, Canberra ACT 0200, Australia 2009, p101.

[17] Vlado Vivoda, China challenges global capitalism, *Australian Journal of International Affairs*, 2009, Vol. 63, Issue 1.

[18] Hugh White, *A Focused Force: Australia's Defence Priorities in the Asian Century*, Lowy Institute Paper 26, April 2009, http://lowyinstitute.richmedia-server.com/docs/White-A-focused-force_exec-summ.pdf.

[19] Paul Dibb, *Australia's Security Relationship with Japan: How much further can it go?* Working Paper No. 407, April 2008.

[20] 澳媒非难华人参与奥运火炬传递，《环球时报》2008年4月25日。

[21] The Lowy Institute Poll 2008, http://www.lowyinstitute.org/Publication.asp?pid=895.

[22] The Lowy Institute Poll 2009, p9. http://www.lowyinstitute.org/Publication.asp?pid=1148.

[23] The Lowy Institute Poll 2009, p29. http://www.lowyinstitute.org/Publication.asp?pid=1148.

[24] Greg Sheridan, Don't kowtow to Beijing bully, *The Australian*, July 23, 2009.

[25] Greg Sheridan, Don't kowtow to Beijing bully, *The Australian*, July 23, 2009. http://www.theaustralian.news.com.au/story/0, 25821436 - 17062, 00.html.

[26] 唐小松、宾科：陆克文“中等强国外交”评析，《现代国际关系》，2008年第10期，第18页。

[27]《陆克文在北大用中文演讲，澳总理期待澳中成“诤友”》，《中国新闻网》2008年4月10日。http://news.sina.com.cn/c/2008-04-10/042013712560s.shtml.

[28] *Defending Australia in the Asia Pacific Century*: *Force* 2030, http://www.apo.org.au/sites/default/files/defence_white_paper_2009.pdf

[29] 胡欣：澳大利亚的战略利益观与“中国威胁论”——解读澳大利亚2009年度国防白皮书，《外交评论》2009年第5期，第133页。

[30] 陆克文回应驻华大使回国：澳中关系充满挑战，《环球时报》2009年8月20日。

# 12

# 悉尼与上海城市更新的发展特征比较——案例分析与启示*

苏　宁　黄烨菁

澳大利亚是一个高度城市化的国家，其主要城市在过去十多年来经历了城市功能完善与转型的历程。2000 年前后澳大利亚最大的城市悉尼进行了较大规模的城市更新，借助奥运会这个重大国际活动实现了城市建设整体性的变迁，成为澳大利亚城市更新的典范。本文选择该城市作为澳大利亚城市更新的典范，与上海 2010 年前后以世博会举办为契机推进的城市功能升级加以比较。由于悉尼与上海都是亚太区域国际化大都市以及所在国的经济首位城市，对这两个城市进行城市更新的案例分析，两个城市的经验对于全球世界城市的更新改造提供了新的思路与探索方向，这个研究也有助于我们进一步深化对世界城市发展规律的认识。

* 本研究得到澳中理事会 2009 澳大利亚研究竞争项目“当代澳大利亚城市更新与中国的借鉴”资助。

## 一、悉尼奥运区域城市更新的主要特点

2000年奥运会不仅是悉尼城市发展中的重要事件，也对西悉尼地区的城市建设起到重要的推动作用。其中，奥运区域的城市更新秉承了此次奥运会作为第一届以“绿色奥运”为主题开展各项建设和组织的原则，在区域功能提升、环境保护、居住区建设方面进行了积极的探索并取得了成效。从整体上看，该区域城市更新的主要特点如下：

### （一）区域功能的整体改变

在悉尼奥运会期间，悉尼政府通过建筑奥运区将离市中心14公里的霍姆布什湾（Homebush Bay）建成比赛场地。这块占地760公顷的地段是从改造原先的一块沼泽地而来，在建成奥运会运动场馆之前，这一区域主要由砖瓦厂、屠宰场和工业垃圾场组成。在筹办奥运会的7年里，悉尼市政委员会花费了3.2亿澳元对它进行了改造。悉尼奥运会的城市更新主要作用在于将该区域从严重污染的垃圾倾倒场转变为一个拥有体育场馆、自然保护资源和公园的以体育、休闲、居住为主要功能的地区。在悉尼奥运之前，该区域曾经进行规划并建设一批体育场馆，但区域的整体功能并未有较大的改变。悉尼奥运会的建设使该地区的发展得到提速。该区域因奥运主办权的获得而取得大量可持续发展资本的投入。悉尼霍姆布什湾无疑比奥运之前拥有了更好的环境条件，这里的公园已经是当地社区重要资源的组成部分。

## （二）城市更新与环境保护的紧密互动

悉尼奥运的城市更新举措体现出与环境保护之间的相互联动。如前所述，悉尼奥运会举办区域原本是环境问题堪忧的“棕色地带”。从20世纪60年代开始，这一区域填埋了900万立方米的生活和工业垃圾，不仅地下埋着垃圾，地上还矗立着数十座由废弃物堆积成的小山，高度在13米至28米不等，在760公顷土地中有160公顷被严重污染。在获得奥运会主办权后，政府决定利用奥运场馆的建设进行城市更新和生态修复，投入23亿澳元进行环境改造，另外还有来自企业赞助的10亿澳元，它就可以带来便捷的通勤并降低了原本十个场馆之间的距离。同时，它也为公众在奥运期间使用公共交通工具的态度产生积极的影响。今天，在奥林匹克公园举行大型活动时，公众已经接受和认可了如下观念：乘坐城铁是更加便捷的方式，并且可以免受停车之苦。

悉尼奥运村中水回用工程是2000年悉尼举办世界奥林匹克运动会实施的样板环保工程之一，是悉尼奥运会倡导的保护资源环境友好活动的一部分。该工程2000年兴建，当年即投入运行，设计处理能力为每天处理7500立方米。中水回用厂的水源来自奥运村污水处理厂，污水处理厂的来水有奥运村景地排水，生活污水和雨水。中水厂出水回用于奥运村和霍姆布什湾公共服务设施的绿地灌溉和冲厕，每年可节省淡水资源200万立方米，价值64万澳元。该厂设计紧凑，厂房面积仅为28×18平方米，厂内基本实现自动化操作，全厂仅需1个人管理，管理人员有半天时间在厂内巡视工作，其他时间厂内无人，系统如有故障，故障信号与管理人的传呼机连接，一般的故障管理人员在家中便可处理。

奥运区域的环保发展，并非只体现在筹办及举办期间。后奥运期间的持续推进，使得环境保护成为这一区域城市更新长期坚持的重要方向。悉尼奥运园区管理局发布的“奥林匹克园区总体规划2030”（Sydney Olympic Park Master Plan 2030 Draft）在规划这一地区未来发展蓝图和规划控制时提出了八项基本原则，其中最重要的一点就是可持续发展（sustainability）。该规划明确指出能源与水系统管理、绿色建筑设计以及良好的经济—环境管理是区域建设的核心原则。[1]

## （三）居住区更新的科学规划与及时调整

在奥运筹办期间，悉尼政府将2000年悉尼奥运村定位为面向社会多阶层的住宅区，耗资达5.9亿澳元（3.4亿美元）。奥运村由660间联排别墅、1400间公寓和500间临时组合房组成，总共可容纳15000名运动员。奥运会结束后，临时组合房被拆除，部分联排别墅被扩建，整个建筑群被改造成为一个全新的居住区。筹办方在设计时，就把以往奥运会一般以宾馆模式建立的运动员村改为单体别墅样式，有利于后续的商业运作，预期在房屋建成后就直接出售。1997年至2007年，经过10年的建设开发，纽因顿村已经建成为一个多样化的新社区，至2007年底所有建成房屋均已售出。然而，在这期间，奥运村的发展也非一帆风顺，主办方对于奥运会结束后将奥运村“一卖了之”的设想在奥运会结束初期并未能如期达到。原因是奥运筹办期间房价不断被推高，吸引了蜂拥而来的投资者，等到奥运会结束，已经过度透支的楼市开始陷入疲软，房价持续下跌，奥运村房子的跌幅明显大于其他城区的房子。这与该房产的地理位置也有很大关系。奥运村所在地区偏僻，周围多是些汽车销售行和修理行，生活不便，且该区域主要的交通线路只有几条，上下班都成问题。

面对这种情况，悉尼奥林匹克管理局在2004年前后对奥运区域的定位进行进一步的调整。其一，将悉尼奥林匹克公园定位为国际大型赛事中心，将有数码大厦的高科技社区变成高科技信息产业基地；其二，将奥运村定位为健康社区，太阳能的使用、环境的保护，使周边居民生活在干净、祥和、优雅的环境当中。在这一调整过程中，纽因顿地区的住房逐渐发展为中等密度的社区了。房地产的更新也改变了地区财富的状况，并向帕尔玛塔（Parramatta）河沿岸延伸，沿河的房地产变得更为抢手，高端新物业不断被开发。奥运会的城市更新使原本被忽视的西悉尼地区成为悉尼大都市区中心城区的新兴地区。[2]通过探索公园式的城市内核与混合用途的发展模式，不断寻找那些需要我们保留和强化的城市中的基础元素，这一带已转化成为具有蓬勃生机的城区中心。2004年年中，体育场馆附近的旅馆平均入住率达到了70%，而此前是30%。2004年年底，奥运村的房子经过改造升级，出售率达到了70%左右。2000～2006年，该区域内商品房的房价上涨了3倍。[3]

## 二、“绿色广场”城市更新项目的主要特点

在2000年悉尼奥运会之后，该大都市区作为国际门户

城市（gateway city）的功能进一步凸显，城市国际化程度不断提升。这一变化趋势对于城市的市区更新提出了新的要求。“绿色广场”项目成为进入21世纪以来悉尼最为引人瞩目的市区更新项目。该项目的实施过程，充分体现了对市区更新理念的许多创新之处。

### （一）轻工业区的整体更新

悉尼的“绿色广场”（Green Square Town Centre）项目是近期澳大利亚最大的市区更新重建项目。这一更新区域位于悉尼的泽特兰（Zetland）区域，项目累计耗资达17亿澳元。泽特兰一带原本是悉尼最古老的传统轻工业区。随着悉尼大都市区的不断扩展和人口的不断增加，这一工业区成为距中央商业区不足4公里的一个非常不协调的功能区域。

为解决该区域的功能提升问题，悉尼市政府将绿色广场作为城市更新的重要项目。在对绿色广场核心区域的功能设定上，目标是将这一区域建设为5500人居住，7000人就业的集住宅、购物中心、商店、餐厅、公园于一体的新兴的现代居民区。在区域更新的目标上，力图将区域总面积达278公顷的绿色广场以及周边地区扩展为3.3万人的居住规模，并提供2.8万个工作机会。在区域的经济与环境功能上，绿色广场区域的绿化环境超过50%，成为悉尼重要的环境优化区域。同时，该区域的经济效应也十分显著，预计在未来30年将给悉尼带来32亿澳元的产值和约2.2万个就业机会。

### （二）商业价值与社会价值的统一

绿色广场项目的城市更新建设中，着力实现区域内商业价值与社会价值的统一。一方面，在商业价值方面，绿色广场通过更新建设，实现了区域商业价值的巨大提升。2010年完工的泽特兰维多利亚广场一带的高档住宅区，主要居民是中央商业区的各大企业年轻白领；绿色广场中心（Green Square Centre）将建成为规模超越悉尼市中心马丁广场的超大型商务/购物中心。此外，绿色广场一带已经建立的商业设施还包括：澳大利亚航空（QANTAS）、P&O CRUISES；法拉利、奥迪、奔驰、保时捷等最负盛名的车行，Gucci Australia、Westfield、Bay Swiss 等著名商铺。另外，澳洲联邦出版社以及 DHL 等运输公司均在该区域开办了门店。众多的商业设施与高档住宅区的建设，使该区域完全摆脱了原本轻工业区的功能定位，成为以商业、服务业为核心的综合性社区。

另一方面，绿色广场项目在建设与规划中，便充分考虑了社会效应，特别强调对社区居民的社会服务以及社会责任。1998 年绿色广场项目向南悉尼管理部门提交的规划，就明确提出需为增长的居民与就业者提供及时的娱乐与社区设施。根据规划中，绿色广场项目在区域中心区提供多样化的社区设施，包括图书馆，文化与社区空间以及为老人服务的空间。同时，绿色广场在住房的类型方面，特别提供了适用房（Affordable Housing）。在住宅的开发中，有 3% 以上的居住性开发面积和 1% 的非居住性开发面积被用于适用房建设。[4]

### （三）充分利用区域的交通优势

绿色广场的成功改造，充分利用了该地区得天独厚的地理位置，同时以基础设施的建设为重要支撑。该区域提出了“10分钟通达”（10 minutes to anywhere!）的口号，表示居住在此地的居民只需要10分钟即可达到悉尼所有最重要的地点：从商业中心到悉尼国际机场，从购物中心到商店街，从大型医院到声名远播的大学。绿色广场的区位十分优越，区域处在悉尼市与机场的走廊之上，与悉尼大学、悉尼科技大学和新南威尔斯大学均相距两公里左右，几个核心社区的邻近城区内皆有大型商场。

同时，绿色广场还着力提高区域的交通基础设施与社区的融合。该区域内的城市轻轨站将进一步扩建，以容纳高速增加的交通流量。同时，泽特兰区域的住宅类型选择也充分考考虑了区域的交通能力。在该区域的住宅项目中，独体住房（House）极其罕有，比例不到1%，与悉尼平均64%的比例差别巨大。而连体住房（Semi）与排屋（Terrace）占23%，较悉尼平均率高出逾一倍；而高容积率的公寓（A-partment）/单元（Unit）占76%，明显高于悉尼平均的22%。这种高容积率，高密集度的住房建设类型，有助于区域形成以公共交通为主要出行方式的集约化交通体系，从而以住宅更新的建设推动了区域的交通体系改良。

## 三、上海世博会城市更新的主要特点

上海世博会的举办为上海城市更新提供了战略性机遇。

从2002～2010年间，在世博会筹办、建设过程中，世博会展馆区域及周边区域的旧区改造、历史文化遗产保护、住房建设、景观建设等领域的更新改造都得到了快速推进。在后世博时期，世博会城市更新对于黄浦江两岸城区功能调整与升级的作用进一步得到凸显。

## （一）异地动迁与集中迁建的相互配合

上海世博会规划红线范围5.28平方公里的土地上，涉及分布在三个区的1.8万余户动迁居民。世博动迁是上海单个项目规模最大、难度最高、要求最严、时间最紧的一次动拆迁。[5]2005年2月，动迁工作在浦东新区率先启动，随后卢湾和黄浦两区的动迁工作也相继展开。2006年6月底，上海世博园会园区居民动迁任务基本完成。[6]世博会原址上居民住宅是上海棚户简屋相当集中的地区。通过此次动迁，市民的生活居住条件得到了较大改善，户均建筑面积达到了75平方米。

世博会区域的城市更新采取居民异地安置的方法，重新规划动迁居民的居住区域。在浦西区域，浦江镇世博会居民定向安置基地“浦江·世博家园”选址位于闵行区浦江镇东南面，主要用于集中安置黄浦区和卢湾区的动迁居民。浦江镇属于上海市“一城九镇”开发项目，规划为现代意大利风貌的城镇，公建配套设施齐全，规划有地铁M8延伸线。浦江·世博家园于2004年11月8日正式开工建设。2005年12月30日，浦江·世博家园首批15万平方米（约1600套）住宅竣工并交付使用。2006年3月和8月，分别有40万平方米（约4660套）和30万平方米（约3400套）

住宅竣工并交付使用。[7]

在浦东区域，上海市世博会动迁定向安置基地主要集中在三林·世博家园区域，该区域位于中环线内的中心城区，地处浦东三林镇境内，地域范围东至春塘河及三林镇域边界，南至华夏西路，西至浦三路，北至南新小区。它靠近世博会会址，主要用于集中安置浦东新区的世博动迁居民。规划居住用地总面积101.23公顷，建设总住宅规模90万平方米，商业及其他公建配套15万平方米。[8]

### （二）对工业遗产的保护与利用

上海世博会场地所在地区是早期的工业发展基地，随着区域功能定位的转变，原有的工厂逐步关闭和搬迁，企业剩余旧厂房均得到重新利用。上海世博会园区保留了近1/6的老建筑，建筑再利用面积约37万平方米，成为世博会可持续发展理念的具体体现。

上海世博会规划对园区内工业遗产的保留与改造提出了三级分类保护原则：一是文物保护单位与优秀历史建筑，二是保留历史建筑，三是其他保留建筑。兼顾建筑自身条件和世博会及城市发展的双向需求，规划采取不同的保护改造策略。[9]江南造船厂、浦钢集团（上钢三厂）、南市发电厂等部分工业老厂房和旧设施实施了改造，成为世博会的展馆和景点。同时，世博园区的一些办公楼、宾馆等也是从旧厂房改造而来。此外，在世博会的用地范围内，共有七处建筑物被列为近代优秀历史建筑，都得到了妥善保护。根据世博会的规划，这些建筑遗产将转变成为具有博览、文化和休闲等多功能的场所。

### （三）后世博期间区域功能的“二次”提升

上海世博会筹办举办期间的城市更新，使世博区域原本以钢铁、船舶制造为主体的生产性功能定位转变为以会展、旅游、休闲为中心的服务性功能。而世博会结束后，该区域的后续开发形成了城市更新的另一高潮。该区域的功能得到了“二次”提升，进一步转变为以高端服务、人居、生态为主的综合性功能。后世博期间，世博会地区的功能定位为：突出公共性特征，围绕顶级国际交流核心功能，形成文化博览创意、总部商务、高端会展、旅游休闲和生态人居为一体的上海标志性市级公共活动中心和世界级新地标。世博会地区结构规划的范围包括世博会红线及协调区，用地总面积约 6.68 平方公里，其中，世博会会展区红线范围 5.28 平方公里。规划形成“五区一带”的功能结构，包括：文化博览区、城市最佳实践区、国际社区、会展及其商务区、后滩拓展区及滨江生态休闲景观带。各片区强调以核心功能为引导，完善配套功能，并塑造与主体功能相适应的各具特色的空间环境。

在世博园区后续规划中，浦西黄浦江一线的“世博滨江文化博览商务区”将与“外滩金融集聚带”连成一体，主要发挥文化博览、创意产业、商务办公三大类的集聚功能。该文博商务区将与知名的“新天地”形成错位发展，前者集中吸引具有核心竞争力的创意设计企业入驻，而“新天地”仍将凸显其国际化的休闲和消费功能。浦东的世博 A、B 片区均改造为高端服务业的集聚区。其中，A 片区以高端商务区为主要改造方向，着力构建知名企业总部聚集区和国际一流的商务街区，并包含相关商业、文化娱乐、酒店公寓等配套功能。在功能上，A片区的目标是成为促进上海城市功能转型和中心城区功能深化提升的重要功能载体。[10]B片区主要以总部办公为核心功能，连接地铁车站和公共活动节点，形成博成路、规划一路公共活动轴线，博成路商务生活轴，沿规划一路下沉广场周边集中配置相应的精品商业、餐饮和休闲娱乐等服务设施，为总部办公人员提供高品质的生活和商务服务，形成综合性总部商务街区。[11]

## 四、悉尼与上海主要城市更新项目的对比与借鉴

通过以上述评不难看出，悉尼与上海作为21世纪前后举办过国际性“大事件”（Big Event）的国际性大都市，在利用相关事件推进城市更新方面均进行了各具特色的探索与实践。二者所经历的城市更新特征比较，为新兴世界城市的城区改造与功能提升提供了很多有益的启示，主要体现在以下几个方面：

### （一）综合性的更新规划对于城区发展而言至关重要

综观各国的城市更新实践，规划上缺乏整体性往往成为影响更新效果的主要因素。而悉尼与上海的“大事件”城市更新，均进行了区域的整体性更新规划，同时，对于更新在不同阶段的重点与主要改造方向进行了谋划。例如，悉尼在奥运区域更新的过程中，从1995年就设定了奥林匹克园区的整体规划，并在2002年进行了进一步修订，目前的规

划已经放眼 2030 年。这种综合性、长时段的规划，对于区域更新的效力长期释放具有重要的引领作用。

### （二）大区域、长时段城市更新需要明确的突破方向

悉尼与上海的城市更新，均设定了明确的目标与主要突破方向。悉尼奥运区域的城市更新选择“棕色地带”改造作为主要目标和推进方向。绿色广场项目则聚焦轻工业区的改造。上海世博会更是创新性地明确提出以中心城区滨水工业区改造作为园区建设的主要精神。这种目标明确的更新策略，绝不仅是为了提升项目知名度的城市营销技巧，而是为城市更新提供具有指向性的抓手，进而在过程中能够起到“纲举目张”之效。

### （三）全面的城市更新需要综合考量经济效应与社会效应的良性互动

20 世纪后半期欧美城市更新运动当中，简单推倒重建、以经济效应为评判标准的更新思路曾经成为主流。这种更新理念对许多更新区域带来了严重的“后遗症”。“贫民窟搬家”，“二次隔离”等问题均频繁出现。在汲取欧美城市经验与教训的基础上，悉尼与上海的更新改造均将社会效应作为重要的衡量原则与推进方向，在建设中充分考虑区域的多样性与社区功能，从而使改造后的区域在经济功能与社会功能上得到统一。例如，悉尼绿色广场项目中对经济适用房比例的规定，上海世博动迁居民异地迁建的集中性社区建设，均反映了对于城市更新可能带来的社会融合问题的不同

思考。

## （四）可持续发展已成为城市更新的重要原则

城市更新曾经被仅仅视为一个城市的空间规划问题，对于更新的目标，也仅限于基础设施的改善与居住条件的提升。而悉尼与上海的更新实践表明，在新的城市更新理念中，可持续发展是城区更新改造不可回避的原则与思路。悉尼奥运区域与上海世博区域的更新过程中，区域的环境领域可持续发展已成为中心环节。当然，可持续发展绝不仅限于环境领域，还涉及建筑、交通、社会等方方面面。绿色广场在提出“10分钟通达”的理念同时，对于轻轨等公共交通的着力建设，便体现出可持续发展在城市更新多领域的渗透与推动作用。

### ［注释］

［1］Sydney Olympic Park Authority. *Sydney Olympic Park Master Plan 2030*, 2009.

［2］李铁北：浅谈奥运的长期影响：以悉尼城市规划为例，《中国城市经济》，2007年7月第20页。

［3］潇琦：奥运前后悉尼房地产变化明显，《北京房地产》，2006年7月第102页。

［4］City of Sydney. *Green Square Urban Renewal Area Background Paper*, 2008.

［5］走进世博新家园·新居篇，《上海世博》，2006年第1期。

［6］孟知行：世博园区居民动迁提前完成，《解放日报》，2006年5月31日第1版

［7］浦江镇，用理想造一座城，《上海世博》，2005年第1期。

[8] 风景这边独好——浦东三林·世博家园规划先睹，《上海世博》，2005 年第 2 期。
[9] 周俭：恩泽于城市长久的未来——上海世博会工业遗产保护与更新探索，《上海世博》，2007 年第 2 期。
[10] 上海市规划和国土资源管理局：世博会 A 片区控制性详细规划（公众参与规划草案），2011 年 9 月 23 日。
[11] 上海市规划和国土资源管理局：世博会 B 片区控制性详细规划（公众参与规划草案），2011 年 5 月 19 日。

## 作者简介

**苏宁**，上海社会科学院澳大利亚研究中心副研究员，主要研究领域为澳大利亚研究。

**黄烨菁**，博士，上海社会科学院澳大利亚研究中心副主任、研究员，主要研究领域为澳大利亚研究、中国对外开放战略。（Email：hyj@sass.org.cn）

# 编 后 记

我是澳大利亚中国友好交流协会会长周泽荣博士20多年的好朋友，这20多年来，作为悉尼市二届的常务副市长、三届新州上议院议员与三任新州州长的助理，我有幸见证了周博士的事业逐年稳健发展壮大，成就了今日侨鑫集团的辉煌。我更开心见证到的是，周博士在个人事业上不断获得进步的同时，一直不忘回馈社会。作为澳大利亚侨领与成功的澳洲企业家，周博士多年来热心支持澳中两国在文化、教育、经贸等领域的交流与合作，受到了澳中两国政府与领导的充分肯定。

我记得，2001年，周先生积极协助双边关系，促成了澳大利亚天然气出口广东的项目，获得了时任澳大利亚总理霍华德的书面肯定；2002年，支持澳大利亚国家博物馆在中国举办中澳建交30周年纪念文化艺术展览，获得时任澳大利亚总督与澳大利亚驻华大使的高度评价；2004年开始，周先生一直赞助澳大利亚新州州长中文教师奖学金计划，支持中文教育事业在澳大利亚的发展；2012年，出资赞助2000万澳币建设悉尼科技大学国际商学院，另设立了500万澳币的澳中学生奖学金，支持澳中两国高等教育的交流合作。

2012年是澳大利亚与中国建立正式外交关系的40周

年，我还记得当年为了澳大利亚经济更好更快发展，周先生多次亲自向时任澳洲教育部长的尼尔森博士（Dr Brendan Nelson）与澳洲移民部长温思瑞女士（Ms. Amanda Vanstone）提议，缩短赴澳中国经贸人士、游客与留学生签证的审批时间。到了今天，中国已成为了澳大利亚最大的海外游客与海外留学生来源国。

在这一具有历史意义的一年，周博士担任会长的澳大利亚中国友好交流协会与中国人民对外友好交流协会一起主办了中澳建交40周年系列活动——中澳沙漠穿越科考环保活动，向中国人民推介了澳洲美丽的内陆风光。

今年初，我与周博士见面。谈话中，我们都感到中澳建交40周年是一件历史大事，如能对这段历史有个回顾，并从思想的高度对中澳两国未来合作交流的发展进行研究，将会是一件很有意义的事情。于是，我接洽了中山大学澳大利亚研究中心主任常晨光教授与中山大学亚太研究院大洋洲研究中心常务副主任喻常森教授，很快就得到中山大学副校长魏明海教授的赞同，并将本研究文集的书名正式定为《中澳关系大趋势：利益共同体的构建与展望——纪念中澳建交40周年》。

经过几个月的辛苦耕耘，此书终于付梓出版。作为澳方的特邀主编，在此我衷心感谢常晨光教授、喻常森教授、魏明海教授为此文集的顺利出版所做的出色工作，也感谢文集的各位作者从学术的高度对中澳关系的发展进行了颇有见地的研究，感谢中国人民对外友好协会李小林会长和中国驻澳大利亚大使陈育明先生亲自为此书作序，感谢澳大利亚外长卡尔同意本书收录他在今年9月发表的《置身中国世纪的澳大利亚》一文，为纪念中澳建交40周年留下重要的思想篇章。

曾筱龙

2012年11月15日

[ English Translation ]

# Afterword

I have been a close friend of Dr Chau Chak Wing, President of Association of Australia China Friendship and Exchange, for more than 20 years. As the former Deputy Lord Mayor of Sydney, MP and Parliamentary Secretary to three Premiers of New South Wales, I have witnessed in the past 20 plus years the gradual growth and development of Dr Chau's business and the prosperity of the Kingold Group. What is most gratifying for me is to see that as his career and business develop, Dr Chau has never forgotten his social responsibility and has always been keen to serve and repay the society. As a leader of the Australian Chinese community and a successful businessman, Dr Chau has been a strong supporter of Australia-China cultural and education exchange and business and trade cooperation, which has won commendation from both the Australian and Chinese governments and leaders.

I still remember that in 2001, Dr Chau's coordination between the two sides facilitated the export of Australian natural gas to Guangdong Province, which was commended by the then Australian Prime Minister John Howard in a written letter. In 2002, with Dr Chau's support, the National Museum of Australia successfully held an art exhibition in China in commemoration of the $30^{th}$ anniversary of China-Australia diplomatic relations, which was highly praised by the then Governor-General of Australia and Australian ambassador to China. Dr Chau started to support the NSW Premier's Kingold Chinese Language Teachers Scholarship from 2004, in order to promote Chinese language education in Australia. In 2012, Dr Chau donated 20 million Australian dollars to build the International Business School of the University of Technology, Sydney. In addition, he set up a scholarship of 5 million Australian dollars to sponsor the student exchange and higher education collaboration between Australia and China.

The year 2012 marks the $40^{th}$ anniversary of Australia-China diplomatic relations. I remember that, in order to ensure the faster and better development of the Australian economy, Dr Chau tried on many occasions to propose to Dr Brendan Nelson, the former Australian Minister for Education, and Ms. Amanda Vanstone, the former Australian Immigration Minister, that the visa approval time of applications from Chinese business people, tourists and students be shortened. Today, China has become Australia's biggest source of tourist revenue and biggest source of international students.

The year 2012 is a year of historic significance. The Association of Australia China Friendship and Exchange headed by Dr Chau and the Chinese People's Association for Friendship with Foreign Countries have co-organized a series of activities in commemoration of the 40th anniversary of Australia-China diplomatic relations, including the Environmental Protection Expedition of Australia-China Desert Adventure, in an effort to introduce the beautiful inland scenery to the Chinese people.

Early this year, I visited with Dr Chau, and we both felt that, as the 40th anniversary of Australia-China diplomatic relations is such an important milestone, it would be very meaningful to review the 40 years of bilateral relationship and conduct research into areas of future cooperation and exchange between the two countries. I then contacted Professor Chang Chenguang, Director of the Australian Studies Centre, Sun Yat-sen University, and Professor Yu Changsen, Deputy Executive Director of the Centre for Oceanian Studies, Sun Yat-sen University. With the strong support from Professor Wei Minghai, the Vice-president of Sun Yat-sen University, we started working on this collection entitled China-Australia Relations: *Towards a Community with Shared Interests – in Commemoration of the* 40$^{th}$ *Anniversary of China-Australia Diplomatic Relations.*

After several months of hard work, the manuscripts are finally ready to be sent to the press. As guest editor of this book, I would like to take this opportunity to express my gratitude to Professor Chang Chenguang, Professor Yu Changsen, and Professor Wei Minghai, for all their efforts to ensure its publication. Thanks also go to all the contributors for their research and academic insights into China-Australia relations. We are especially grateful to Ms Li Xiaolin, the President of Chinese People's Association for Friendship with Foreign Countries, and His Excellency Ambassador Chen Yuming, who have each written a preface for this volume. Special thanks are due to Senator the Honorable Bob Carr, the Foreign Minister of Australia, who agreed to have his speech "Australia in the China century", a speech delivered in September this year at a conference, included in this special collection, which is an important highlight of this commemoration volume.

The Honorable Henry Tsang OAM

November 15, 2012